Why Didn't

I Think of That?

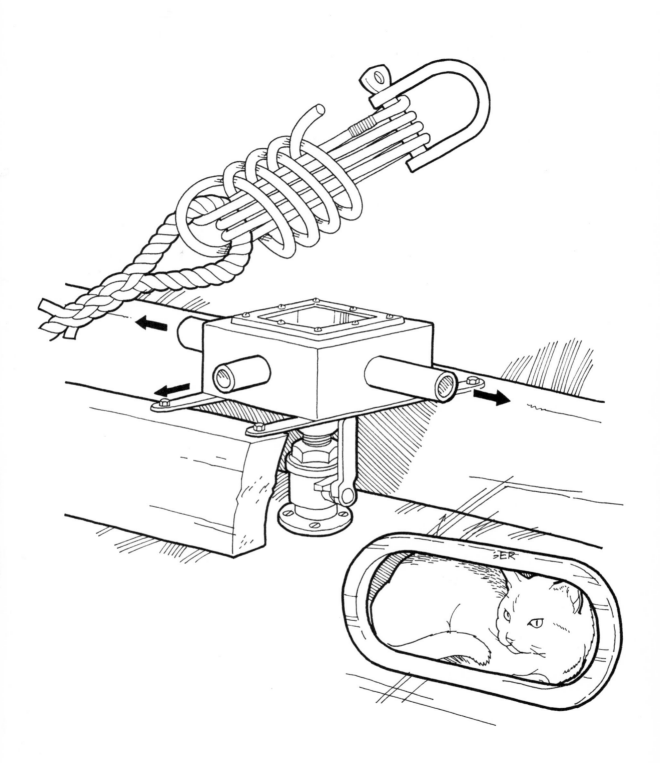

Why Didn't I Think of That?

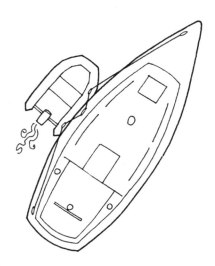

John and Susan Roberts

Illustrations by Jim Sollers

International Marine
Camden, Maine

International Marine/
Ragged Mountain Press

A Division of The McGraw·Hill Companies

10 9 8 7 6 5 4 3 2

Copyright © 1997 by International Marine,
a division of The McGraw-Hill Companies.

Library of Congress Cataloging-in-Publication Data
Roberts, John, 1938–
    Why didn't I think of that? / John and Susan Roberts.
       p.   cm.
   Includes index.
   ISBN 0-07-053222-2 (hardcover). – ISBN 0-07-053221-4 (paperback)
    1. Boats and boating—Equipment and supplies.   I. Roberts, Susan,
1948–   . II. Title.
VM321.R635   1997
623.8'6—dc21   97-5422
                                                 CIP

Questions regarding the content of this book should be addressed to:
   International Marine
   P.O. Box 220
   Camden, ME 04843

Questions regarding the ordering of this book should be addressed to:
   The McGraw-Hill Companies
   Customer Service Department
   P.O. Box 547
   Blacklick, OH 43004
   Retail customers: 1-800-262-4729
   Bookstores: 1-800-722-4726

✹ *Why Didn't I Think of That?* is printed on 60-pound Renew
   Opaque Vellum, an acid-free paper that contains 50 percent
   recycled waste paper (preconsumer) and 10 percent postconsumer
   waste paper.

Why Didn't I Think of That? is set in 10 point Adobe Garamond
   with Helvetica Black headings.

Printed by R.R. Donnelley, Crawfordsville, IN
Design and Production by Dan Kirchoff
Edited by John Kettlewell, Jane Crosen, Tom McCarthy

Contents

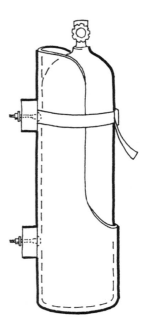

Food

Life Afloat

Maintenance

Major Equipment and Systems

Introduction

This book had its origins several years ago when we were visiting cruising friends Bruce and Sheryl Segovis on their boat near Fort Myers, Florida. We'd moved aboard our 36-foot cutter *Sea Sparrow* and begun full-time cruising about three months earlier and, in conversation, remarked on how stiff the pump for our head had become.

"Oh, don't you know the oil in the head trick?" asked Sheryl. The blank looks on our faces answered the question, so she explained. "Once a week or so, you put about a tablespoon of vegetable oil in the head and pump it through. The oil lubricates the pump and makes pumping a breeze." As soon as we got back to *Sea Sparrow*, we got out the vegetable oil. And we've been getting out the vegetable oil ever since!

Three years and many more tips like that from fellow cruisers plus a few lessons learned the hard way ourselves, and the idea for this book was born in Susan's mind—a sort of *Heloise's Hints* for boaters who like to cruise, whether for weekends, weeks, months or years.

Since the tips we could generate by ourselves would be limited to our own experience, we decided to pick the brains of fellow cruisers through a series of interviews with people we met as we sailed from the British Virgin Islands to Puerto Rico, the Bahamas, and up and down the U.S. East Coast between Florida and Maine. As a result, although this book has two authors, it is not an exaggeration to say that it was written by the crews of 120 cruising boats from the United States, Canada, the United Kingdom, Belgium, Holland, Sweden, Germany, Switzerland and Australia. Collectively, the 222 men and women we interviewed have more than 900 years of cruising experience. Some had been cruising for less than a year when we spoke with them. Others had been cruising either full-time or part-time for more than ten years. Sixteen people—including one woman and one 76-year-old man—were singlehanding. Four couples had sailed around the world, one of them twice! The crews of 18 boats were part-time cruisers. That is, they cruised for periods ranging from one to nine months a year and had been doing so for several years. The remainder were what we called full-time cruisers: they were cruising for at least one full year. And finally, while most of the people we met were sailors, seven of the interviews were with cruisers on motorboats. And, yes, we discovered, sailors can pick up some useful ideas from "stinkpotters"!

What all of these people have contributed to the following pages is nearly 1,200 hints to help make your cruising easier, safer or more pleasant. Their suggestions range from tips about anchors and anchoring to advice about the weather. Whether for weekend sailors, liveaboard cruisers or anyone cruising between those two extremes, there is a wealth of tips in the pages that follow.

Note: Tips accompanied by illustrations are so noted by ☞, which will point you in the right direction.

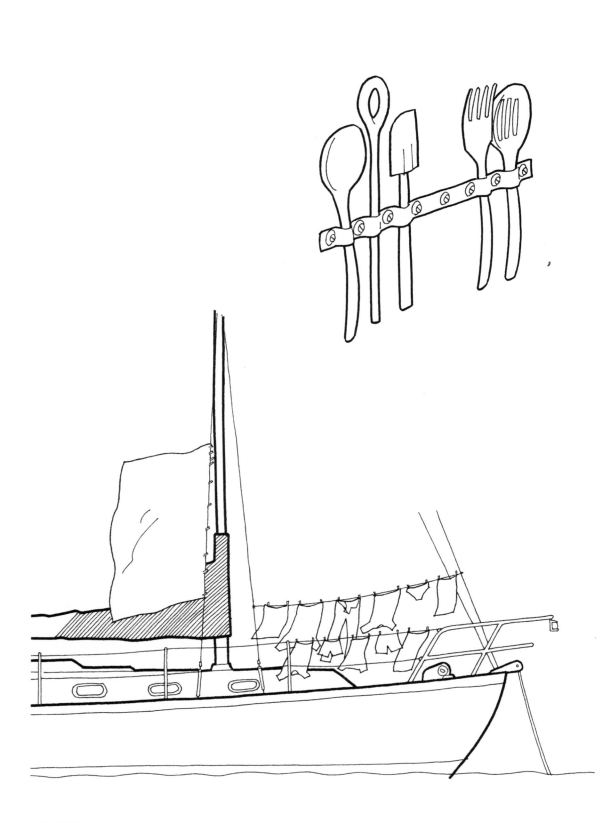

Above Deck

Cockpits

A boat's cockpit often has a split personality. It must be highly functional because—on small craft, at least—the cockpit is the center of action when you are underway. At the same time, the cockpit is frequently the most used "room" on the boat. It's where you sit in the evening to watch the sunset. If friends come by to visit, most often the visiting is done in the cockpit. In warm weather, many cruisers also eat and sleep in their cockpits. The tips that follow reflect the multiple-use character of cockpits. (See also Tip 102, "Awnings.")

General Tips

Engine instrument panel cover   1

Using Plexiglas or other clear plastic sheeting, make a hinged cover to protect the engine instrument panel from the weather and spray. Unprotected, the panel will begin to show effects of exposure, including corrosion, particularly in a saltwater environment.

Ignition key lubricant   2

To keep your ignition switch in good working order, squirt a bit of Boeshield T-9 waterproof lubricant into the slot for the ignition key every two or three months. After squirting, insert the key and turn the ignition on and off several times.

Increasing cockpit space   3

On a sailboat with wheel steering, consider trading your large-diameter wheel for a smaller wheel. The original wheel on Darby Jones's *Seco '44* was so large that he had to climb onto the cockpit seats to get around it. He exchanged it for a smaller-diameter wheel that allows him to get around the steering pedestal more easily.

Nonskid for cups   4

For a secure spot to put cups in the cockpit, try using oversize coasters cut from a roll of rubber nonskid mat, sold in marine stores. We keep our cups on these nonskid coasters next to the sliding companionway hatch.

Beds

Leeboards for cockpit sleeping offshore   5

Install short vertical pieces of genoa track on the cabinhouse and aft coaming or bulkhead at each end of the cockpit seats. With a car and eye on each piece of genoa track, you can attach a small Forespar pole fore-and-aft and adjust the height so that the pole acts as a leeboard along the inside edge of the seat. When sailing offshore at night and sleeping in the cockpit, Bob and Sally Greymont on *Gypsy Spray* say these "leeboards" keep them securely on their cockpit seat berths. Remove the track cars when not in use.

Queen-size cockpit bed   6

If you have tiller steering and can lift the tiller out of the way, Art and Lynne Bourne on *Suits Us* have found an easy way to convert your cockpit into a large bed. First, install wood cleats (strips) on the sides of the cockpit seats ⅝ inch below seat level. Next, cut two pieces of ⅝-inch plywood that will fit into the cockpit well, resting on the wood cleats. With the plywood in place, bring out cushions from below to form a comfortable, queen-size bed. Finger holes in the plywood make for easy removal when it's time to put the bed away. A coating of West System epoxy will seal the plywood. ☞

Cockpit Grates

Grate design   7

When making a cockpit grate, use parallel teak slats 2 inches wide running fore-and-aft instead of the traditional crossed pattern. The slat design is

Darby Jones on *Seco '44*

At age seventy-six, Darby Jones on the 44-foot sloop Seco '44 was the oldest of the single-handers we interviewed. Darby, who had been cruising three years when we met him in the British Virgin Islands, sailed singlehanded from Florida to the Bahamas and down the Thorny Path (the often difficult island-hopping route to the Caribbean against strong winter winds) to the Dominican Republic, then took on a crewman for the last leg of the trip. He had been in the British Virgin Islands a year and a half.

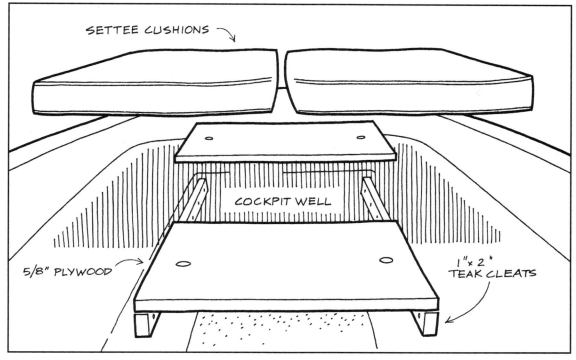

Queen-size cockpit bed (Tip 6).

much more comfortable to stand on with bare feet. We have a traditional grate in *Sea Sparrow*'s cockpit and can certify that it is not intended for bare feet—unless, of course, your feet are much tougher than ours.

Vibration damper   8

Try putting foam weather-stripping on the cross-pieces of the cockpit grate. It will put a stop to any vibration and provide a bit of cushioning—much like carpet underlayment. The foam must be replaced periodically, but it's inexpensive.

Cockpit Screens

Fitted screen   9

Considering the area from the front of your dodger to the back of your bimini as if it were a table top, make a cover for it using a light polyester/cotton sheet fabric. Next, sew mosquito netting to the four edges of the fabric so that the netting will drape with an excess onto the deck.

Finally, stitch together any seams in the mosquito netting so that it forms a continuous screen around the cockpit. Drapery weights, fishing weights, or small bags of washed sand sewn into the hem will hold the sides down.

Free-form screen   10

A large mosquito net that can be draped over the bimini and dodger to hang on the deck on all sides will provide an inexpensive and effective cockpit screen. Use enough mosquito netting that there is an excess all around on the decks. As in the fitted screen above, use weights in the hem to hold the net down.

Cushions

Cockpit cushion alternative   11

As an alternative to cushions, Holger and Christa Strauss use indoor-outdoor carpet on *Golem*'s cockpit seats.

Cockpit cushion nonskid

Nonskid material such as Scoot-Gard, sold in rolls in marine stores, will usually keep cockpit cushions from sliding off the seats when the boat heels. Alternatively, a strip of Velcro on the bottom of cushions will hold them in place. By putting the Velcro near the outboard edge of the cushion, the mating strip on the cockpit seat will be out of the way.

Cockpit throw cushions `13`

Old polyester-filled bed pillows in zippered plastic pillow cases make handy throw cushions for the cockpit. Use terrycloth for inexpensive, comfortable, and easy-to-wash cushion covers.

Covers for cockpit cushions I `14`

Ruth and Earl Freeman on *Mowgli* used plastic mesh fabric, sold for patio cushions, on the top and bottom and Sunbrella marine fabric on the sides of their closed-cell-foam cockpit cushions. The mesh lets the cushions dry quickly and is comfortable to sit on even in hot weather.

Covers for cockpit cushions II

As a variation of the plastic-mesh idea, Steve and Donna Thompson on *Donna Jean* suggest using plastic mesh fabric only on the bottom of your cockpit cushions and Sunbrella fabric on all other surfaces. The mesh fabric on the bottom lets the cushions breathe, and the Sunbrella on the top protects the foam from solar UV—particularly important in the tropics.

Covers for cockpit cushions III `16`

Whatever material is used to cover your cockpit cushions, Rick and Carol Butler on *TranQuility* recommend using bright yellow, orange, or red fabric so that the cushions can be seen more easily in a man-overboard situation.

Improving Visibility

Runt board I

Art and Carole Prangley on *Somewhere* first introduced us to the concept of a "runt board." On *Somewhere*, Art has installed a folding step aft of the wheel so that Carole can see over the bow when

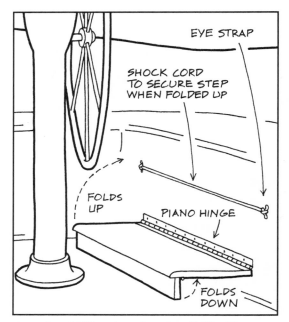

Improving visibility using a "runt board" (Tip 17).

Holger and Christa Strauss on *Golem*

Holger and Christa Strauss on their 42-foot ketch *Golem* were one year into their second circumnavigation when we met them in Beaufort, North Carolina. On their first round-the-world cruise, they had sailed from their home in Berlin, Germany, in 1978 and completed the trip in 1987. After working for several years to replenish their cruising funds, they had set out once again from Berlin and had been exploring the U.S. East Coast before heading to the Panama Canal.

she's steering. When Carole's at the helm, the step folds down for her to stand on. When Art takes over, he flips it up and out of the way. They've also installed runt boards as needed down below to make it easier to open and close overhead hatches.

Runt board II · 18

As an alternative to a built-in folding step, cut down the ends of a 2 x 8-inch board to fit rubber fenderboard end pieces designed for 2 x 6s. This "fenderboard" should be just long enough (or short enough) to be placed athwartships on the cockpit sole at the steering station, where it will provide a steering platform about 3 inches high.

Seating

Backrest I · 19

A 2 x 4 with upholstered cushioning attached and fitted with two hooks, such as those sold in marine stores as "boathook holders," makes an excellent backrest. Use the hooks to hang the backrest from the stern rail. The cushion can be attached to the board using Velcro, snaps, or screws.

Backrest II · 20

On *Sheldro*, John Robinson used 1½-inch nylon webbing to fabricate a ladder-like backrest that runs from port to starboard between the lifelines or sides of the stern rail. The backrest consists of two long horizontal lengths of webbing held about 15 inches apart by short, vertical webbing pieces spaced at roughly 1-foot intervals.

Companionway seat · 21

A seat that fits in the companionway so that the person on watch can sit under the dodger is worth its weight in teak in raw weather. On *Flyway*, Dave and Phyllis Carroll made their seat from a ¾-inch board about 7 inches wide and just long enough to fit across the bottom of the companionway. (The fraction ¾ is lumber terminology denoting a board

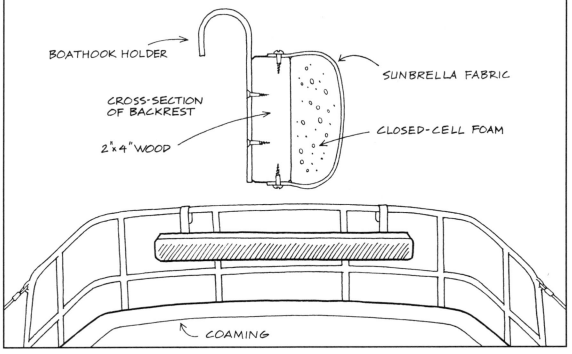

A cockpit backrest that hangs on the stern rail (Tip 19).

BOATHOOK HOLDER

CROSS-SECTION OF BACKREST

2"x4" WOOD

SUNBRELLA FABRIC

CLOSED-CELL FOAM

COAMING

Cockpit backrest made with nylon webbing (Tip 20).

that measures a full 1¼ inch thick.) Cleats across the bottom hold it in place. We needed to sit higher on *Sea Sparrow*, so we modified the Carrolls' design by cutting a piece of wood to fit in the companionway like a short hatch board to raise our seat. Cutouts in the ends of the seat fit around the sides of the companionway to hold the seat in place. For extra comfort, we added a piece of 2-inch closed-cell foam covered with fabric and held in place with snaps.

Stowage

Binocular box   `22`

A binocular box on the forward side of the wheel-steering pedestal keeps binoculars handy and safe. Just remember to take them below at night in an anchorage or dockside. Also, be sure there are drain holes in the bottom of the box, even if it has a lid.

Cockpit bags I   `23`

On *Decatur*, Mike McGivern has two Sunbrella cockpit bags measuring about 10 by 12 inches that

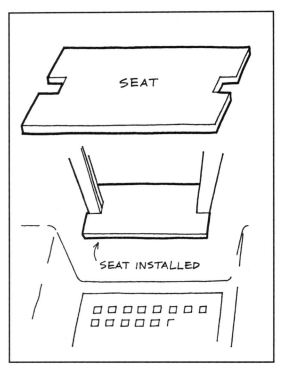

Companionway seat (Tip 21).

John and Petra Kowalczyk on *Ragtime Duet*

In 1983, John and Petra Kowalczyk on the 46-foot cutter *Ragtime Duet* started sailing from their Chesapeake Bay–area home every fall to spend all or part of the winter in Florida, the Bahamas, or Mexico. When we met them in Beaufort, North Carolina, they were making their tenth trip south and beginning to think about retiring to the boat to cruise full-time.

can be snapped onto the coaming in a position accessible to the helm. Mike uses these bags to hold his deck log, sunglasses, sunscreen, and other items. When he has a guest aboard, he assigns the guest a pouch.

Cockpit bags II   24

Another approach to cockpit bags uses Sunbrella pouches about 12 inches wide and 16 to 18 inches deep that hang from the lifelines inside the weather cloths. With grommets in the four corners, they can be secured to the upper and lower lifelines with light line.

Cockpit box   25

John and Petra Kowalczyk on *Ragtime Duet* have installed a box about 12 inches wide and 14 inches deep between the wheel-steering pedestal guardrail and the bridge deck. They use the box to stow docklines. Including its top, the box should be about the same height as the bridge deck and secured to both the bridge deck and the steering-pedestal guardrail.

Cockpit coamings   26

The wide, fiberglass coamings of many sailboats contain space waiting to be used. By installing deck plates in the cockpit side of the coaming, you can use that space for cockpit stowage. *Note:* You may have to install a bottom to your coaming lockers.

Hatch boards I   27

What to do with your hatch boards? Begin by making a Sunbrella bag with dividers that form separate pouches for each hatch board. A flap over the top of the bag can be held closed with Velcro. Then fasten the bag in the cockpit well against the bridge deck.

Hatch boards II   28

A somewhat simpler suggestion: Using eye straps, install a piece of ¼-inch shock cord to hold the hatch boards snugly against one side or the other of the cockpit well. Alternatively, use the same system to hold them snugly against a bulkhead down below—but where they will be out of the way.

Locker divider   29

If you have a large cockpit-seat locker, install a vertical divider running fore-and-aft about 6 inches outboard from the inside edge of the locker. On *Packet Inn*, Jack and Terry Roberts use this 6-inch-wide space to hang their docklines so that they are always available for immediate use.

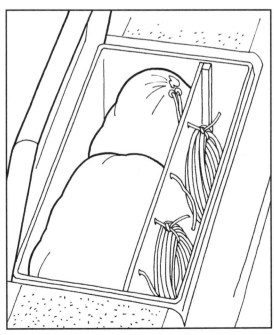

Locker divider eases dockline stowage in large cockpit lockers (Tip 29).

Mesh bags 30

Use large mesh bags to organize hoses, shore power cable, docklines, snorkel gear, and spare anchor rodes in cockpit lockers or the lazarette. According to Mike McGivern on *Decatur*, the mesh bags save digging around through a lot of loose gear to find what you want. By getting different-colored bags, you can also color-code them for content—say, yellow for shore power, red for docklines, and so on. Buy them in an Army/Navy store or where camping gear is sold.

Weather cloth pockets 31

Pockets sewn onto the inside surface of your weather cloths can also provide handy stowage. While the pockets are best constructed with a top flap secured with Velcro to keep water out, it's still a good idea to provide a couple of drain holes by installing small grommets. We've seen weather cloth pockets as large as 15 by 24 inches. If you'll be keeping heavy items in the pockets, the weather cloths should be reinforced where the pockets are sewn to them.

Tables

Double-duty table 32

For a table that doubles as a propane tank locker, see Tip 747, "Propane storage I."

Table size 33

If you have a choice, a cockpit table in front of your wheel-steering pedestal guard should be sized to fit a BBA Chart Kit or a folded chart—particularly for traveling inland waterways or in harbors where frequent reference to the chart is needed.

A piece of ⅛-inch Plexiglas that fits on top of the table to protect the chart is an added touch of convenience. Fiddles port and starboard on the table will keep both the chart and Plexiglas in place. The absence of fiddles at the two ends of the table allows rain to drain off and makes it easy to lift the Plexiglas.

Equipment

General Tips

Anchor rode fairlead 34

On *Dublin Dragon*, a collar on the bowsprit forward of the bobstay fitting provides a base for mounting a ⅜-inch stainless steel rod bent to form U-shaped hooks at each end. After the anchor is set, the rode is put into one of the U-hooks to keep it from banging and chafing on the bobstay.

Emergency motor mount 35

On *Star Cruiser*, Robert and Carol Petterson have mounted an outboard-motor bracket on the transom, positioned so they can use their dinghy's 9.9-horsepower outboard for emergency auxiliary

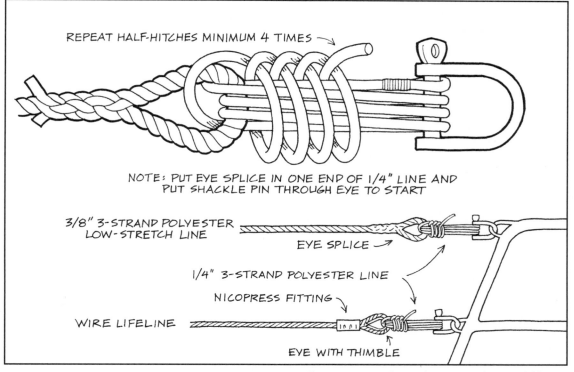

REPEAT HALF-HITCHES MINIMUM 4 TIMES

NOTE: PUT EYE SPLICE IN ONE END OF 1/4" LINE AND
PUT SHACKLE PIN THROUGH EYE TO START

3/8" 3-STRAND POLYESTER
LOW-STRETCH LINE

EYE SPLICE

1/4" 3-STRAND POLYESTER LINE

NICOPRESS FITTING

WIRE LIFELINE

EYE WITH THIMBLE

Alternative means for attaching rope and/or wire lifelines to the bow and stern rails (Tips 36 and 37).

power in the event of a main engine failure. We've seen similar mounts on several other boats as well.

Rope lifelines 36

As an alternative to wire lifelines, John Robinson on *Sheldro* suggests using ⅜-inch, low-stretch polyester three-strand line. Stainless steel eye-straps welded to the outside of stanchions will accommodate the rope lifelines. With small eyes spliced at each end, the lifelines can be attached to the bow and stern rails with shackles. By making the finished lifeline about 8 inches too short, it can be tensioned from one end using several turns of ¼-inch line to connect the eye to the shackle. Replace the ¼-inch line every eighteen to twenty-four months.

Jim and Ronelle Cromeenes on *Dublin Dragon*

After living for three years aboard their 37-foot pilothouse cutter *Dublin Dragon* in northern California while they were working, Jim and Ronelle Cromeenes packed up the boat and shipped it to Florida to go cruising. When we met them, they'd been cruising for six months along Florida's east coast and in the Bahamas, where we shared an anchorage.

Wire lifelines 37

Instead of connecting your lifeline ends to the bow and stern rails with turnbuckles, put an eye and thimble in each end of the lifeline wire and use several turns of ¼-inch three-strand polyester line to secure the lifeline to the bow and stern rails, as described in the previous tip. If you need to drop the lifelines quickly, a sharp knife can be used to cut the polyester rope securing the lifeline ends.

Boarding Ladders

Boarding ladder 38

If your boat does not have a permanently mounted boarding ladder, consider getting one. It's more than a convenience. A ladder that is immediately available enables you to respond quickly when there is need to go into the water, or to get someone out of the water. For emergency use—such as man overboard—a midship ladder is safer than a transom ladder.

Canoe-sterned boats/ midship ladder 39

It is often difficult to find a sturdy boarding ladder for a canoe-sterned boat, especially if the boat also has a slotted aluminum toerail. However, Metal Design, Inc. (296 Taugwonk Road, Stonington, CT 06378) manufactures a stainless steel ladder specifically designed to be hung from either a slotted toerail or genoa track atop the wood caprail. Each ladder is made specifically to fit your boat and folds up into your lifelines or lifeline gate. We purchased one soon after seeing them on three boats in our survey, and have been delighted with it.

Emergency boarding steps 40

Singlehander Dick McCurdie on *Pelagic Vagrant* reports that folding mast steps installed on the transom (or near the end of a canoe stern) make a good emergency "ladder" if you do not otherwise have a ladder immediately available and there is no one on the boat to put a ladder down.

Midship boarding ladder 41

An alternative to a custom boarding ladder may be a ready-made ladder sold by various marine chandleries. To use one of these ladders, Guy and Joan Brooks on *Orca* mounted the ladder brackets on a teak board long enough to overlap the two gate stanchions. With the board lying flat against the toerail and overlapping the gate at both ends, the ladder is hung from those mounts. The mounting board, which can be used on either side of the boat, is stowed with the ladder when not in use.

Rubber ladder feet 42

To keep the white rubber cups on the ends of your ladder's legs from disintegrating in the sunlight, wrap them with rigging tape. With the tape to shield them from solar UV, the rubber cups on *Sea Sparrow*'s ladder have lasted as long as two years in the tropics.

Boarding Steps

Boarding step I 43

A fender board hanging about 12 inches below deck level makes a handy step for people climbing from a dinghy to your boat. Secure the fender board to the gate stanchions or to your slotted toerail.

Boarding step II 44

A piece of teak 5/4 x 12 x 8 inches makes a simple, easy-to-stow step to assist people boarding from a dinghy. First, drill 7/16-inch holes about 1½ inches from the board's edges at each corner. Use two pieces of 3/8-inch line to form a loop at each end. Then tie figure-eight knots in the line ends under the step.

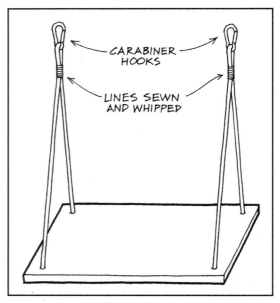

Boarding step (Tip 44).

The line (loop) length is determined by where you want to hang the step. Use carabiners or snaphooks to hang the step from your slotted toerail. Alternatively, wrap the loop end around the gateway stanchion bases and hook it back on itself using carabiners or snaphooks. With the step hanging level and adjusted for height, use whipping twine to bind off small eyes in the ⅜-inch line where the carabiner hooks are positioned so that they stay in place.

Boathooks

Boathook saver   `45`

A boathook is one piece of equipment that will inevitably wind up in the water at least once in its lifetime. For that reason, William and Edna Baert on *Liebchen* suggest securing a light line to the handle end of the boathook and fastening the free end of the line to a cleat or stanchion when getting ready to use the hook. This way, when the boathook slips or is pulled from the crew's grip, it is still attached to the boat.

Extra-long boathook   `46`

A small-diameter telescoping whisker pole or awning pole fitted with a boathook end-piece (available from marine store catalogs) makes an extra-long, lightweight boathook.

Put-or-take boathook   `47`

How many times have you tried to use your old-fashioned boathook to put a line out over a piling,

William and Edna Baert on *Liebchen*

William and Edna Baert on their 37-foot sloop *Liebchen* had been making an eight-month cruise from Massachusetts to Florida, across to the Bahamas, and back to their home in Massachusetts every other year for ten years when we met them in Vero Beach, Florida. This was the sixth time they had made the voyage south for the winter.

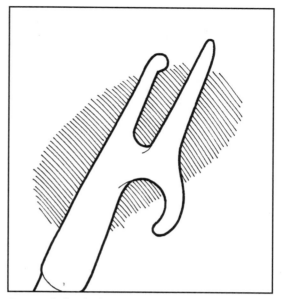

Put-or-take boathook (Tip 47).

only to have the line fall off the end of the hook short of the piling? The put-or-take boathook is designed to eliminate that frustration, by letting you put a line out or pull one in. One supplier of a sturdy put-or-take design is MB Associates, Inc. (Legacy Lane, Box 66, Aspers, PA 17304). Lighter-weight variants on the put-or-take design are shown in various marine equipment catalogs.

Cockpit-Exit Grab Bars

Grab bar I   `48`

Several boats in our survey had grab bars on the sides of their dodgers, bolted or welded to the dodger frame. Short (12-, 18-, or 24-inch) stainless steel handrails with studs welded in the ends and suitable for installation on dodger frames are sold by some marine chandleries. Of course, the dodger canvas must be modified to accommodate the handles, and the entire frame must be made of stainless steel tubing and well anchored. ☞

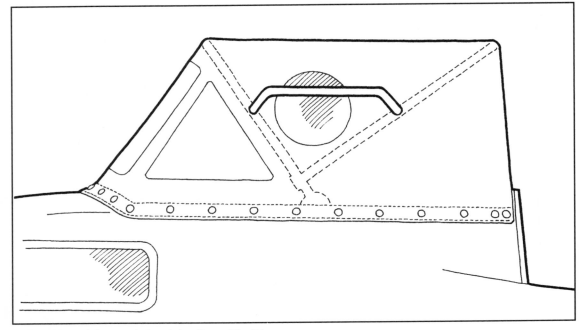

Cockpit-exit grab bar attached to dodger frame (Tip 48).

Grab bar II 49

A sturdy boom gallows just forward of the cockpit that arches over the dodger provides double service: It supports the boom when you're not sailing and provides a secure handhold when going out of or into the cockpit.

Fenders and Fender Boards

Dinghy fenders 50

You will occasionally need small (4-inch-diameter) fenders to protect your dinghy from a seawall or bulkhead. Also, a small fender hanging from your lifeline provides a buffer between your dinghy and topsides when the dinghy is lying alongside.

Fender board gangway 51

On *Mooneshine*, one of Ron and Kathy Trossbach's two fender boards is a 5-foot 2 x 6 that serves double duty as a gangway when they are Med (Mediterranean) moored (see Tip 386).

Fender boards 52

Fender boards are particularly useful for keeping a boat away from a piling because they allow for some fore-and-aft movement. Preferably, a fender board should be either a 2 x 4 or a 2 x 6 between 4 and 6 feet long. In use, hang the fender board over two 6-inch-diameter cylindrical fenders hung vertically.

Recommended fenders 53

Carry the largest fenders you can stow—a minimum of one for each 15 feet of boat length. You may also need additional fenders for your fender boards.

On-Deck Stowage

Treated-lumber tie rail 54

Frank and JulAnn Allen on *Carpe Diem* fastened a ¾ x 3-inch plank of salt-treated lumber to two forward stanchions a few inches below the lower lifeline using stainless steel U-bolts. Jerry cans and bicycles can be strapped to the board.

Propellers

Feathering propellers   `55`

One of the most important maintenance requirements of a Max-Prop or similar feathering propeller is providing sufficient zincs to prevent electrolysis damage to the propeller. The Max-Prop itself is equipped with a special zinc that is quite expensive. On *TranQuility*, Rick and Carol Butler also put two doughnut zincs and two bullet zincs on the prop shaft, replacing them each year. By using these extra zincs, Rick reports, they were still using the original Max-Prop zinc after four years, and it was still 90 percent intact.

Lobster-pot shield   `56`

Fish trap, crab trap, and lobster pot lines are a frequent hazard to the propellers of fin-keeled sailboats. Alan Campbell and Joan Normington use a length of ⅛-inch stainless steel rigging wire with a small eye at each end to shield *Acamar*'s propeller from lobster pot lines. One end of the wire is

Alan Campbell and Joan Normington on *Acamar*

After vacation-cruising for twenty years, Alan Campbell and Joan Normington were taking advantage of Alan's retirement to spend the four summer months every year cruising in Maine on their 37-foot sloop *Acamar*. When we met them anchored at Frenchboro, they had been spending their summers this way for eight years. They had also sailed *Acamar* south for a winter in Florida.

attached to the boat bottom forward of the propeller shaft by a panhead screw through the eye; the other end is attached using another panhead screw on the bottom of their rudder near the axis of rotation. Errant lobster pot lines are fended away from the propeller by this wire.

Gadgets: Exterior

General Tips

Chafe protection   `57`

Lines are not the only things that can be chafed. Coamings and caprails are frequent victims of chafe from sheets, docklines, and fender lines. For chafe protection, John and Petra Kowalczyk installed curved half-oval stainless steel strips at strategic places on the rounded edges of *Ragtime Duet*'s coaming and caprail.

Midship cleats   `58`

Sturdy mooring cleats amidships port and starboard, through-bolted with large backing plates, are among the most useful cleats on a

Dave and Vickie Johannes on *Westward*

Dave and Vickie Johannes, along with Hannah, ten, and Zachary, eight, had been cruising for just three months on their 31-foot ketch *Westward* when we met them in Vero Beach. They had set out from the Chesapeake Bay planning to cruise for two years, but were leaving open the possibility of staying on the boat longer. This first winter, they were bound for the Bahamas.

boat. Use them as an attachment point for a boom vang/preventer and, of course, for spring lines forward and aft when coming to a dock or slip.

Stern-rail gate 59

On *Westward*, Dave Johannes used a pipe cutter to make a gate in their stern rail for use when moored stern-to. Underway, the opening sections of rail are secured by stainless steel sleeves that slip over the rail ends and are held in place with clevis pins.

Viewing bucket I 60

A glass-bottomed bucket—for sightseeing underwater without getting wet or, possibly more important, for checking your anchor from the dinghy—is an easily made and handy item to have aboard. Simply cut most of the bottom from a mid-size plastic bucket, leaving a one-inch bottom lip around the edge. Cut a piece of ⅛-inch or thicker Plexiglas so that it will fit securely on the bucket's bottom lip. Bed the Plexiglas well with silicone sealant and let it cure.

Viewing bucket II 61

For easier stowage, use a collapsible canvas bucket to construct your viewing bucket. However, before cutting out the bottom of the bucket (leaving a 1-inch lip as described above), coat the circle to be cut with a thin layer of a polyurethane adhesive/sealant on both sides of the canvas,

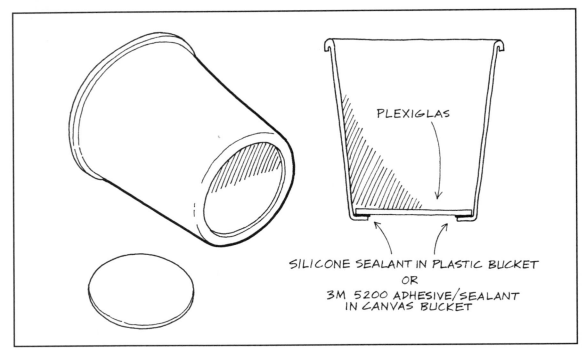

Viewing bucket (Tips 60 and 61).

rubbing the adhesive into the canvas. When the adhesive/sealant has cured thoroughly, you can cut out the bottom without the canvas fraying. Use the same adhesive/sealant to bed the Plexiglas bottom, allowing it to cure thoroughly before collapsing the bucket. 🐟

Cargo Booms

Cargo boom I   62

A Forespar davit mounted by the stern rail can be used to lift the outboard and other heavy items from your dinghy by using a four-part block and tackle. The boom swings out over the water and back over the deck, and can be disassembled and stowed in a small bag when not needed. All parts needed to mount the boom come with it. The unit is available from various discount marine outlets.

Cargo boom II   63

Here, the boom itself is made of 1½-inch stainless steel tubing bent to form an L. The boom is then

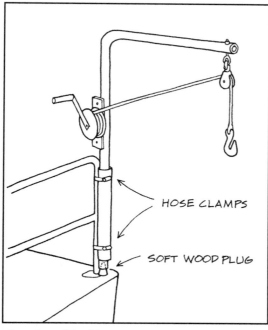

Cargo boom (Tip 63).

equipped with a standard trailer winch with crank. The long part of the L fits into a vertically mounted stainless steel tube welded or fastened to the stern rail with hose clamps. A wood plug in the bottom end of the tube protects the deck against scarring. The rope from the winch runs through a block at the end of the boom. 🐟

Masts and Rigging

Halyard saver   64

A 2- to 3-foot piece of light line with a loop on one end to fit over your wrist and a sturdy spring clip on the other end can keep your halyard from getting loose. Before unfastening the halyard, slip the halyard saver's spring clip over your halyard and the loop over your wrist. If you suddenly need both hands, you can let go of the halyard without losing it up the mast.

Low mast steps   65

Eugene Henkel and Bill Zeisler on *Sea Fever* say that two folding mast steps about 2 feet above deck level will take all of the tip-toes and stretching out of reaching the head board of the mainsail and putting on the sail cover.

Mast-climbing system   66

Singlehander Alex Quintard on *Cetus* uses a four-part block and tackle with a cam cleat to go up his mast. In fact, he sands and varnishes his wood spar using this system, sanding on the way up and varnishing on the way down. The upper block is raised to the top of the mast with a halyard. With the halyard secured, Alex can pull himself up the mast in his bosun's chair. We have adopted a similar system on *Sea Sparrow*, using a ratchet block along with the cam cleat.

Organizers

Line organizers · 67

Begin with a 2-foot piece of ³⁄₁₆-inch line having a brass snaphook at one end and an eye at the other. Tie the line to the stern rail with a clove hitch so the snaphook hangs barely 2 inches below the rail. Use the longer end of the line to hang coiled running rigging or docklines by securing the eye end of your line organizer into the snaphook.

Velcro straps · 68

Glue the two halves of Velcro back-to-back, cut to length, and use them to secure things to your lifelines or stern rail. Just wrap the Velcro around on itself.

Winch handle holder I · 69

A 1-foot length of PVC pipe 1¾ or 2 inches in diameter makes a cheap and effective winch handle holder. Cut the pipe at a 45-degree angle at the top and fasten in place with a hose clamp or screw. Dwight and Karen Rettie on *Tarwathie* note that these holders are open at the bottom and don't collect dirt—unlike store-bought winch handle holders.

Winch handle holder II · 70

If your Dorade vents are close to your mast, they make a handy stowage place for the winch handle. Just put the handle into the Dorade vent, business end first. It will stay put in the roughest weather and is always handy when needed.

Winch handle holder III · 71

You thought winch handle holders were just for winch handles? Not necessarily. Earl and Ruth Freeman on *Mowgli* say they also make good holders for any item that fits—such as bilge pump handles, pencils, and cockpit tools.

Dwight and Karen Rettie on *Tarwathie*

When we met them in Beaufort, North Carolina, Dwight and Karen Rettie had been cruising on their 42-foot ketch *Tarwathie* for five years. In that time, they had explored the U.S. East Coast and most of the islands—including Bermuda—from the Chesapeake Bay to Grenada in the Windward Islands.

Washdown Systems

Freshwater washdown I · 72

To provide a freshwater washdown on deck, Bob and Chesley Logcher installed a garden hose fitting teed into *Cygnet*'s pressure water system with an on/off valve. The fitting is accessible through a cockpit locker.

Freshwater washdown II · 73

When water conservation is important, use a garden sprayer for your freshwater washdown. Win Smith on *Rosinante* said he needs only two gallons of water to rinse off his 34-foot sloop with the garden sprayer, which does double duty as *Rosinante*'s shower.

Saltwater washdown · 74

On *Sunrise*, John and Maureen La Vake have installed a saltwater washdown system notable for its simplicity. They mounted a Jabsco Water Puppy pump in the chain locker and attached a flat hose that's kept in a nylon bag in the chain locker. The saltwater feed is teed off the head intake. The pump is turned on with a manual switch.

Masts and Rigging

General Tips, 75–83
Safety, 84–85

General Tips

Backup headstay   75

On *Stage Sea*, Tony and Jenny Collingridge have a second headstay as a backup to the roller-furling jib should it fail, or for use with a storm jib. The backup headstay is removable at the bottom. A hook-like fitting at the spreaders secures the stay when it is led aft for storage.

Flag halyards   76

To help keep flags away from your sails, seize a sturdy nylon ring to the upper shrouds a foot or so below the spreader and run one lead of the flag halyard through the nylon ring. Then, hoist the flag to the nylon ring.

Halyard security I   77

Instead of using snap shackles to attach your halyards to the sails, use a bowline knot. There's no struggling to open the shackle to get it onto or off the sail. There's also never any question as to whether the shackle is closed securely and, since you've always got your hands on the line to tie or untie the knot, there's less risk of letting go the line. The clincher: bowlines are also much less expensive than snap shackles.

Halyard security II   78

To keep a halyard end from getting lost inside the mast, tie a figure-eight knot a foot or so from the sail end and about 6 feet from the winch end of the halyard. The knots will keep the halyard ends outside the mast.

Leaks around the mast   79

Bill Wittenfeld on *Runinfree* solved his problem of water leaking where his mast passes through the deck by using an adhesive bedding compound to hold the wedges in place. *Caution:* Do not use a polyurethane adhesive/sealant for this purpose, or removing the wedges will be extremely difficult.

Re-reeving a lost halyard   80

If a halyard gets lost down the mast, you can use a spare halyard—if you have one—to run a messenger for re-reeving the lost halyard. The idea is to run the messenger line over the sheave for the missing halyard, tie it to the spare halyard inside the mast, and use that to pull the messenger down through the mast.

First, provide several feet of slack to your spare halyard. Next, use your mainsail halyard (or mast steps) to go up the mast, taking a messenger line and a piece of rigging wire with you. Working from the opposite side of the mast from your spare halyard, use the rigging wire to reach into the mast truck to snag the halyard inside the mast and pull a small loop of halyard out to you. Next, use the

Bill Wittenfeld on *Runinfree*

Singlehander Bill Wittenfeld sailed from his home in Washington state on his 40-foot sloop *Runinfree* some fifteen months before we met him in Beaufort, North Carolina. His course took him down the Pacific coast of the United States and Central America to Panama, through the Canal, and to Jamaica before making his way to the Bahamas. From there, he cruised to the Chesapeake Bay, before turning south at the approach of winter.

wire as a fish to run the messenger line over the sheave for the missing halyard and through the mast truck so that the messenger line emerges right alongside the loop of spare halyard. Now, secure the messenger to the spare halyard with a series of clove hitches and have the crew on deck pull the spare halyard and messenger gently into the mast. After returning to the deck, secure a downhaul line to the sail end of the spare halyard and pull the messenger line down through the mast. Use a wire fish to snag the messenger at the bottom of the mast and pull it out through the correct opening. At this point, you can use the messenger to replace the halyard. We know firsthand that this system does work; we've had to do it. That's why we now have knots in our halyards as suggested above in Tip 78, "Halyard security."

Running new halyards   81

To rig a new halyard, sew the ends of the old and new halyards securely end-to-end with whipping twine or sail-repair thread. (As an alternative, some cruisers suggest using duct tape to tape the two lines end-to-end.) It's then a simple matter to pull the new halyard up to the top of the mast, over the masthead sheave, and down through the mast.

Swaged fittings   82

To prevent corrosion within the fitting, heat it gently with a small torch and melt wax or anhydrous lanolin down into the fitting. (See Tip 979, "Anhydrous lanolin.")

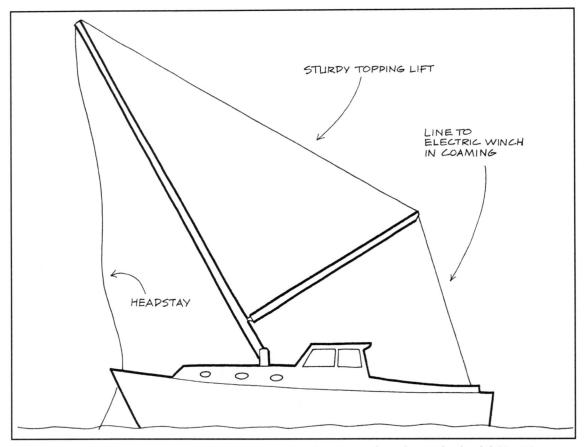

STURDY TOPPING LIFT

LINE TO ELECTRIC WINCH IN COAMING

HEADSTAY

Lowering a tabernacle mast shorthanded (Tip 83).

Tabernacle masts 83

Jack and Margaret Eady have developed an easy system for lowering *Grand Marjac*'s tabernacle mast so that they can pass under a low bridge near their home base. The system has three key components: (1) a quick-release lever on the backstay; (2) an electric boat trailer winch permanently mounted inside the coaming at the back of the cockpit with a deck plate for access; and (3) a sturdy topping lift for the boom. The line from the trailer winch attaches to the end of the boom, with the topping lift completing the linkage to the masthead. After removing the aft lower shrouds and slacking off on the remaining shrouds, the backstay is disconnected and the winch used to lower the mast forward onto the bow rail. ✒

Safety

Boom vang/preventer 84

Rig a four-part block and tackle with a jam cleat between a mid-boom bale and the leeward midship cleat. If you do not have a midship cleat, attach it to a genoa track car. Whenever you change tacks, move the vang/preventer to the other side. Alternatively, rig separate vangs for each side. While not a true preventer, this arrangement not only functions as a vang to flatten your mainsail, but will act as a preventer to hold your boom safely in place if the wind gets behind your mainsail as you roll downwind. It also helps secure your boom when taking down and furling the mainsail. Of course, this tip assumes you've got a sturdy boom and not a featherweight boom for racing that might buckle in severe conditions. (*Note:* A true preventer runs from the boom end to a forward cleat.)

Lifeline gate latch 85

The pelican hooks typically used in lifeline gates are known to open accidentally. However, pelican hooks with snap shackle latches provide a positive latching mechanism that makes your lifeline gate more secure. In fifteen years of service, ours have needed only occasional lubrication—and have kept our gates secure. We've seen them in the West Marine and Defender catalogs.

Sail Plan

General Tips, 86–88
Roller-Furling Sails, 89–92
Storm Sails, 93–94

General Tips

Bobstay 86

To keep their anchor rode from chafing on the bobstay, Dave and B. K. Bennett on *Blue Ribbon* installed PVC tubing over the bobstay, allowing a few inches at the forward end so they can slide the tubing up to check the lower turnbuckle pins and shackle.

Downwind gear 87

If you will be sailing on large bodies of water with significant waves, a whisker pole and boom vang/preventer are critical to downwind sailing, particularly in light to moderate air. Otherwise, the rolling will collapse your jib and may even cause accidental jibes.

Lazyjacks 88

Rig your lazyjacks to be pulled forward to the mast when they're not needed so that they can't rub against the sail. Particularly if you're sailing long distances, the continual light chafe from lazyjacks can weaken the stitching along a sail's seams.

Roller-Furling Sails

Bent extrusion | 89

If you bend your roller-furling jib extrusion, you may be able to correct the problem temporarily by cutting out the bent section—only the few inches that are actually bent—and reassembling the extrusion. If the reassembled extrusion is too short for your full jib, it may still be long enough for a smaller jib—assuming you carry one.

Furling line | 90

Gunnar Dahl on *Sandra* reports that the rigger installing their roller-furling jib removed the core from the part of the double-braid line that rolls up around the furling drum. As a result, the line rolls up flat around the drum, making jams unlikely. At the same time, they have the full heft of the line to grab with their hands or to put around a cockpit winch when it's time to furl the sail. Reportedly, this is now standard practice among many riggers.

Maintenance | 91

Kirk Chamberlain on *Moxie* suggests servicing your roller-furling system annually—more frequently if you sail year-round—following the manufacturer's instructions. Servicing should include partial disassembly to inspect for water damage to bearings and seals and checking the extrusion to be sure it is not candy-caned (twisted).

When to roller-reef | 92

As in reefing any sail, take in part of your roller-furling jib or mainsail as soon as you begin to think about it. If you wait too long, the pressure on the sail may bow the luff extrusion or rod, making the sail difficult to furl. Easing halyard tension makes it easier to roll up the sail.

Storm Sails

Mizzen reefs | 93

By making provision for two reefs in your mizzen, it's possible to balance a ketch under jib and jigger going upwind, even in heavy winds. You may have to persuade your sailmaker to do it, though; reefed mizzens are not common.

Storm jib with roller-furling gear | 94

On *Bowstring*, John Halley rigged an inner stay that can be set up about 2 feet aft of the headstay in heavy weather. He used a smaller-diameter wire for the inner stay so the headstay still carries the major rigging loads. The inner stay, which runs from the masthead to a chainplate secured to a below-deck bulkhead, is reserved exclusively for the storm jib.

John Halley on *Bowstring*

John Halley had been cruising on his 43-foot double-headsail sloop for a year and a half when we met him in the British Virgin Islands. He was not singlehanding, however. Instead, John, an insulin-dependent diabetic, was joined by one or two friends as crew at various times. Since leaving his home in England, John and his friends had sailed *Bowstring* to the Mediterranean, then across the Atlantic to Barbados and up the island chain to the Virgin Islands.

Weather Protection

General Tips, 95–101
Awnings, Biminis, and
Dodgers, 102–105

General Tips

Companionway storm door I 95

Used in place of your hatch boards, a piece of clear vinyl like that used in dodger windows makes a handy storm door for the companionway hatch. Cut the vinyl 4 or 5 inches wider than the companionway and long enough to hem top and bottom. Use snaps in the top hem to attach your storm door to a length of ¾-inch-square teak cut to fit at the top of the hatch-board slots. A second piece of teak slipped into the bottom hem will help hold the storm door in place. Two snaps down each side will secure it in windier conditions. You can also trim the edges of the vinyl with Sunbrella fabric. ☞

Companionway storm door II 96

Cut a piece of clear, soft vinyl large enough to drape over the open companionway hatch, leaving several inches of excess at each end. Sew four to six ounces of No. 8 birdshot or lead fishing weights in pockets at all four corners by turning over the ends of the vinyl. In use, the vinyl is draped over the open hatch and the weights hold the top and bottom in place.

Companionway window 97

Use ⅝- or ¾-inch Plexiglas to make a replacement hatch board for your companionway. With the hatch boards in place, the Plexiglas hatch board lets you see into the cockpit or down into the cabin without opening the hatch.

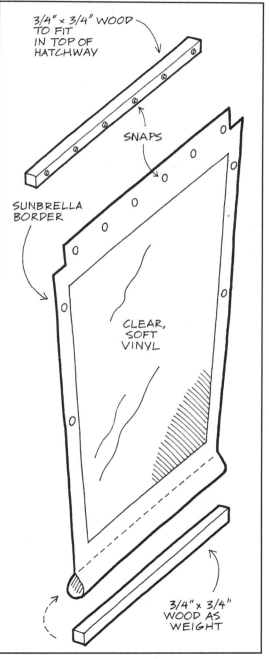

3/4" × 3/4" WOOD TO FIT IN TOP OF HATCHWAY

SNAPS

SUNBRELLA BORDER

CLEAR, SOFT VINYL

3/4" × 3/4" WOOD AS WEIGHT

Companionway storm door (Tip 95).

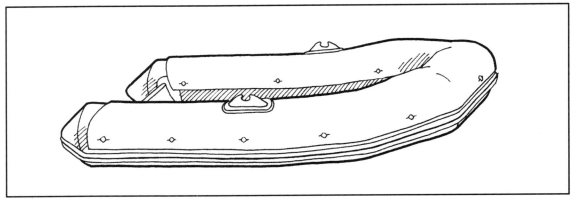

A Sunbrella cover for your inflatable dinghy's tubes (Tip 98).

Dinghy cover 98

A form-fitting Sunbrella cover for your inflatable dinghy's tubes can extend your inflatable's life expectancy by shielding the tubes from solar UV. Jeff and Donna Tousley on *Keramos* made a dinghy cover that fits over the top half of the tubes and is attached with button holes fitting over rubber buttons like those used for fastening a dodger to the dinghy. Jeff and Donna added a few buttons down each side of the tubes. *Note:* Dinghy covers are especially useful for PVC inflatables, which are much less resistant to solar UV than are Hypalon dinghies. ✐

Jeff and Donna Tousley on *Keramos*

Jeff and Donna Tousley had been cruising on their 37-foot double-headsail sloop *Keramos* for more than three years when we met them in Elizabeth City, North Carolina. They started out from Puget Sound and made their way slowly south to Panama. After transiting the Canal, they crossed to Colombia before heading north along the Caribbean coast of Central America and crossing to Key West to begin exploring the U.S. East Coast.

Jerry can covers 99

Rick and Carol Butler on *TranQuility* suggest using your old mainsail cover to make covers for your plastic jerry cans to protect them from solar UV. Particularly in the tropics or subtropics, continuous exposure to sunlight shortens the useful life of these containers. Several cruisers, in fact, reported having plastic jerry cans fail from sun damage.

Plastic gas tank covers 100

Protect your plastic gasoline tanks from the weakening effects of solar UV by making covers for them.

Sunscreen 101

Use Chapstick with SPF 15 sunblock on your nose as well as on your lips to prevent sunburn. Elaine Quayle on *The Glass Lady* says the Chapstick tends to stay where you put it and to resist perspiration better than conventional sunscreens.

Awning, Biminis, and Dodgers

Awnings

If you live in the North but are planning to go south, wait until you are in tropical or subtropical areas before getting an awning made for your boat. Canvas shops in these areas usually have considerably more experience in designing and making awnings for a wide variety of boats than do their northern colleagues.

Bimini or dodger-top window `103`

If you want windows in your bimini or the top of your dodger so that you can watch your mainsail more easily, Steve and Donna Thompson on *Donna Jean* say to keep those windows small—no larger than a foot square—and fit them with Sunbrella covers held in place using snaps or Velcro to keep the sun out when you don't want it. Large or uncovered overhead bimini or dodger windows act like a greenhouse roof and can make the cockpit very hot.

Dodger and bimini straps `104`

Put a pair of D-rings near the top of your dodger and bimini straps to make adjusting the tension easier. Most dodger and bimini straps are designed to be adjusted before you hook them in place.

Waterproofing fabric `105`

Use Thompson's Water Seal to waterproof your canvas. Although made for use on masonry and wood, it works well on fabric and is often recommended by canvas shops. You can even use it on the seams of your foulweather gear. Apply using a squeeze spray bottle or brush, and clean up overspray or drips with mineral spirits. You can find it in most hardware stores.

Below Deck

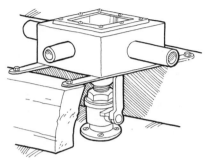

Bugs and Vermin

"If all you see are baby cockroaches, that means you brought eggs aboard and they are hatching. If there are adult roaches, they'll come out to get food for the babies and you won't see the little ones."
—Tom and Cheryl Whitaker on *Sun Shine*

General Tips

Containing bugs 106

To keep undetected bugs from spreading, keep grains, sugar, eggs, and other food staples in plastic containers with tight-fitting lids so that if bugs are in one item, they don't get a chance to move into others.

Prevention 107

In the subtropics and tropics, dip fruits and vegetables in salt water before bringing them onto the boat. If pollution makes dipping impractical, inspect fruit and vegetables carefully for bugs, removing outer leaves of leafy vegetables.

Ants

Prevention and control 108

Beware of bringing clumps of grass onto your boat. Jeff and Mary Ann Lawlor brought clumps of grass aboard *Passport* for their pet hermit crab and found it a quick way to an ant problem. They report, however, that D-Con ant traps and spray solved the problem.

Cockroaches

Prevention I 109

Do not take paper bags or corrugated cardboard boxes onto your boat—ever. Roaches and/or roach eggs may be unwelcome passengers. If, for some reason, you must bring paper bags or cardboard boxes onto the boat, unpack them immediately in the cockpit and take them ashore promptly for disposal.

Prevention II 110

In known cockroach areas, check for bugs under the eggs in egg cartons while still in the store.

Dealing with roaches 111

Ken and Penny MacKay on *Take Two* were the first of several cruisers to offer a simple but effective way to get rid of cockroaches. Mix boric acid powder with honey or sugar (add a bit of water if using sugar), forming the mixture into small balls. Put each ball on a piece of tin foil and place one or two in areas where roaches are known or suspected. As an alternative, many grocery stores and hardware stores in the United States sell small boxes of roach tablets—a mixture of boric acid (40 percent) and sugar. We can vouch for the fact that they work.

Leaving the boat I 112

Before leaving your boat for an extended period, dispose of all food items not stored in cans, bottles, or plastic containers with tight-fitting lids.

Leaving the boat II 113

Before leaving your boat for an extended period, put boric acid tablets/balls and roach traps in places where roaches might go.

Roach eggs 114

People concerned about roach eggs sometimes remove the labels from canned goods. Instead, leave the labels alone and keep one or two boric acid tablets or balls in the lockers with your cans.

Ken and Penny MacKay on *Take Two*

Canadians Ken and Penny MacKay on their 35-foot sloop *Take Two* had been cruising more than four years when we met them in the British Virgin Islands, where they had paused to work and thereby replenish their cruising kitty. For most of those four years, they had been visiting anchorages down the Caribbean island chain to Venezuela and back up to the British Virgin Islands.

If roaches do hatch, the boric acid tablets/balls will take care of the potential problem.

Roach traps 115

Put roach traps in likely places for roaches and change the traps religiously every three or four months. This way, if you do bring roaches aboard, you have a chance of getting them before they can multiply.

Flying Insects

Insect repellent 116

If using Avon's Skin-So-Soft as an insect repellent, be sure you get the oil, not the lotion. The lotion does not repel insects. Dilute the oil with equal parts of rubbing alcohol and water. Apply using a small finger pump bottle like those sold in drugstores.

No-see-ums 117

A product called Screen Pruf made by Protexall Products, Inc. of Longwood, Florida, is sold in RV stores and many hardware stores to keep no-see-ums away from your screens. The product is sold as a spray, but Philip and Marilyn Lange on *Kuan-yin* say you'll get more mileage by spraying it onto a cloth and then wiping it onto *both* sides of the screen. If sprayed, the mist goes through the screen and casts an oily sheen wherever it settles. The Langes say that one application is effective for three or four days when wiped on the screen. The Protexall Products telephone number is (407) 830-7775.

Red lights 118

At night in mosquito or gnat country, use your red interior lights (installed for keeping your night vision) for lighting the cabin. In our experience, the red lights don't attract flying insects to the same extent that white lights do.

Philip and Marilyn Lange on *Kuan-yin*

Philip and Marilyn Lange, whom we met in the British Virgin Islands after they'd been cruising for about two years, had helped build their 37-foot, cutter-rigged trimaran *Kuan-yin* from three bare hulls while living in Florida. When she was launched, they moved aboard to ready her for cruising before setting sail for the Caribbean.

Rodents

Keeping rats off the boat 119

If you must take a line ashore in an anchorage, thread the line through a metal funnel (large end facing the shore) to keep rodents from using the line as a bridge to your boat. The funnel should be near enough to your boat that if the line dips into the water, the funnel will stay dry; otherwise, the rodent can swim around the funnel and climb back onto the rope bridge. Plastic funnels won't work; a determined rodent will eat its way past a plastic barrier.

Rat traps 120

A rat can be relatively easy to get rid of if you have a trap. As Bob and Sally Greymont on *Gypsy Spray* learned, however, the hard part of the job may be finding a rat trap if you are cruising away from the United States. Their advice? Be sure to include a rat trap among your stores. As for baiting the trap, they found cheese more effective than peanut butter. The Greymonts' rat apparently came aboard via a stern line to shore. (See the previous tip, "Keeping rats off the boat.")

Weevils

Preventing weevils I   121

Put one or two bay leaves in flour, rice, cornmeal, pasta, and other dry staples to prevent weevil infestation. We don't know why it works, but we've not seen a weevil since we started doing it more than five years ago, and we did have problems before then. If we can't open and reseal a package with a bay leaf inside, we put the unopened package in a Ziploc bag with one or two bay leaves.

Preventing weevils II   122

If you have access to a microwave oven, "nuke" your grains and pastas in the microwave to kill any weevil (or other) eggs. Using a plastic container, put about a pound of the flour or grains in the microwave under high power for about 20 seconds. Then put the flour in a storage container with a bay leaf, and seal.

Decor and Decoration

"It's important to make the boat into your home, and the easiest way to do that is to decorate the interior."
                    —Nancy Hauswald on *Annie D*

General Tips

Interior woods   123

If interior wood surfaces in your cabin are dark, you can brighten the cabin by removing the varnish and using teak cleaner and bleach before recoating with a clear varnish. If the cabin is filled with dark wood, you might also consider painting some surfaces white. On a rainy or gray day, a light interior helps keep moods bright.

Plants   124

Bill and Heidi Cornell on *Ho Bo V* brightened their cabin with an African violet growing in a two-handled soup mug secured just below a cabin-top hatch by a piece of shock cord.   ☞

The mast   125

If your keel-stepped mast is exposed in the cabin, wrapping it with Ultrasuede makes the mast considerably less obtrusive visually, helping it blend into the decor by softening its surface. The Ultrasuede cover also deadens sounds from the mast. Use rubber cement to apply the Ultrasuede so you can remove it relatively easily when it needs to come off.

A two-handled mug flowerpot (Tip 124).

The personal touch I 126

On *Annie D,* Nancy Hauswald and Jon Cheston have a variety of small, lightweight decorations

Bill and Heidi Cornell on *Ho Bo V*

Bill and Heidi Cornell and Heidi's fourteen-year-old son Bob Atkinson were just two months into a planned two-year cruise to the Bahamas and Europe on their 36-foot cutter *Ho Bo V* when we met them anchored in Virginia's Great Wicomico River. It was the second cruise for the three of them. Ten years earlier, when Bob was four years old, they had sailed from their home in Ontario, Canada, to the Bahamas for fourteen months.

Jon Cheston and Nancy Hauswald on *Annie D*

After several years of living aboard and cruising on two different sailboats, Jon Cheston and Nancy Hauswald were making their first cruise south on their new 36-foot lobsterboat cruiser *Annie D* when we met them in Vero Beach. Their previous cruising had taken them from Nova Scotia to the Bahamas and the eastern Caribbean.

ranging from family photos to a dried flower arrangement that can be stowed quickly when they get underway, but which come right out again when they are at anchor or dockside.

The personal touch II 127

Chesley Logcher on *Cygnet* has a collection of owls, some of which grace the cabin interior, epoxied in place on a shelf behind the settee.

The personal touch III 128

Plastic plates and cups make a lot of sense on a moving boat. Some cruisers, however, like to bring out stoneware or china plates and mugs when sitting at anchor or securely in a slip, to add a touch of elegance to their dining.

The personal touch IV 129

In a similar vein, several cruisers noted they use cloth napkins rather than paper napkins—not only a touch of elegance, but a space saver since you don't need to carry paper napkins, and a trash saver, too.

Displaying Photos and Pictures

Changing photos 130

Changing the photos in hanging picture frames is one way of keeping your decor fresh and upbeat. To make photo-changing easy, make or purchase a frame of a size to hold standard color prints. The same frame will also accommodate postcards or the front page of some greeting cards, though these may have to be trimmed to fit. The frame should be open on the top or one side so that photos can be slid in or out without removing the frame from the bulkhead.

Hanging pictures without frames 131

Use an adhesive putty made specifically for sticking pictures onto a wall. Blu-Tac is one brand.

Mounting frames I 132

Mount wood picture frames on bulkheads, sides of lockers, and other interior surfaces using No. 8 bronze wood screws (bronze chosen for the color) countersunk just enough to make the screw head flush with the frame surface. Put one screw at the midpoint of each vertical side of the frame. Two screws should be sufficient for all but very large frames.

Mounting frames II 133

As an alternative to screwing picture frames to the bulkhead, hang the frame with a picture hook and put two small screw eyes into the bulkhead so that they will fit tightly against each side of the picture about an inch above the bottom. The hook will hold the frame up; the screw eyes will hold it in place.

Mounting frames III 134

Glue round spots of Velcro on the back of the picture frame near the corners. Measuring carefully, glue the mating spots onto the bulkhead and, after letting the glue dry for twenty-four hours, hang your frame.

Warning: For safety, do not use glass in any picture frame on your boat. If you must use something to protect the picture, use Plexiglas or the clear plastic used in dodger windows.

Rugs and Carpets

Carpeting 135

If you sail in salt water, remove your carpeting periodically for cleaning to remove any salt accumulation in the pile or backing. Since salt absorbs moisture, this will help prevent problems of mildew and mustiness which may occur in hot, humid environments. (For more on preventing and dealing with mildew, see Tips 199–207, "Mildew and Mold.")

Replacing carpet hull liner 136

Kees Oudt and Margaretha Christoffersen on *Ahoy* removed the carpet-like fabric on the hull above their berths when the fabric mildewed. In its place, they epoxied vertical strips to the hull, glued closed-cell foam between the furring strips as insulation, and covered it all with 2-inch-wide horizontal teak strips fastened to the furring strips.

Throw rugs 137

Put down a throw rug to add a touch of warmth, coziness, and color to your main saloon. Used with rubber nonskid, it will stay put. (See Tip 147, "Nonskid mats.") The advantage of throw rugs over carpets is that they are easily taken up and stored when headed offshore or in wet weather. If they do become damp, they can be hung out in the sun. Some can even be washed in fresh water and sun dried. We cruised nearly two years in the Caribbean with a wool throw rug in *Sea Sparrow*'s saloon, and it worked out well— aesthetically and functionally.

Upholstery

Protecting upholstery I 138

Terrycloth covers—essentially oversize towels—provide excellent protection for settee or dinette cushions. They are particularly useful when offshore or in windy conditions when wet crew may bring seawater below. They also help protect cushion upholstery when you've been swimming from the boat. The terrycloth covers can be washed and dried easily.

Protecting upholstery II 139

Put towels on cushions to protect them from salt, suntan lotion, and spills.

Upholstery design 140

Vinyl and cloth upholstery fabrics can be combined in slipcovers that help make the interior cozy most of the time, but provide protection from salt water when the spray is flying and the crew gets wet. Made of vinyl on the cushion's bottom and three of the four edges, with cloth upholstery fabric for the top and front edge, the cushions are placed fabric-side-up at rest. Underway, they are turned so the vinyl sides are exposed and the upholstery fabric is out of sight, therefore protected.

Windows and Hatches

Hatch curtains 141

Hatch curtains made with a liner of blackout fabric will block out sunlight and help keep the cabin cooler, assuming you have adequate ventilation or air conditioning. You can use snaps or Velcro to hold them in place. Ruffles around the edge may add decorative value.

Window curtains I 142

Curtains can be fastened to windows with snaps at the four corners. Lined on the outside (the side nearest the window) with blackout fabric, they will show a white side to the outside world and block out the sun's rays completely. To open the curtain, unsnap the bottom, roll it up, and use a piece of Velcro to hold it in place.

Window curtains II 143

Rather than using snaps to hold up your window curtains, try affixing small round spots of Velcro.

Window/hatch shades 144

As an alternative to curtains, Frank and JulAnn Allen on *Carpe Diem* installed sunscreen window shades (sold in the automotive section of discount department stores). They made small teak knobs that will accept the shade's handle when they want it to stay pulled down. The shades can also be mounted so that they are pulled horizontally across a window or mounted on the overhead for use as hatch shades.

Venetian blinds 145

Still another alternative to curtains is venetian blinds, usually made for use in homes ashore. Cruisers reported they were able to order blinds made to the width they wanted, and then simply shortened them. Brackets provided with the blinds will hold the bottom in place so it doesn't swing away from the window. The amount of light (or privacy) desired is simply a matter of adjusting the slats. The cost reportedly ranges between ten and thirty dollars per blind.

Frank and JulAnn Allen on *Carpe Diem*

When we met Frank and JulAnn Allen, they had been cruising and living aboard their 34-foot sloop *Carpe Diem* for a bit more than two years. They had sailed from their home in up-state New York to the Florida Keys, and back up to the Chesapeake Bay, stopping for part of that time in Hilton Head, where Frank had a twelve-month consulting job.

Gadgets: Interior

General Tips

Gas lighter 146

To light your stove, Skip and Gerri Smith on *Yellow Bird* suggest using the long-nosed gas lighters sold for lighting fires in a fireplace. The long-nosed lighter is also easier to use for melting rope ends than a regular lighter, which gets too hot to hold.

Nonskid mats 147

Multipurpose nonskid mats are sold in small, paper-towel-width rolls in marine chandleries. They are lacy in appearance, available in different colors, and—most important—very effective. Use them under throw rugs on the cabin sole, on countertops and shelves—wherever you want to keep things from sliding around in a seaway. (See also Tip 653, "Gimbaled counter space II.") Mats cut to plate or mug size make excellent "coasters" to keep dishes from sliding on the table.

Seawater manifold 148

A manifold to distribute seawater enables one through-hull fitting to do the work of several. On *Star Cruiser*, the seawater manifold is mounted

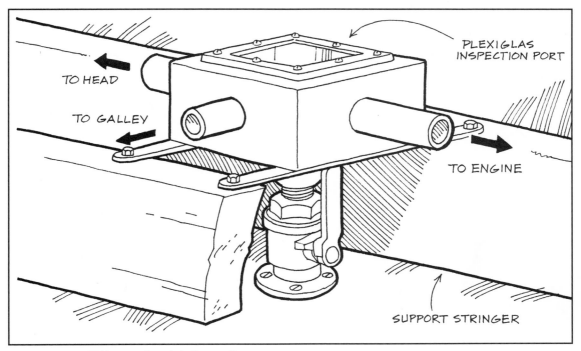

A seawater manifold lets one through-hull serve all seawater needs (Tip 148).

on a 1½-inch through-hull with seacock and distributes seawater to the engine for cooling water, the galley sink, the watermaker, and the head. A clear Plexiglas inspection port on the top of the manifold lets you look right down through the open seacock and through-hull fitting to check for any obstructions. 〜

Sliding bulkheads   149

In some boats, the top third of one or more bulkheads has been omitted to provide a sense of space below decks. The result can also be a loss of privacy. To enjoy the best of both worlds, space *and* privacy, install a movable section that slides under the side deck or into a cabinet when put away, but will fill the top section of the bulkhead when pulled out to close off an area. Because it has no structural role, your "sliding bulkhead" can be made of thin, veneered plywood. You could also use a curtain for the same purpose. *Note:* Never remove any part of a bulkhead yourself without consulting with your boat's builder to be sure you do not compromise the hull's structural integrity.

Wire fish   150

A piece of flexible stainless steel wire—³⁄₃₂- or ⅛-inch 1 x 19 rigging wire, for example—makes a useful fish when you need to run electrical wires or clear clogged hoses or pipes. The wire fish should be at least 10 feet long.

Cleaning

Vacuum cleaner   151

A good-quality 12-volt, automotive vacuum cleaner is worth its weight in gold for keeping the inside of your cabin clean. It's sometimes surprising how much dust there is in clean salt air!

Whisk brooms   152

An old-fashioned whisk broom is handy for cleaning upholstery—especially along the cording—and for getting into small corners.

Holders

Clothes hooks   153

It's easy to make teak clothes hooks that fold against the wall when not in use. All you need are scrap pieces of ¾-inch teak, a sharp knife (plus a whetstone to keep it sharp) for whittling, sandpaper, some small brass hinges, a few screws, and a bit of time and patience. Whittle a clothes hook (shaped somewhat like an upside-down comma), sand it smooth, and fasten it to the bulkhead or cabinet with a hinge. If the bulkhead or cabinet wall won't let you use ¾-inch or longer wood screws, use flathead machine screws, flat washers, and lock nuts to fasten the hinge to the wall. 〜

Liquor rack   154

To hold liquor bottles that are in use, try mounting a bar rack (used in bars to hold the bottles upside down for easy dispensing). *Blue Swanny*'s bar rack

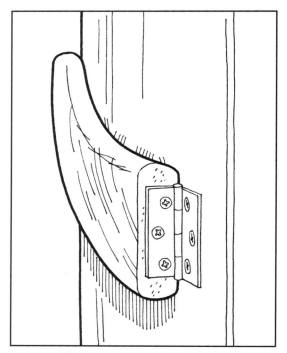

Hand-carved teak clothes hook folds flat when not in use (Tip 153).

holds five bottles and is mounted out of the way on a galley bulkhead. The bottles are held securely even in heavy weather.

Trash drawer 155

On boats where the chart table is across from the galley, the footwell for the chart table is often much larger than needed, providing a handy place for a pull-out drawer for your galley wastebasket. It's a relatively simple job to prefabricate the drawer and its own cabinet and slip the unit under the chart table. Then, with the drawer removed, fasten the cabinet securely to the cabin sole and the bulkhead at the forward end of the footwell. If possible, it's preferable to size the drawer to hold a standard kitchen wastebasket.

Lifters and Pullers

Companionway hatch puller 156

Install a bell rope on the underside of the companionway hatch to make it easier to pull the hatch open and closed.

Floorboard lifter 157

Paul and Barbara Wolter on *Economy* use an accordion-style bathroom plunger to lift floorboards or hatches in the cabin sole. Paul said the bathroom plunger works so well they have not had to put lift rings or finger holes in the cabin sole.

Mattress lifter 158

Lifting and holding up large mattresses to get into lockers under berths is often a challenge. Bob Greymont on *Gypsy Spray* met this challenge by devising a plywood "lifter" for his V-berth mattress. Using a piece of ¼-inch plywood only a little smaller than the mattress, Bob drilled a hole in the end of the plywood near the inboard corner, attached a small line, and secured an S-hook in the line's free end. When he wants to get into the lock-

ers under the mattress, he simply lifts the inboard edge of the mattress and plywood until he can hook the line to an overhead eye. The mattress is held securely while he rummages around in the lockers.

Paul and Barbara Wolter on *Economy*

When Paul Wolter retired from his longtime job as the professional skipper of a large sailing yacht, he and his wife Barbara were able to begin cruising on their own schedule on a 39-foot sloop that Paul had built from a bare hull. Summers were spent in Maine, and they sailed south every year for the winter. When we met them in Beaufort, North Carolina, seven years after Paul's retirement, they were on a new boat, *Economy*—a 32-foot lobsterboat cruiser that Paul had finished out from a hull and deck.

Heads

"You're going to be rebuilding your head more often than you expect. So you need to carry spares for spares."

—Karl Jensen on *Lorelei*

General Tips

Hanging towels · 159

Towel bars use a lot of wall space. In their place, Ron and Kathy Trossbach on *Mooneshine* suggest

Ron and Kathy Trossbach on *Mooneshine*

Ron and Kathy Trossbach began cruising more or less full-time on their 39½-foot cutter *Mooneshine* more than three years before we met them in Vero Beach. They had sailed *Mooneshine* from the Chesapeake Bay to New England and Canada and across the Atlantic to explore the coasts of Ireland, Great Britain, France, Portugal, and Spain, before crossing to the Caribbean with a stop in Madeira along the way. After cruising in the eastern Caribbean, they returned to the United States via Bermuda.

putting up shallow hooks, sewing loops onto the edge of your towels about midway down the long side, and using the loop to hang the towels on a hook. In this way, you can hang two or three towels in the space taken by one towel bar.

Toilet overflow · 160

Even toilets mounted above the waterline can let seawater siphon into the boat through the head outlet hose when sailing heeled well over. To prevent back-siphoning, make certain the head outlet hose loops high up under the deck, and install a vented loop (vacuum relief valve) at the high point of the hose. In addition, if the head outlet seacock is accessible, get into the habit of keeping it closed when the head is not in use. *Note:* You will need to clean the vacuum relief valve on your vented loop periodically.

Toilet seat lid · 161

One problem when using the head in a seaway is keeping the toilet seat lid from banging you in the back. A piece of shock cord permanently installed so that you can slip it over the lid to hold it open easily takes care of that problem. You can also simply remove the lid.

Ventilation · 162

A closed head can become very stuffy. Installing a long hook on the inside of the head door lets you secure the door mostly closed, but holds it open enough to allow ventilation. Alternatively, consider replacing the door with a curtain that can easily be left open except when needed.

Cleaning Agents

Chlorine bleach · 163

Do *not* use Clorox or other chlorine bleaches in heads having leathers in the pump—or you will soon have no leathers. Instead, use only cleaners recommended by the toilet manufacturer.

Lysol and pine oil cleaners 164

Do *not* use Lysol or pine oil cleaners in heads having rubber seals, valves, and/or piston rings; these cleaners will damage the rubber parts. Chlorine bleach, on the other hand, will not harm rubber parts and can be used safely, but should not be left in the head system more than one hour.

Holding Tanks

Controlling odors 165

Even with the Y-valve turned to direct the head discharge overboard (where it can be done legally), there may be a small amount of seepage into the holding tank—not enough to accumulate significantly, but enough to create odors. For that reason, you may need to flush and deodorize the holding tank periodically even though you're not actively using it. Alternatively, you can rinse and deodorize the holding tank by adding water and bleach through your holding tank deck plate. Chlorine bleach is by far the best holding tank deodorant we've found.

Portable holding tank 166

To make a portable holding tank, Pierre Angiel on *Defiance* suggests using a five-gallon jerry jug with a sturdy vent nipple and screw-on cap. Run a vent tube just as you would for a fixed tank, and adapt the head output hose to fit the spout. To empty the tank, disconnect the vent and head hoses, put caps on the spout and vent, and carry the tank off the boat to a disposal facility. It's just like carrying a jerry jug of water. . . . Well, almost.

Lubrication

Lanolin 167

A dab of lanolin on the head pump shaft will help extend the life of your shaft seal. Tubes of refined

lanolin are available from your pharmacist. Best, however, is anhydrous lanolin, which is much thicker in consistency and more water resistant. (See Tip 979, "Anhydrous lanolin.")

Silicone grease 168

A good silicone grease is an alternative to lanolin for lubricating the shaft of your head pump.

Vegetable oil 169

Lubricating your head pump every few days by putting a couple of tablespoons of vegetable oil into the almost empty toilet bowl and pumping it through the system will keep your head easy to pump and extend the life of the piston ring. Use the cheapest oil you can find. Pump it through with the intake water turned off. For heads with leathers, see the next tip.

Wilcox-Crittenden heads 170

A product called Sea Lube is recommended for lubricating heads with leathers. Kirk Chamberlain and Sherrie Rausch on *Moxie* say that lubricating their Wilcox-Crittenden head with Sea Lube twice a year does the trick.

Kirk Chamberlain and Sherrie Rausch on *Moxie*

Kirk Chamberlain and Sherrie Rausch had been cruising for more than ten years on their 30-foot ketch *Moxie* when we met them anchored off the island of Culebra, roughly halfway between Puerto Rico and the U.S. Virgin Islands. In that time, they had cruised the waters from Nova Scotia to Venezuela, stopping to work as needed to replenish their cruising funds.

Maintenance

Calcium deposits I   171

In tropical waters, calcium deposits form in the head system. In heads containing rubber (no leather) parts, flushing a quart of vinegar through the head on a monthly basis will help keep calcium deposits under control. With the head intake off, pour the vinegar into the bowl, pump just enough to get the vinegar into the system, and let it sit for a couple of hours. Then flush the vinegar out. Vinegar is also an effective deodorizer.

Calcium deposits II   172

Muriatic acid also can be used to clean calcium deposits from your head system, but is much more aggressive than vinegar. Add one part muriatic acid to ten parts water. Pour the acid-water mixture into the empty toilet bowl and pump the dilute acid into the head system. Let sit for about fifteen minutes, then pump it through a little farther. After another fifteen minutes, flush it through the system. *Caution: Be certain you add acid to water.* If you pour water into the acid, there will likely be a violent chemical reaction that spatters acid in all directions. *Also, do not use muriatic acid* if your head has any leather, nylon, or aluminum internal components.

Clogged head I   173

If your head appears clogged and you are using your holding tank, check to see if the holding tank is full. It may be that pumping out the holding tank will solve your problem.

Clogged head II   174

If your head system is clogged, Art and Carole Prangley on *Somewhere* suggest that you not over-look the obvious—a bathroom plunger. Before using the plunger, however, Art suggests the following: First, check all hose clamps on your head discharge hose to be sure they are firm and snug. Next, raise the piston in the head pump to its highest position so that the path from the toilet bowl to the discharge hose is open. Then, begin working the plunger gently to dislodge the stoppage.

Warning: A toilet plunger can create a lot of pressure—pressure that can pop a head discharge hose loose or rupture an inadequately vented holding tank if you overdo it. So, use the plunger judiciously and with patience.

Odors I   175

If the head smells despite your best efforts to clean and deodorize it, consider the possibility that the head intake hose needs cleaning. After closing the intake seacock, disconnect the hose at the seacock and immerse the hose end in a gallon bottle of water containing chlorine bleach (a cup of bleach to a gallon of water). Slowly pump the bleach mixture through the hose until it reaches the toilet bowl. Stop pumping and let the bleach sit in the system for fifteen minutes. Reconnect the hose end to the seacock and pump the bleach out of the system.

Odors II   176

If head odors persist after cleaning both the head and the intake hose, get someone with a sensitive nose to smell the outer surface of the head outlet hose. Over time, this hose will absorb sewage odors until the hose itself begins to smell. (See Tip 182, "Preventing smelly hoses.") When this happens, the only way to get rid of the odor is to install new hose. In fact, we now carry spare head outlet hose as part of *Sea Sparrow*'s stores.

Spare parts   177

At the least, you should have the spare parts kit offered by your head's manufacturer. Additionally, you can telephone the manufacturer and ask the technical service people what spare parts they suggest you carry along with those in the spare parts kit. It may be, for example, that you should carry three or four of a particular seal, but the spare parts kit includes only one. Then, every time you use one of your spare parts, replace it at first opportunity.

Troubleshooting   178

When all else fails, read the owner's manual for your head. The answer to your problem may be right there in black and white.

A light touch, but a serious message (Tip 179).

Using Your Head

Gentlemen—please be seated

179

On *Dolly,* Jack and Rowena Baltar have a standing rule: Everyone—men and boys included—sits down to use the head. On *Mooneshine,* the Trossbachs instruct crew and guests to sit or kneel when using the head. As these and several other cruisers have emphasized, the head on a small boat is no place for men to practice their marksmanship. In fact, there is a framed needlepoint sign in *Sea Sparrow's* head that reads: "Gentlemen: please be seated."

Guests

180

Type up instructions for using your head, laminate them in heavy plastic, put them in the head where they're readily available, and point them out to all guests.

Preventing clogged heads

181

Many cruisers—ourselves among them—have house rules about the amount of toilet paper used in any one wad. The amounts we've heard about range from three to six squares of paper at a time. Such a rule is particularly useful with guests, who may not appreciate how easily a wad of paper can stop up a marine head. Also, be sure everyone knows to pump the head clear of fecal matter before adding toilet paper. Most clogs reportedly are caused by the fecal matter and toilet paper being compressed into a solid mass.

Preventing smelly hoses

182

To help keep your head outlet hoses from picking up sewage odors, pump at least twenty-five to thirty times after all solid matter has left the bowl to be certain the head discharge lines are clear. *Note:* This tip may be impractical if you are using a holding tank.

Jack and Rowena Baltar on *Dolly*

Jack and Rowena Baltar had been taking a two- to three-month cruise every summer for more than ten years when we met them in Tenants Harbor, Maine, aboard their 38-foot sloop *Dolly.* Although the Baltars, whose home is in Florida, usually spent their summers in the Bahamas, they had sailed north to cruise the Chesapeake Bay four years earlier, and northeast that year to sample Maine's cruising waters.

Heating and Cooling

"If you have a cabin heater, hang onto it even if you think you'll never need it . . . because you will someday."

—Mike Carlson on *Ariadne*

Cabin Heater

Alcohol heater   183

For something to take the chill out of the cabin in the morning, Ron and Jayne Demers suggest a simple heater using jellied alcohol (Sterno). *Adelante*'s alcohol heater was enough to extend their New England sailing season and make their autumn trip down the Intracoastal Waterway more comfortable. *Note:* Insofar as such heaters are not vented to the outside, they should not be used with the boat closed up tight or left burning while you sleep.

Bulkhead insulation   184

On *Runinfree*, Bill Wittenfeld was concerned about heat from his cabin heater affecting the wood bulkhead behind the heater. By laying ceramic tile within a teak frame on the bulkhead behind the heater, he eliminated the source of his concern and made the heater installation more attractive. A piece of stainless steel sheet will also do the job, though it is less attractive.

Carbon monoxide warning   185

If you have a cabin heater that is not vented directly to the outside, or if you use your stove

Ron and Jayne Demers on *Adelante*

Ron and Jayne Demers were nearing the end of a one-year "between careers" cruise when we met them in Northeast Harbor, Maine. They had sailed from Connecticut on their 30-foot sloop *Adelante* the previous fall, heading for Florida, crossing to the Bahamas, and going as far south as San Salvador before turning around. Although they were planning to return to land at summer's end, they were uncertain about their future activities.

and/or an oil lamp as your cabin heater, consider buying and installing a carbon monoxide detector. It is relatively inexpensive and works much like a home smoke detector.

Heater fan   186

A 12-volt cabin fan will help circulate the warmth from your cabin heater so that your legs don't freeze while your upper body feels toasty warm.

Heater smokestack   187

Don't try to save a few dollars by using aluminum tubing instead of stainless steel for your heater smokestack. As Rick and Carol Butler on *Tran-Quility* learned, the aluminum dissipates the heat so fast that the exhaust gases cool down too much to go up the stack efficiently. In other words, aluminum smokestacks don't work.

Kerosene heaters   188

Some people have difficulty lighting kerosene heaters (and stoves) without flareups. There's a simple solution that takes all of the worry out of lighting kerosene burners. It's called a Tilley wick, and it works every time. (For detailed information about Tilley wicks, see Tips 741 and 742, kerosene "Preheating burners.")

Cabin Heater Alternatives

Companionway storm door | 189

In cold weather, a clear plastic companionway door that allows the sun to shine into the cabin will make a significant difference in warmth. The storm door can consist of Plexiglas hatch boards or a piece of flexible plastic with a fabric edge that hangs over the companionway. For additional details about making companionway storm doors, see Tips 95 and 96.

Flower pots | 190

Some cruisers carry a heavy clay flower pot that they can put upside down over a burner to serve as a radiant heater. As the pot heats up, it radiates heat from the stove into the surrounding air. *Caution:* Use potholders to remove the flower pot from the stove—even if you think it's no longer hot. The clay will retain heat much longer than you expect it to, and you cannot tell whether the flower pot is hot by looking at it.

Rick and Carol Butler on *TranQuility*

On their 42-foot ketch *TranQuility*, Rick and Carol Butler had been exploring new anchorages and revisiting their favorites—from New England to the Chesapeake Bay, down the Intracoastal Waterway to Florida, and in the Bahamas—for three-and-a-half years when we met them in Vero Beach.

Ovens | 191

Several cruisers mentioned that they do a lot of baking in cold weather because the oven helps warm the boat. However, the boat should not be closed up tight when baking, because exhaust gases may build up dangerously.

Trawler lamps | 192

A large, hanging kerosene (oil) lamp will give out a considerable amount of heat—enough to take the chill out of the cabin in a cold snap. However, you need to ensure adequate ventilation to guard against carbon monoxide poisoning—especially if the lamp is on for long hours. (See also Tip 185, "Carbon monoxide warning.")

Condensation

Preventing interior condensation | 193

A common difficulty when cruising in cold weather is formation of condensation on windows, hatches, and sometimes the interior surfaces of the hull and cabinhouse. While it's difficult to prevent condensation on windows and hatches, Paul Wolter has found that a woven hull liner fabric made by Ozite Corporation can reduce or prevent such condensation. On *Economy,* he glued the fabric directly to the fiberglass hull and cabinhouse.

Cooling the Interior

Anchoring | 194

Assuming there is at least some air moving, a boat at anchor will usually be more comfortable in hot weather than a boat at dockside because more of the breeze will blow through the cabin—unless, of course, the boat at dockside is air-conditioned!

Awnings 195

A good awning—even a makeshift one (we used spare bedsheets once)—will make a noticeable difference in interior comfort in hot weather by shading the cabinhouse from the sun. Also, though we can't prove it, we are convinced that we get more breeze in light air through *Sea Sparrow*'s cockpit with the awning up. It's as if the awning creates its own breeze.

Exterior colors 196

If you will be cruising in the tropics, or in hot summer weather, the color of your boat will make a large difference in the interior temperature. The best color is white. Even a colored covestripe running below the toerail will soak up solar heat and radiate it into the boat. You can feel this heat by opening lockers located high up under the deck: the inside of the locker will be noticeably hotter than the surrounding area.

Fans 197

Small 12-volt fans to keep air circulating can be a big help in cooling your boat. The best fans we and many of the cruisers we interviewed have found are the Hella Turbo Fans sold by many marine discount stores. Although they are relatively expensive, a major attraction of these fans is their low power consumption. They also move an impressive amount of air. (See also Tip 264, "Electric Fans.")

Window curtains 198

Sun shining through your windows provides delightful warmth in cold weather but unwanted heat in hot weather. Light-colored window curtains—if they are drawn—will help keep the interior cooler by blocking out the sun's heat energy, while letting some of the light filter through. (See also Tips 141–145, "Windows and Hatches.")

Mildew and Mold

General Tips

Exterior canvas 199

In tropical areas—especially in rivers—mildew can be a problem on bimini and dodger fabric. To combat mildew, spray affected areas of the bimini or dodger (wetting the fabric thoroughly) with a mixture of chlorine bleach and water (three tablespoons of bleach to a quart of water). Let the fabric soak for a few minutes, then rinse it completely. While chlorine bleach will generally not harm Sunbrella fabric, it may degrade the waterproof coating. (See also Tip 105, "Waterproofing fabric.")

Fenders 200

Use Tilex bathroom cleaner to clean mildew from fenders.

Mildew and mold removal 201

Clean mildewed surfaces with a solution of either vinegar and water or chlorine bleach and water. If using vinegar, mix one part white vinegar with one part water. For chlorine bleach, mix three tablespoons of bleach with a quart of water.

Boat Storage

Homemade fumigant 202

If leaving your boat in tropical or subtropical regions for more than a few days, wipe down all interior surfaces with a mixture of either vinegar and water or chlorine bleach and water. If using vinegar, mix one part white vinegar to four parts water; if chlorine bleach, two teaspoons bleach to a pint of water. Then, before closing up the boat, mix two cups of white vinegar and two cups of chlorine bleach in a plastic bowl in the galley sink as a fumigant. After ensuring that all compartment doors are open, close up the boat. We tried this system when leaving *Sea Sparrow* in Florida for a month and were delighted to find the boat mildew free upon our return. *Note:* When returning to the boat, assume that the atmosphere inside the cabin is not user-friendly and air out the interior thoroughly before spending any significant time down below.

Store-bought fumigant   203

To prevent mildew when storing your boat, Dave and Lynn Cunningham on *Genie* recommend a commercial product called Mildew Gas, which consists of a small fabric bag containing a granular substance that evaporates slowly through the bag fabric. To use, hang the bag in a holder provided and close up the boat. A bag will last from two to three months. We've bought Mildew Gas in grocery and hardware stores and have found it effective.

Dave and Lynn Cunningham on *Genie*

When we met Dave and Lynn Cunningham anchored off the Puerto Rican island of Culebra, they had been cruising for nearly a year and were on their way to Venezuela for hurricane season. *Genie*, a 43-foot cutter, had survived close calls in Charleston where they were living when Hurricane Hugo struck, and in Narragansett Bay two years later when Hurricane Bob came ashore nearby. Dave and Lynn were not anxious to try their luck with hurricanes a third time.

Preventing Mildew and Mold

Environmental control   204

Since salt absorbs moisture, you'll need to make a serious effort to keep salt out of the cabin. For example, give swimmers and their bathing suits a freshwater rinse before drying. Wear different clothes on the boat from those you use to go ashore, since going-ashore clothes often get wet. If you get doused with salt spray while sailing or in the dinghy, remove your wet clothes and dry off in the cockpit before going below. And keep deck hatches closed when going to windward!

Interior surfaces   205

Wipe all interior surfaces (the overhead, bulkheads, cabinets) every two or three months with a mixture of either one part white vinegar to four parts water, or two teaspoons of chlorine bleach to one pint of water.

Leather goods   206

Leather goods—particularly shoes—provide an excellent medium for growing mold. You'll need to remove leather items from their lockers at least monthly, wipe them with a vinegar-and-water solution, and air-dry them in the sun to keep them free of mold. (See also Tip 826, "Shoes.")

Lockers   207

Clean lockers thoroughly about every six months, wiping all surfaces with the same vinegar-and-water or chlorine bleach-and-water mixtures used for wiping interior surfaces. (See Tip 205, "Interior surfaces.")

Miscellany

General Tips

Door curtains   `208`

Mike Weizenegger and Deb Bair on *Anna* suggest using curtains in place of solid doors. Curtains provide privacy when needed, but can be taken down, rolled up, or pushed aside to allow maximum ventilation. Small Velcro tabs will serve to keep door curtains closed when desired. We can second Mike and Deb's suggestion. *Sea Sparrow*'s crew and guests have been well served by door curtains for the head and forward cabin over the years.

Interior modifications   `209`

When altering the interior arrangements in your boat, make sure that you do not block access to such vital points as through-hull fittings, hose connections, electrical wiring, and backing plates for various deck fittings.

Rattles and Bangs

Noisy doors and   `210`
door hooks

To silence those noisy cabinet and passageway doors, glue small felt pads to the corners of each door where they meet another surface. To keep door hooks from rattling, banging, or swinging back and forth when not in use, purchase extra eyes for each door hook and mount them so that

Mike Weizenegger and Deb Bair on *Anna*

Mike Weizenegger and Deb Bair were nine months into a planned one-year cruise on their 22-foot sloop *Anna* when we met them in the Abacos. They sailed from Burlington, Vermont, on Lake Champlain down the Champlain Canal and Hudson River to New York City and up into Long Island Sound before heading south to the Chesapeake Bay and the Intracoastal Waterway to Florida, where they crossed to the Bahamas.

the hook can be secured out of the way when not being used to hook the door.

Porthole dogs   `211`

If the dogs on your opening ports are marring the finish of your cabinhouse, Jim and Ronelle Cromeenes on *Dublin Dragon* suggest inserting sacrificial trim under each dog. Using the thin (approximately $\frac{3}{32}$-inch) mahogany plywood sold at hobby shops for making engine mounts on model airplanes, cut pieces to fit under each port, stain and/or varnish as desired, and glue them in place. As an alternative, you could screw small brass plates under each dog.

Securing Items

Books   `212`

On *Yellow Bird*, Skip and Gerri Smith stretch a length of $\frac{1}{4}$-inch shock cord across the face of their bookshelves to keep books where they belong while sailing. We've used the same system on *Sea Sparrow* and found it works well—even in heavy weather.

Hanging lanterns 213

Large hanging lanterns in the main cabin are handy for light and warmth. When the going gets at all rough, however, hanging lanterns can be a problem if they're not well secured. Try using sail ties or ¼-inch shock cord to secure your hanging lantern to fixed table supports or a grabrail.

Towels 214

Use clothespins to keep towels from falling off towel bars in a seaway. Clip the clothespin to the two edges of the towel just below the towel bar.

Odors

General Tips, 215–217
Bilge Odors, 218–221

General Tips

(See also Tips 165, 175, 176, and 179 for suggestions for controlling odors in the head.)

Deodorant 215

Jack and Terry Roberts on *Packet Inn* recommend an all-purpose deodorant, Nodor, whose principal commercial use is getting rid of dead-fish odors in bait wells and on boats that take people day fishing. Jack and Terry have used Nodor to get rid of a sour-milk smell in the refrigerator as well as for fish smells. It is also advertised to get rid of fuel and holding tank odors. The product is sold by the Nodor Chemical Co., Inc., Island Heights, NJ 08732.

Drawers and lockers 216

Put cedar blocks or chips in drawers and lockers to help keep them smelling fresh.

Sinks, drains, and shower sumps 217

Bill and Betz Hartge on *Alegria* were the first of many cruisers to recommend putting chlorine bleach in sink drains and shower sumps to prevent or get rid of odors. For sink drains, close the seacock and pour a quarter cup of bleach into the drain, then add water up to sink level. Let it sit about fifteen minutes before reopening the seacock. For shower sumps, pour about a half cup of bleach into the sump (add water if the sump is empty) and pump it clear after fifteen minutes. The bleach will kill any odor-causing bacteria.

Bilge Odors

Bilge odor 218

Turn off the automatic bilge pump. Add a quart of liquid chlorine bleach to a bucket of seawater and pour it into the bilge, followed by one or two more buckets of seawater. Allow the bleach-seawater mixture to slosh around in the bilge for several hours, then pump the bilge dry. Add two or three more buckets of seawater and pump that clear. This is best done on a breezy day with a bit of wave action in the anchorage so that the boat motion will help move the bleach mixture around the bilge.

Diesel fuel odor 219

Pour white vinegar into the area contaminated by diesel fuel. The vinegar clears out the diesel odor.

Preventing bilge odor 220

On *John Martin*, Pete and Yvonne Seddon use a toilet bowl brush to scrub the bilge area between their water tank and the engine with a bleach solution, roughly once a month.

Shower drains to bilge 221

Several cruisers report that draining their showers to the bilge caused an odor problem until they routinely began adding chlorine bleach to the shower-bilge water.

Screens

When sunset draws near and the mosquitoes or no-see-ums emerge, having screens in your boat can make the difference between enjoying a lovely anchorage and spending a hot summer evening huddled down below with all hatches closed. Screens need not be elaborate or expensive, but you've got to have them to use them.

Companionway

Screen I 222

Cut a larger-than-needed piece of mosquito netting, and sew several weights into one hem. Put the weighted end of the netting on top of the sliding hatch and drape the remainder over the open hatchway. Made large enough, the screen can be used with the sliding hatch open or closed.

Screen II 223

Cut nylon screening oversize to cover the vertical part of the companionway, allowing enough top and bottom for pockets to contain lengths of ¾-inch doweling. Hem all four sides so that the screen won't unravel. At the top, fold over and sew the screen material to form a pocket for a length of dowel cut to fit snugly at the top of the hatch-board slots; sew a similar dowel pocket at the bottom of the screen. The excess screening

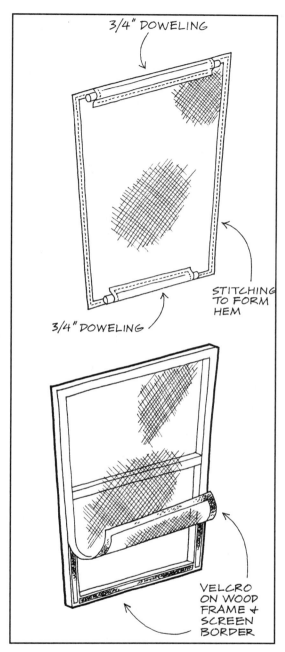

3/4" DOWELING

STITCHING TO FORM HEM

3/4" DOWELING

VELCRO ON WOOD FRAME + SCREEN BORDER

Companionway screens (Tips 223 and 224).

on the sides will overlap the companionway's vertical trim. The screen replaces your hatch boards and, with the top of the companionway closed, will keep insects outside.

Screen III 224

Make a frame that will fit in the opening normally filled by your hatch boards. Put one or two cross-pieces in the frame for security. Then either staple screen material to the exterior side of the frame using stainless steel staples, or glue and staple Velcro to the frame, sewing (and gluing) the mating half of the Velcro to your screen material with a backing strip of sturdy fabric. With this screen door in place of the hatch boards, you can close and lock the companionway sliding hatch from the inside at night, and sleep with both ventilation and security. An advantage of the Velcro system is that you can remove the screen itself from the frame for safe storage when you are not using your screen door. ☞

Dorade Vents

Screen I 225

Many marine chandleries sell round screens with flexible rubber rims made to fit in Dorade vents. You will not regret having them. Water may not enter your boat through Dorade vents, but mosquitoes will.

Screen II 226

To make screens for your Dorade vents, glue strips of Velcro to form a square frame around the vent opening. Cut nylon screen material to size. Cut strips of sturdy fabric to serve as a backing for the screening for sewing purposes. Glue and sew the mating Velcro strips to the nylon screening and backing strips.

Overhead Hatches

Screen I 227

Make a wood frame, using two thicknesses of ¼-inch x 1-inch strips from a lumberyard. Fit the frame snugly up into the hatch. Using contact cement, glue an oversize piece of nylon screening between the two frame layers. Trim away excess screening. Use turn-tabs forward and aft to hold the screen in place.

Screen II · 228

Make a sturdy wood frame to fit snugly in the hatch. Then have an aluminum-frame screen made to fit tightly within the wooden frame, using an adhesive/sealant to secure the aluminum screen in the wood frame. Use turn-tab door latches to hold the screen assembly in the hatch. The aluminum frame makes the screening easy to replace if it is damaged. The wood frame protects your hatchway from scratching and can be made to fit rounded corners.

Screen III · 229

Use mosquito netting or nylon screening with Velcro edges to make screens for overhead hatches. The noise Velcro makes when being removed has an added advantage of sounding a "burglar alarm" if someone tries to remove the screen to enter the boat while you're asleep.

Stowage

General Tips

Ceramic mugs · 230

Donna Tousley on *Keramos* used leftover fabric to make baggies for their coffee mugs to protect against breakage in a seaway. She notes also that if one of the mugs is broken, the baggie will contain the sharp fragments so they don't wind up on the floor or in a locker where someone could get hurt.

Hooks · 231

Use low-profile brass clothing hooks on bulkheads or the sides of lockers in the head, sleeping cabins, and near the companionway to hang clothes, towels, washcloths, foulweather gear.

Magazine racks · 232

Plastic magazine racks, sold at discount department stores, can be mounted out of the way on bulkheads or locker sides to hold magazines and cruising guides. These inexpensive, maintenance-free racks are solid plastic along the bottom and two sides, and latticed on the front and back.

Minimizing onboard trash · 233

As you bring provisions onto the boat, Jack and Carly Dethorn on *Jacarde* suggest taking them from their boxes or other bulky packaging materials and stowing them in plastic containers. Dry foods packaged in strong plastic bags inside a box can be stowed in the bags and the box discarded. Then, take the unneeded packaging materials ashore for proper disposal before starting or continuing on your cruise.

Securing drawers I · 234

If you have drawers with heavy items in them, install hooks and eyes or barrel bolts to secure the drawers so they can't come open in a rough seaway.

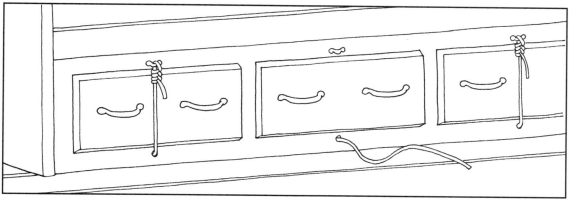

Securing drawers (Tip 235).

Securing drawers II 235

Even though drawers have notches or finger latches to keep them from opening accidentally, Gunnar Dahl and Marie Louise Sterno on *Sandra* found that they can be jolted open in a seaway. To prevent accidental openings, they suggest drilling a hole in the frame below the drawer. With the drawer removed, put a line through the hole and tie a figure-eight knot on the inside line end. Replace the drawer. Install a small padeye or mini-cleat above the drawer. With the line drawn tight across the face of the drawer and made fast at the top, the drawer will be secure even in heavy going.

Small-diameter line 236

Use the core from paper towel rolls to wind up lengths of small-diameter line for neat stowage.

Toilet paper and paper towels 237

Use a vacuum sealer made for packaging food (see Tip 781, "Seal-A-Meal") to vacuum-pack toilet paper and paper towels after first crushing the cardboard core. The rolls of paper will be greatly compressed and take up much less space. Vacuum sealers are sold in department stores and some marine stores.

"Where is it?" 238

Create a separate inventory notebook to list where each item is stowed. Develop a series of broad subjects—tools, spare parts/engine, spare parts/electrical, ropes/lines, paper products, soaps/detergents, medicines and medical supplies, maintenance supplies, etc.—so that all crew members can find what is needed quickly and accurately.

Jack and Carly Dethorn on *Jacarde*

Jack and Carly Dethorn on *Jacarde*, a 41-foot sloop, cruised along the east and west coasts of Florida and in the Bahamas before following the Thorny Path to the Caribbean. When we met them anchored at the Puerto Rican island of Culebra, they had been cruising for about two years and were heading east and south along the island chain.

Bedding and Towels

Pillow shams 239

Pillow shams are handy for stowing extra towels, bedding, and winter clothes, with the stuffed shams serving double duty as decorator pillows. When you have company, the pillow shams that previously held your guests' towels and bedding can be used to stow their clothing.

Settee pillows 240

Use spare sleeping pillows to stuff small cushions made of your settee upholstery fabric. When you have guests, retrieve the spare bed pillows from the upholstered cushions and put the covers away till the guests depart.

Sleeping bags 241

Use king-size pillow cases to stow rolled-up sleeping bags, using them as bolsters on your berth by day. At night, if you don't need the sleeping bags, just move the bolsters out of the way.

Throw pillows 242

Make bolster covers or throw pillows for use in the saloon from appropriate fabric, and stuff the bolsters or throw pillows with spare towels or blankets. Some cruisers use throw pillows to stow their everyday bedding, taking it out to make the bed in the evening, and putting it back into the pillow covers in the morning.

Clothing

Hanging lockers I 243

If you use hanging lockers for clothes, Robin and Pat Bowden on *Tournel of St. Mawes* suggest installing shock cord that you can stretch around the clothing to hold it snugly against the side of the locker. Clothing allowed to hang free in lockers will chafe if not secured against swinging when the boat rolls.

Hanging lockers II 244

To convert your hanging locker to shelf space, purchase racks of sliding wire bins from a closet outfitting store for installation in the locker. The coated wire baskets resist rust well, and the ability to slide them out makes for easy access.

Hanging nets 245

Hang small hammock nets from the overhead adjacent to the hull as additional stowage space for your clothing or for guests'.

Keeping lockers fresh 246

Put a fabric softener sheet—one of those intended for use in automatic clothes dryers—in each locker to keep it smelling fresh.

Vacuum bags 247

If you have a device for packaging food in vacuum-sealed bags (see Tip 781, "Seal-A-Meal"), Jim and Kay Stolte on *Siris IV* suggest using it to vacuum-seal clothes you won't need for a while. By drawing a vacuum on the bag, the clothes will be compressed into surprisingly small packages.

Creating Stowage Space

Bookshelves 248

Outboard lockers behind settees often are quite tall and wasteful of space. On *Lyra*, Ralph and Doris DeGroodt found they could put that wasted space to good use by installing a bookshelf against the hull across the top half of these lockers.

Bunk bags 249

Single saddlebags made of fabric, bunk bags can be hung securely against the hull along the sides of the V-berth or quarter berth and used for stowing light-weight items of clothing and other personal gear.

Drawers I 250

Drawers are convenient but often inefficient users of space. By converting drawers to lockers, you can usually increase stowage space significantly. When possible—for example, when converting drawers under a settee—make the new lockers open from the top. By removing the drawer front from the drawer itself, you can glue and/or screw it in place to close the opening left by removing the drawer. A new access panel can be provided under the settee cushion. *Note*: When converting drawers to lockers, be on the lookout for wires or hoses that

Ralph and Doris DeGroodt on *Lyra*

Ralph and Doris DeGroodt on the 31-foot cutter *Lyra* were neighbors at our marina in the Chesapeake Bay before we started cruising. When we saw them in Vero Beach, they had begun cruising every other year and were making their second trip from the Chesapeake to Florida and the Bahamas. They were also making shorter summertime cruises, and had sailed to Bermuda and New England twice.

have been run behind the drawer. You might need to shield them from the new locker's contents.

Drawers II 251

Drawers on boats often do not extend all the way out to the hull, leaving potentially usable stowage space. You can utilize this space by making auxiliary drawers that you put in first, followed by the regular drawers.

Drawers III 252

If you have drawers under your settees, there is probably space between the cabin floor and the drawer bottom that you can use to store flat items. Simply remove the drawers, stow the items, and re-place the drawers. (See also Tip 765, "Wine cellar.")

Hanging lockers I 253

Putting nets in the back of hanging lockers lets you make use of otherwise wasted space.

Hanging lockers II 254

You can often install shelves in the back of your hanging lockers, behind the hanging clothes. How-ever, be sure to use fiddles and/or shock cord to keep things from falling from the shelves when the boat heels.

Head space 255

If your boat is equipped with a shower and molded-in shower seat, ask the builder whether any use is made of space under the shower seat (say, for a holding tank). If the space is unused, John and Petra Kowalczyk on *Ragtime Duet* suggest cutting a hole in the front of the seat and installing a 5- or 6-inch deck plate so that you can stow supplies underneath the seat.

Offshore stowage 256

If your V-berth will not be used for sleeping off-shore, use that area to stow your deflated and rolled-up inflatable dinghy and other large items normally carried on deck. First, however, cover the berth with a large plastic tarp to protect your cush-ions. And finally, secure your V-berth cargo so that it cannot fall out of bed.

Pilot berth stowage 257

If you have one or more pilot berths, fit stowage bins over the foot end of the berth(s), leaving about 12 inches of vertical clearance for the sleeping crew's feet. By making the bin open aft (or forward, whichever the case may be), contents are less likely to spill in a seaway.

Shoe bag stowage 258

Shoe bags made for hanging from the closet door in your house are useful "hold-alls" on boats as well. Hang one on any bulkhead where it will be out of the way, but accessible.

V-berth 259

A small shelf over the forward third of the V-berth can provide space for such things as small sails, bedding, or paper products. Netting or "lifelines" will be needed, however, to keep everything on the shelf in rough water.

Organizing Large Lockers

Locker dividers 260

Install removable vertical locker dividers spaced to contain plastic milk crates. You can organize things in the milk crates so that they won't tumble around in a large locker.

Organizing food lockers I 261

Use plastic tubs to hold cans of food in large lockers so that the cans do not become a jumbled mess.

Organizing food lockers II 262

Mesh bags with drawstrings make excellent organizers for food lockers. Use different colors to keep like items—canned vegetables, meats, beer, and so on—together and easy to find.

Ventilation

General Tips

Deck hatch dodgers 263

If your deck hatches are reversible so that they can be opened aft, a simple dodger that snaps or hooks in place along the two sides and forward edge of the hatch box will keep light spray and rain out of the boat when going to windward or at anchor. Made of Sunbrella fabric, the dodger should fit so that the sides are taut when the hatch is open about 45 degrees.

Electric fans 264

In hot weather, one or more electric fans can make the difference between comfort below and a sweatbox. With electricity at a premium if the fans must run off the battery, Terry and Nancy Newton on *La Esmeralda* recommend Hella Turbo

Deck hatch dodger (Tip 263).

Fans. They draw from 0.2 to 0.5 amp, depending upon the fan speed—a fraction of the electrical requirements of most other 12-volt fans. We took their recommendation more than two years ago and are happy to second it.

Windscoop I 265

Install snaps on the bottom of your Windscoop and on the *outside* of the deck hatch box where you'll be using it. When rigging the Windscoop, snap the bottom of the scoop to the outside of the hatch box so that the hatch opens inside the scoop. This lets you open and close the hatch without taking down the Windscoop—very handy when a sudden shower comes up.

Windscoop II 266

Install twist fasteners or boat-cover hooks on the inside of the deck hatch where you will use the Windscoop. Similarly, install sockets for the twist fasteners or loops for the boat-cover hooks around the hem of the windscoop. Use these to secure the bottom of the Windscoop when it's in use.

Terry and Nancy Newton on *La Esmeralda*

Terry and Nancy Newton had just begun their second ten-month cruise on their 37-foot cutter *La Esmeralda* when we met them in Wrightsville Beach, North Carolina. In their first cruise three years earlier, they had sailed from their Florida home north to the Chesapeake Bay for the summer and south to the Bahamas for the winter. They were following a similar itinerary this time as well.

Cruising and Seamanship

Advice: General

"If you would have a life of carefree leisure, never marry a man who has a boat." From the comic strip "Hagar the Horrible"
— provided by Helen Roderick on *Lady Helen*

General Tips

Boat handling 267

Anytime things don't go the way they should when anchoring, docking, changing sails, reefing, and with other maneuvers, sit down afterward with the crew to review what you did, what seemed to go wrong, and what you might do differently the next time to avoid repeating the same mistakes. In other words, do not try to assign fault. Instead, use the problem as a learning opportunity.

Charts 268

Always have charts for a wide range of alternative ports, particularly if cruising along the coast or making offshore passages. Among the boats in our survey, for example, *Sea Wolf* left Beaufort, North Carolina, for the British Virgin Islands and limped engineless with almost dead batteries into San Juan, Puerto Rico. *Yeti* also left Beaufort for the British Virgin Islands, but was forced by weather to the Bahamas. Many others headed for the Caribbean from the mid-Atlantic states have made unplanned stops in Bermuda because of equipment failures or weather.

Lauren and Fran Spinelli on *Club Cheer*

Lauren and Fran Spinelli on the 41-foot ketch *Club Cheer* were on their way back to the Chesapeake Bay and the end of a one-year sabbatical cruise when we met them in Mile Hammock Bay (Camp Lejeune), North Carolina. They had made their way down the Intracoastal Waterway from the Chesapeake Bay to cruise Florida waters during the winter, but were now making plans to cruise full-time in the not-too-distant future.

Old bull/young bull 269

Lauren and Fran Spinelli on *Club Cheer* tell a story about an old bull and a young bull in a field of cows to make their point: Take it slow and easy. Don't try to see the world in two weeks. Instead, do a little at a time. Like the old bull in the Spinellis' story, you'll get a lot more from your cruising experience and enjoy it more, too.

Planning your cruise 270

Plan where you want to go, but allow for much flexibility. It's often wise to adjust your schedule and itinerary to the wind and weather—easily done if you have not made arrangements that lock you into a set plan.

Sea stories 271

Believe only a third of what you hear—and then, only the best third. The reason: people's perceptions vary. For example, Rick and Deanna Helms on *Themroc* said they have been within a mile of boats who reported having 60 knots of wind and 30-foot seas when *Themroc* was sailing in 25 knots of wind and 8- to 10-foot seas. We've had similar experiences.

Shore officials 272

Do not let yourself be intimidated by harbor officials into doing something you feel is unsafe. If an official wants you to do some paperwork before your boat is secure at anchor or dockside, tell him politely that you'll be happy to take care of it as soon as the boat is secure.

Cruising Lifestyle

Meeting other boaters 273

Take the initiative to meet other boaters by going over to their boat in your dinghy to say hello, or stopping them on the dinghy dock to introduce yourself. The people you meet are one of the best parts of cruising.

Sharing the burdens | 274

It is usually not enough to divide responsibility on a cruising sailboat. You often need to share burdens or responsibilities as well, such as cooking, dishwashing, laundry, shopping, steering, watches, maintenance, cleaning. This way, you avoid having any crewmember feel as though he or she has to do most of the "scut work."

Cruising Readiness

Acquiring useful skills | 275

If you are working on a long-term plan for cruising, take night school courses at your community college or technical high school to learn about diesel engines, refrigeration, electrical systems, canvaswork, carpentry, cabinetmaking—all skills that can be very useful while cruising.

Boat sea trials | 276

Before departing home waters, take your boat out for sea trials lasting several days to be sure that everything is in working order. Better to have things fail during a sea trial while you are still in your home waters than after you've started your cruise. The sea trials should include ten to twelve hours of straight motoring at cruising rpm.

Crew sea trials | 277

If your cruising experience is limited to weekends and short vacations in home waters, save up vacation time for a minimum four-week cruise well away from your normal sailing area. Bareboat charters are available in many of the popular cruising areas, and this will give the entire crew opportunity to sample the cruising lifestyle before you've made serious commitments to long-term cruising.

Foul weather | 278

Unpleasant—sometimes rough—weather is a part of cruising, whether you are underway or at anchor. Before casting off your shore lines for an ex-tended cruise, get out on weekends or during vacation in foul weather to learn what it's like to sail, come to anchor, and spend the night and maybe the next day or two hanging on the hook under adverse weather conditions. In this way, you can greatly reduce crew anxiety over the weather when you begin longer-term cruising. Just be sure you've learned to anchor securely in good weather before anchoring in foul weather.

What do you need? | 279

Before you go off cruising, get away from the dock for several weeks, spending most of your nights at anchor to find out what you really need to live this lifestyle—and what you don't need.

Fitting Out the Boat

Oversize gear | 280

Certain gear is critical in that failure can cause real difficulty. Anchors, anchor chain, and—for long-distance cruisers—wind vanes and autopilots fall in this category. To reduce the potential for failure of critical equipment and systems, many cruisers buy this gear in sizes or models one step larger than recommended for their boat size.

Purchasing decisions | 281

When considering whether to make a major purchase, Hal and Katie Ritenour on *Equinox* suggest living without it for a while before deciding to spend the money. You may just find that you don't need it after all.

Sails | 282

Start with good sails. Several crews commented that they had sails blow out in their first year of cruising, leading to major unexpected expense.

Used equipment | 283

If you start looking well ahead of your need, and are patient, you can buy a lot of good equipment used, including sails. Good sources range from stores specializing in used gear, to marine flea markets, to classified ads in local boating publications.

Record Keeping

Boat file
284

Sarah and Reade Tompson on *Sarasan* suggest using a 3 x 5-inch card file with alphabetized dividers to keep file cards on every cruising boat (and its crew) that you meet. Update the cards each time you encounter a boat. The file cards are handy reminders when you see a familiar boat several months or even years later. This is another of the many tips we've found particularly helpful.

Boat journal
285

Bill and Joanne Weston on *Hummingbird* are among several cruisers who recommended keeping a "boat journal" in which you record all work done on your boat, including the names and affiliations

Reade and Sarah Tompson on *Sarasan*

Reade and Sarah Tompson on the 36-foot ketch *Sarasan* are former neighbors of ours who started cruising in the early 1980s for about nine months each year, following the seasons between North Carolina and the Gulf Coast of Florida, the Keys, and the Bahamas. When we took a mooring next to them in Vero Beach to ask them for cruising tips, they were making their eleventh cruise south for the winter.

of people who do the work and comments as appropriate about the work. Also include repairs, maintenance, and installations done by your own crew.

Anchors and Anchoring

"So many people seem to be afraid of anchoring and staying at anchor overnight instead of going into a marina. But if you anchor right, you don't need to be afraid of it."

—Christian Le Roye on *Blue Swanny*

General Tips

Bow rollers
286

If your anchor rode streams over a bow roller, there should be a heavy-duty pin or rod to keep it from jumping out of the roller. If your boat is not so equipped, have the omission corrected, even if it means modifying or replacing the roller assembly.

Chafing gear
287

Always put chafing gear around your rope anchor rode or rope chain snubber where it goes through a chock or from your bow roller. We've found clear vinyl hose very effective as chafing gear and have slipped 2-foot lengths of this onto our nylon anchor rodes as permanent parts of those lines. Use light line to lash the chafing gear in place. In serious conditions, you can supplement your normal chafing gear by using duct tape to wrap a towel or other heavy fabric around the rode wherever it might chafe.

Personal space 288

As individuals, we all try to preserve our own personal space. Moreover, if someone invades our personal space, we become uncomfortable. Pete and Yvonne Seddon on *John Martin* point out that this same sense of personal space applies in an anchorage. So, when anchoring, avoid intruding upon other cruisers' personal space by giving their boats plenty of room.

Protecting the foredeck 289

Problem: Anchor chain coming off the bow roller to a windlass in a foredeck chain locker drags across a section of the deck, damaging the surface. *Solution:* Install a thin sheet of stainless steel on the deck between the stemhead fitting and anchor well. Bed the stainless sheeting well with polyurethane adhesive/sealant and fasten the edges with self-tapping panhead screws.

Securing your anchor on a bow roller 290

Use a bowline to tie a 3-foot piece of 5/16-inch line to the crown of your anchor. With the anchor on the roller, secure this line to the bow rail so that the anchor cannot go overboard unless that line is untied. When anchoring, use the same line to attach an anchor buoy with its line to the anchor.

Anchoring

Anchor buoys 291

Problem: Knowing how long to make the line on your anchor buoy. *Solution* (as provided by Guy and Joan Brooks on *Orca*): Using a light line as long as the depth of the deepest water you will anchor in, attach one end to the anchor, run the line through a shackle on your anchor buoy, and attach a one-pound weight—say, a heavy shackle that won't slip through the anchor buoy's shackle—to the free end

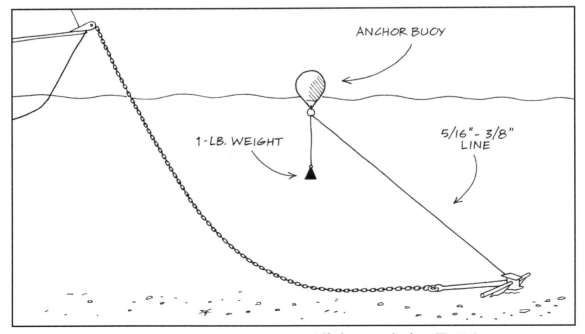

ANCHOR BUOY

1-LB. WEIGHT

5/16" - 3/8" LINE

Self-adjusting anchor buoy (Tip 291).

Guy and Joan Brooks on *Orca*

When we met Canadians Guy and Joan Brooks at Cumberland Island, Georgia, they were headed back to their home in Ontario after a one-year "sabbatical" cruise on their 35-foot cutter *Orca*. After following the New York State Barge Canal System and Hudson River to New York City, they had sailed coastwise and down the Intracoastal Waterway to the Florida Keys before crossing to the Bahamas.

of the buoy line. As the anchor is lowered, the line will run freely through the buoy's shackle to adjust to the water's depth with tension maintained by the weight on the free end. The line will also adjust automatically to tidal changes.

Anchoring in soft mud   292

A Danforth-type anchor will usually hold better than a plow anchor in soft mud because of the broad, flat surface area presented by the anchor's flukes. We've also found that being able to adjust the flukes to a deeper angle, as on a Fortress anchor, is helpful and that "heavier" is better than "lighter" in mud. Sometimes, letting the anchor work itself in for an hour or so before trying to back down on it is more effective than using the engine to dig the anchor in initially. In any case, dig the anchor in gently.

Preventing keel wraps   293

Skip and Gerri Smith on *Yellow Bird* have found that using a sentinel—a weight lowered down their nylon anchor rode to increase its catenary (curve)—keeps the rode from wrapping around their boat's fin keel. However, the sentinel must be fairly heavy—ten pounds or more.

Using plow anchors   294

To dig in a plow anchor, back down gently at first, gradually increasing power to 75 or 80 percent of your cruising rpm. If you back down hard right away, the plow may not dig in.

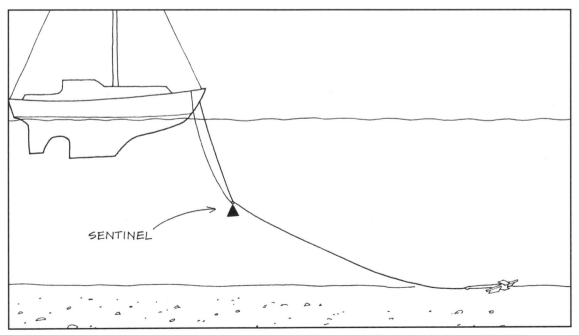

SENTINEL

Using a sentinel to prevent keel wraps (Tip 293).

Anchor Lights

Anchor lights/safety 295

Use a deck-level anchor light instead of or in addition to a masthead anchor light. From a short distance, a masthead anchor light may not be seen by boat operators looking for water-level obstacles.

Solar-powered anchor light 296

A relatively inexpensive patio light made by Siemens comes equipped with its own small solar panel, rechargeable batteries, and a photovoltaic cell to switch the light on and off as needed. Fill the stake portion with sand as ballast and seal it with epoxy. You can then hang the light above deck as an anchor light.

Anchor Rodes

Chain snubbers 297

A galvanized chain hook (from any hardware store) tied with a bowline knot to a 25-feet length of ½-inch three-strand nylon makes a worth-while snubber. Use a 3- or 4-foot piece of ⅝-inch reinforced clear plastic water hose as chafing gear for the snubber. In fair conditions, keep the snubber short; but when the wind pipes up, let the snubber out for much of its length, with a large excess of chain to ease stresses on the anchor and the boat.

Cleaning anchor chain/rode I 298

In subtropical and tropical waters, grass, scum, and barnacles will begin to grow on your anchor chain or nylon rode within a few days—but only on the first 20 feet or so below the water's surface. By putting out 20 to 30 feet more chain or nylon than needed when you first anchor, you can take in and let out those 20 to 30 feet of chain/nylon every couple of days so that the marine life doesn't become established on your

rode. This will greatly ease the task of cleaning your anchor rode when you get ready to leave the anchorage.

Cleaning anchor chain/rode II 299

If you have been anchored in one place for several days or more, check the anchor rode for marine growth two days before your planned departure. If the rode will need cleaning, do it ahead of time. It's no fun being all set for an early start only to find that you have a three-hour job of cleaning the rode before you can raise the anchor.

Marking chain length I 300

John Russell and Mary Fellows on *Joint Venture* cleaned 3-foot sections of their anchor chain at 40-foot intervals by dipping it into a bucket of phosphoric acid (OSPHO, sold at hardware stores and marine chandleries) to remove rust. Next, they spray-painted each section to mark off the 40-foot intervals, alternating the colors red, white, and blue to make it easy to tell how much chain is out.

Marking chain length II 301

Use white plastic wire ties to mark chain length. For example, at 50 feet, use one large wire tie; at 75 feet, one large and one small; at 100 feet, two large; and so on. We've used this tip for nearly three years and found it works well for us. However, be sure to carry spare wire ties; they do need replacing occasionally.

John Russell and Mary Fellows on *Joint Venture*

John Russell, Mary Fellows, and their daughter Kate were enjoying their annual month-long cruise when we met them aboard their sailboat *Joint Venture* in the British Virgin Islands. Kate was ten years old at the time. The rest of the year, they lived in their Oregon home.

Spare anchor rodes | 302

To bundle the chain leader of spare anchor rodes, fasten one end of a 3-foot length of ¼-inch line to the shackle joining the chain to the eye of the nylon rode. Thread the other end of the small line through links of chain at 18- to 24-inch intervals until you reach the end of the chain and loop it back through the shackle, making it fast. The small line secures the chain and makes it easy to move the rode and chain around.

Stowing anchor chain | 303

Always put clean chain into the chain locker. Crud from a fouled anchor chain can quickly clog the chain locker drain; it can also generate strong odors.

Stowing nylon anchor rode | 304

Dry your nylon rode on deck before putting it in the anchor locker—particularly if your anchor locker opens into the forward cabin—by laying it out in a large coil on the foredeck and lashing the coil in place if necessary. Leaving the rode out in the sun longer than necessary for it to dry, however, will shorten the nylon's useful life.

Twisted rodes | 305

When lying to two anchors in tidal waters, it's common for the rodes to get twisted. To simplify untwisting the rodes, Dave and Phyllis Carroll on *Flyway* suggest using a two-part rode joined in the middle by a shackle as your secondary rode. To untwist the rodes, pull in (or let out) the secondary rode till you reach the shackle, remove the shackle, and untwist the lines. Before removing that shackle, however, be sure that you've secured the part of the rode attached to the anchor with another line fastened below the twist, so that you don't lose it if you happen to drop the loose end.

Retrieving Stuck Anchors

Using an anchor buoy to retrieve an anchor | 306

An anchor buoy with a ⅜-inch line attached to the anchor crown provides a ready-rigged system for pulling your anchor out backwards if it becomes stuck. First, tie another line onto the buoy line to make it long enough for a good pulling angle. Then, use a snorkeling mask or viewing bucket to see how the anchor is lying. If necessary, buoy the bitter end of the anchor rode and let it all go overboard for retrieval later; alternatively, put the anchor rode in the dinghy and set the dinghy free while retrieving the anchor. Finally, position the boat to pull in the desired direction and add power as needed to free the anchor. *Note:* Dinghies with outboards usually do not have the power needed to free a stuck anchor.

Using a collar to retrieve an anchor | 307

If you do not have an anchor buoy rigged and your anchor is stuck, you can pull it out backwards by sliding a collar down the anchor rode and slipping it over the shank of the anchor up to the crown. You can use either a very large shackle (the size of your hand) or a loop of heavy chain about 6 inches in diameter. The shackle or chain loop must have the towing line attached. The procedure is as follows:

First, pull your anchor rode in tight, till it is straight up-and-down. Then put the shackle or chain collar around the taut anchor rode and lower it to the anchor. You may have to play with the collar to get it onto the shank of the anchor; you should be able to feel what's happening through the rope. Confirm using a snorkeling mask or viewing bucket that the collar has slipped onto the anchor's shank. Ease off on the anchor rode, and either let it go overboard with the end buoyed or put it in the dinghy (as described in the previous tip).

Position the boat to pull in the desired direction, working the collar down the shank of the anchor as needed. Finally, put tension on the retrieval line and increase power as needed to free the anchor.

Stern Anchors

Stern anchor rode stowage   308

On *Sunrise*, John and Maureen La Vake have installed a chain pipe in the after deck with a sturdy nylon net bag attached underneath to catch their stern anchor rode. The net bag provides a discreet "chain locker" in the lazarette and keeps the rode ready for use. Dry the anchor line after use before feeding it into the lazarette.

Stern anchor stowage   309

Using hose clamps, fasten a 15-inch length of 4-inch PVC drain pipe to a vertical section of the stern rail. Stow your stern anchor upside down with the anchor's shank in the pipe and rode attached, ready for use. The rode should lead out the top of the PVC pipe.

John and Maureen La Vake on *Sunrise*

John and Maureen La Vake were beginning their second year of cruising on *Sunrise*, a 31-foot cutter, when we met them in Annapolis. The year before, they cruised down the Intracoastal Waterway to Florida and across the Gulf Stream to the Bahamas before heading north in the spring.

Using Two Anchors

Putting out a second   310
anchor with your dinghy

First, hang the anchor over the dinghy transom so that it is 4 or 5 feet below the surface. "Fake" or coil the anchor chain/rode in the dinghy, taking on 30 to 40 feet more than you need for adequate scope. After cleating the rode on the bow cleat of the mother boat, take the dinghy out in the desired direction, paying out the rode from the dinghy. When all of the rode is out, put over the remaining chain and release the anchor. From the mother boat, take in the slack and allow the boat's motion to set the anchor. Using this system, we have on many occasions successfully put out a 45-pound CQR anchor with 20 feet of $\frac{3}{8}$-inch chain as a second anchor—sometimes rowing the anchor out, other times using the outboard on the dinghy.

Upstream/downstream   311
anchoring

When setting a downstream anchor first, run the rode through a large shackle near the stern to help keep it clear of the propeller(s). Avoid excessive slack in the line. When anchoring is completed, remove the shackle so that both rodes lead from the bow. On *Sea Sparrow*, we hang the shackle from the base of a lifeline stanchion a bit ahead of our canoe stern using a short piece of $\frac{3}{8}$-inch nylon line which acts as a shock absorber. On a boat with a squarer stern, the shackle could be hung from a stern cleat.

Caribbean Boat Boys

"Boat boys are a pain in the [neck]. There are some places we will never go back to because of them."
—Jim Cazer on *Mariah*

"Boat boys" seem to be an eastern Caribbean phenomenon, and even there they are found mostly in the Windward Islands. Generally, they are young men ranging in age from the early teens to thirty years or more who make their living by providing some real or imagined service to cruisers. Many will come out to your boat in small boats, on cast-off sailboards, or on anything else that floats (we've seen one boat boy paddling a log!); others will greet you as you go ashore, sometimes competing with each other to help you land your dinghy. All are attempting to find some way they can make a buck from you.

As Jim Cazer's comment illustrates, boat boys in the eastern Caribbean often evoke strong negative feelings among cruisers. But those who spend much time there either learn to live with boat boys or bypass islands where they've had unpleasant experiences with them. We found the tips—and insights—that follow helpful in our dealings with boat boys.

General Tips

A boat boy primer 312

Mike Hamilton and Barbara Davis on *Wild Duck* offer what is in effect a primer on dealing with boat boys. (1) Leave behind any feelings that you should not have to pay someone else to do something you can do yourself. (2) Recognize that boat boys are a part of the local economy, their role

being to provide services to visiting yachtsmen. (3) Understand that the boat boy business is highly competitive on some islands and that's why the boat boys are so aggressive in trying to get your business. (4) Think of money you spend with boat boys as one of the normal expenses of visiting those islands. (5) Understand that, as in any business, there are rules to the game. If we as visitors are going to participate, we need to know and follow those rules

Rule 1—A new boat is fair game for any boat boy.

Rule 2—Once a particular boat boy has gotten a boat as his customer, the other boat boys will leave the boat alone—so long as you let them know that John Doe is your boat boy.

Rule 3—Once you agree to give one boat boy your business, you should not use any other boat boy for anything. You cause problems that way.

Boat boy costs 313

During *Sea Sparrow*'s two-month cruise south to Venezuela, the total paid to boat boys, from our first one in Nevis to our last in the Grenadines, was $19.43 (U.S. dollars). That included buying fruits, vegetables, and ice, having a stern line taken ashore in a couple of anchorages, local guide service, and dinghy watching. Payment was in local currency.

Dealing with Boat Boys

Choosing your boat boy 314

Be cautious about choosing either the most or least aggressive among the boat boys. The most aggressive may become a pest simply because he's found that persistence pays. The least aggressive may not be respected enough among his peers to keep others from pestering you. Dave and Jan Miller on *Jewell* say the

Dave and Jan Miller on *Jewell*

Dave and Jan Miller were among the seven crews we interviewed who cruise on motorboats. We came across *Jewell,* a 51-foot semi-displacement cruiser, in the British Virgin Islands where the Millers were enjoying their third year of cruising three months a year—but this year with a new boat. They had taken delivery of *Jewell* only three weeks earlier.

best approach seems to be choosing a moderately aggressive boat boy and then doing some early business with him to cement his position as your man.

Garbage | 315

Your boat boy may offer to take your garbage ashore for you. Suggest instead that you take it together so that you can learn where it goes and that he can carry it. If you accompany your garbage ashore, it will probably wind up in an appropriate disposal place. Otherwise, it could wind up dumped overboard or behind the nearest shrub.

Learning from boat boys | 316

On some islands, your most intense contact with local people will be with your boat boy. While boat boys may know little about the world beyond their horizons, they have a lifetime of knowledge about their own country and will be delighted to tell you about themselves and their island—if you will but ask.

Negotiating prices I | 317

Most boat boys will try for the highest price possible—a price which by U.S. standards may seem cheap, but which can throw local economies out of kilter if you pay it. So, don't hesitate to negotiate down prices which seem high by local standards. For example, when a boat boy wanted too much money from us for spending half an hour to show us around town, we gave him about one-fourth of what he requested, explaining that what he asked

was more than we paid the bus driver for the two-hour minibus ride we took to get to his town. He huffed and harrumphed about it, but he also accepted it. The important point is to avoid a situation in which boat boys are paid more than skilled laborers, or minibus drivers.

Negotiating prices II | 318

To avoid misunderstanding, make sure you and your boat boy agree ahead of time on the price you'll pay for his service.

Provisioning | 319

Use your boat boy to purchase local fruits and vegetables. Frequently he'll sell you fruits that he picks himself. If you buy ice from him, it may cost you a bit more, but he'll bring it out to the boat. He can also help you find things ashore—a service worthy of a small tip.

Securing your dinghy | 320

Always secure your own dinghy—that's the advice of Jeff and Mary Ann Lawlor on *Passport.* Boat boys sometimes don't like it, but you can explain that it is your responsibility as captain to be sure the dinghy is tied up correctly. They may have suggestions about where to tie it based on their local knowledge, and, if so, you should listen. Ideally, then, you would hire the person who wanted to be helpful to watch your dinghy. (See Tip 321, "Watching your dinghy.")

Watching your dinghy | 321

Getting paid to watch visiting yachtsmen's dinghies is a time-honored way of making money for eastern Caribbean boat boys. Three keys: Agree ahead of time on the price you'll pay and what you expect from the boat boy—that your dinghy will be safe and as clean when you return as it is when you leave; pay only upon your return to the dinghy; and, pay only if your dinghy is as you left it. If, for example, local children have been playing in it and gotten it full of sand and water, you should explain to the boat boy that he didn't do his job and refuse to pay him.

Supermarket Boys

Venezuela and Colombia 322

In a variation on the theme of boat boys, you may find "supermarket boys" who approach while you're shopping to make you understand they will be at a particular checkout counter and want to push your cart to your dinghy (through the sand) and help you load your dinghy—for a tip, of course. Alternatively, you can ask the person who bags your groceries if he will push the cart to your dinghy. It's a nice service, particularly when doing a major provisioning.

Communications

Amateur (Ham) Radio

Emergency communications 323

In an emergency involving people or property, an amateur radio license is not required to transmit on ham frequencies.

Obtaining an amateur radio operator's (ham) license 324

Any electronics store selling amateur radio equipment or parts (such as Radio Shack) can provide information about obtaining an amateur radio license. Also, there are ham radio operators wherever cruisers gather, and since the hams themselves do the testing for licensing purposes, it is relatively easy to find someone to administer licensing exams.

Ham and Single-Sideband Antennas

(See also Tip 992, "Single-sideband emergency antenna.")

Low-cost antenna 325

You can make an efficient antenna for a single-sideband or ham radio from components readily available at Radio Shack for less than twenty dollars, according to Alex and Diane Allmayer-Beck on *Ariel III*. Materials include two small egg insulators and 35 feet of copper antenna wire. Attach an egg insulator at each end of the copper wire, using a small Nicopress tool to make secure fittings on the antenna wire.

Using the topping lift or spare main halyard, raise the antenna wire. Secure the lower end of the antenna and tension the wire using a length of ¼-inch line from the stern rail, through the egg insulator, and back down to the rail. Clamp the wire from your antenna tuner to your antenna, and you're in business. This antenna is easily taken down and stowed when not in use.

High Seas Telephone and Marine Operators

Credit card calls and purchases   326

Do not make credit card telephone calls or purchases over your marine radio. Make only collect calls. If ordering parts or equipment, have them sent C.O.D. The world is listening to your conversation!

Emergencies   327

If you are unable to raise the U.S. Coast Guard on your radio in an emergency situation, you can call the Coast Guard or seek emergency medical assistance through the High Seas Operator, and there is no charge for the service. Simply call the High Seas Operator, report that you have an emergency, and ask them to connect you with the U.S. Coast Guard or to a specific medical service.

Making and receiving radio telephone calls   328

Before leaving your home waters, set up an account with one or more of the High Seas telephone services, so that you can easily make calls from your boat using the single-sideband radio. At the same time, be sure that one or two friends or family members ashore understand how to use the High Seas Operator to call you should the need arise. *Note:* It is imperative that people ashore who may try to call you through the High Seas Operator understand that there are many possible reasons why you may not receive or re-

Alex and Diane Allmayer-Beck on *Ariel III*

In their first two years of cruising, Alex and Diane Allmayer-Beck on the 31-foot cutter *Ariel III* had sampled the waters from Maine to the Florida Keys and up to the Great Lakes. When we met them in Beaufort, North Carolina, they were once again headed south with plans to cruise in the Bahamas. More recently, they were planning to extend their cruising range into the Caribbean.

spond to the call, and that they should not worry about your safety simply because they have difficulty reaching you.

Single-Sideband Radio

Long-distance cruising   329

If you will be cruising in remote areas or crossing oceans and are not a ham radio user, a marine single-sideband radio can help relieve separation anxieties both for crewmembers and family left ashore. Why? Because it offers a means of communications in the event of family or personal need.

Unlike amateur radio, the marine single-sideband is intended only for marine communications. It provides a relatively simple way of maintaining contact with other boats and with coastal authorities anywhere in the world. It also enables use of the High Seas Operator for making telephone calls from your boat. Single-sideband radios often are easier to use than ham radios. In some models, authorized frequencies are preset so that the user selects channel numbers rather than dialing in radio frequencies. Single-sideband radios can be used to listen to amateur radio frequencies (you can listen to ham nets, for example), but are not intended for transmitting on those frequencies.

Telephone and Fax

International telephone calls 330

For better control over long-distance telephone costs, avoid billing calls to your credit card—it's too easy to run up a large bill, because you don't know how much you're spending. Instead, use the local telephone system to make your calls, paying as you go; that way, you know exactly how much you have spent each time you make a call. In countries where phone cards are used, you can limit the length of each call to the value of one phone card—making it easy to say good-bye because the connection will be broken when the phone card is used up.

Ordering parts 331

A fax offers perhaps the best way to communicate when ordering parts. The dealer can send you parts diagrams and lists as well as installation instructions and diagrams so that you can identify exactly what you need to install the parts correctly. Fax messages also are secure, so that you can safely communicate credit card information for billing.

Personal business calls 332

Before leaving your home area, Kathy and Conrad Johnson, Jr. on *Copasetic* suggest that you obtain the 800 numbers for any businesses or services you will be dealing with regularly. If they do not have an 800 number, many companies—such as telephone and credit card companies—will accept collect calls. Most banks and financial institutions will also accept international collect calls from their customers. Check with them to see whether they have specific procedures and/or special telephone numbers for you to use when calling collect.

Rotary-dial telephones I 333

In some areas, you will find either rotary-dial telephones or push-button phones that work differently than the touch-tone dialing system common in the United States. If you have an answering machine or use a bank or other service requiring a touch-tone system to provide proper access codes, Robert and Carol Petterson on *Star Cruiser* suggest buying a Radio Shack Pocket Tone Dialer (about ten dollars). After making your initial connection, place the Pocket Tone Dialer over the telephone mouthpiece and enter the required codes. It really does work. We bought one.

Rotary-dial telephones II 334

When placing long-distance calls from a rotary-dial telephone, use a Pocket Tone Dialer (see the previous tip) to enter your telephone credit card number to be sure you get direct-dial rates.

Telephone alternative 335

If you are frustrated when telephoning friends and family by getting answering machines or by finding those you want to speak with not at home, David and Valerie Wraight on *Dutch Maid* suggest using public fax services for your communications in lieu of the telephone.

VHF Radio

(See also Tip 993, "VHF antenna backup.")

Antenna location 336

Most sailboats have their VHF antenna mounted at the masthead to obtain maximum range. However, masthead antennas are vulnerable to lightning and other hazards. Earl and Ruth Freeman on *Mowgli*, for example, had their masthead VHF antenna broken by a bird. As a result, Earl relocated his antenna to their bimini frame—a change he recommends enthusiastically. The only loss, he says, is a small reduction in range. *Sea Sparrow's* VHF antenna has been mounted on the stern rail since the radio was installed ten years ago. We're still using the same antenna, even after being hit by lightning twice!

Troubleshooting I 337

If you have trouble transmitting—perhaps the radio thinks you are transmitting, but nobody hears you or there is a squeal when you transmit—check the antenna cable connection at the radio, at the antenna, and at any junction between those two ends. Unscrew the connections, clean the male end with emery cloth or fine sandpaper (330 or 440 grit), wipe it with alcohol, spray both male and female ends with WD-40, and re-assemble, tightening well. If that solves your

Ruth and Earl Freeman on *Mowgli*

In six years of cruising seven to eight months a year, Ruth and Earl Freeman had sailed their 38-foot cutter *Mowgli* from the Chesapeake Bay to Florida, throughout the Bahamas, and to Mexico and Central America, returning each spring to their Chesapeake Bay home. We found *Mowgli* and the Freemans in Vero Beach.

problem, wrap the connections well with electrical tape to help protect them from moisture. If that does not solve your problem, go to the next tip, "Troubleshooting II."

Troubleshooting II 338

If you have cleaned the connectors in your antenna wire and still have trouble transmitting, either take your radio to a technician to have it checked or find a friend with a similar radio (in good working order) and install your radio on his boat to test it yourself. If your radio checks out okay, start looking at the cable between your radio and your antenna. Before pulling your mast to replace the antenna cable (if you have a masthead antenna), however, make two final checks. Rig an emergency or spare antenna on the stern rail and run a cable through the cabin and cockpit to the stern rail antenna. See if you can transmit. Assuming that you can transmit using the stern rail antenna, replace your masthead antenna with the spare from the stern rail to see if a new antenna solves the problem. If so, the problem was your antenna. If not, the problem is in the antenna wire between your radio and the masthead.

Troubleshooting III 339

If you are having trouble transmitting, have cleaned the antenna connectors, need to test your radio, and have neither a radio technician nor another boat with similar radio available to do the testing, there are two ways you can test your system if you have the materials aboard.

1) Connect your fully charged handheld radio (assuming you have one) to your boat's VHF antenna system using a short adapter cable as described in Tip 994, "Handheld VHF radios." If the handheld is able to transmit through the larger radio's antenna system, the problem is almost certainly in your radio. If the handheld cannot transmit through this antenna system, most likely the problem is in the antenna or antenna wire. Before deciding that, however, we suggest the second test.

2) Rig a spare or emergency antenna on the stern rail and connect it to your radio using an an-

tenna lead that you have tested previously. If the radio will transmit through this antenna, you know the radio is okay. If it will not transmit through this antenna, you can assume the problem is in the radio. If your handheld (using the adapter cable) will transmit through the new antenna system and your big radio will not, the problem is clearly in the radio.

VHF radio range · 340

In general, the maximum range of a marine VHF radio is about 20 miles. You can estimate your radio's range by using the following formula: 1.4 times the square root of your antenna height plus 1.4 times the square root of the receiving radio's antenna height. For example, if your boat's antenna at masthead is 50 feet above the water and another boat's antenna on the stern rail is 6 feet above water, figure the maximum VHF range between your two boats by adding the square root of 50 (approximately 7) to the square root of 6 (approximately 2.5) and multiplying the sum (9.5) by 1.4 to obtain the approximate theoretical maximum range—about 13.3 miles. If the antennas on both boats were at masthead (50 feet), theoretically the maximum range between the two radios would be just under 20 miles.

Dinghies

"Cruising is sailing from place to place about 10 percent of the time. The other 90 percent of the time you're at anchor. . . . You need a good dinghy."
—Tom Owen and Patricia Baily on *Licole*

General Tips

Hard-dinghy alternative · 341

As an alternative to carrying a hard dinghy on a small sailboat during offshore passages, Alex Quintard on *Cetus* suggests buying or building an inexpensive hard dinghy when you reach your cruising area. When you are ready to move on, you can sell it to someone else.

Keeping things dry · 342

Always carry one or more large plastic garbage bags with you when going ashore to shop, do laundry, and run other errands. On the return trip, put your goodies in the garbage bag(s) and tie the tops to keep things dry. The bags can be reused many times.

Securing your dinghy I · 343

Always tie your own dinghy painter, whether going ashore, visiting another boat, or returning to your own boat. This way, as Jeff Lawlor on *Passport* points out, you are not depending on someone else's knot.

Alex Quintard on *Cetus*

Singlehander Alex Quintard helped build his 32-foot wooden cutter *Cetus,* then moved aboard to cruise. When we anchored next to him in Annapolis, Alex had been cruising for six-and-a-half years, visiting anchorages from Maine to South America and stopping to work periodically in such different places as the Virgin Islands, Bonaire in the Dutch West Indies, and Annapolis.

Securing your dinghy II   `344`

When keeping a dinghy next to your boat, hang a small fender over the side of the mother boat from the lifeline so that the dinghy snuggles against the fender rather than your topsides.

Two dinghies   `345`

Tony and Jenny Collingridge on *Stage Sea* advocate cruising with two dinghies, for a number of reasons.

For example: (1) If you go ashore in one dinghy, the second one—left behind with the boat—can enhance security by making your boat look occupied. (2) If part of the crew uses one dinghy to go visiting or ashore, the rest of the crew is not stuck on the boat. (3) If you have guests or children aboard, two dinghies provide opportunity for them to get off by themselves without isolating the others. (4) If you have a hard dinghy to go with your inflatable, you can land places where rocks, coral, or shells would quickly deflate your inflatable. (5) If you have the misfortune of having one dinghy stolen or punctured, you are not left high and dry.

Wood deck for inflatables   `346`

On *Runner*, John and Diane Rapp used a piece of ⅜-inch plywood with a reinforcing rib underneath and a fiddle across the after end as a splash rail to make a sturdy foredeck for their inflatable. To secure it to the dinghy, they drilled ¼-inch holes about an inch from the edge so they could lace the deck to buttons glued to the dinghy's inflatable sides. The plywood is sealed with epoxy. After using the deck for several weeks, they noted where it was

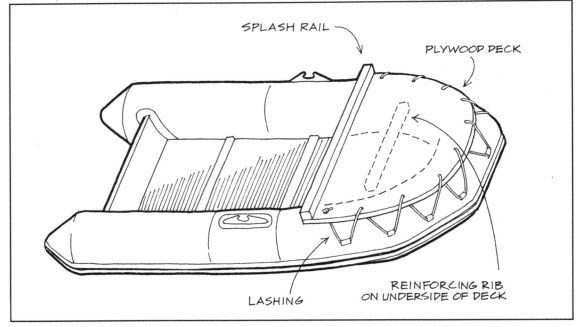

SPLASH RAIL

PLYWOOD DECK

LASHING

REINFORCING RIB ON UNDERSIDE OF DECK

A wood deck for your inflatable (Tip 346).

rubbing on the dinghy tubes and used their repair kit to apply patches as sacrificial chafe guards.

Anchoring

Anchor availability | 347

Carry your dinghy anchor with you routinely; it can't do you any good if you don't have it with you. You'll need the anchor to fish, swim, snorkel, or scuba dive from your dinghy and—most often—to hold your dinghy away from a dock, a shell-covered bulkhead, or a shell-covered beach when going ashore.

Anchor rode | 348

Fifty feet of ⁵⁄₁₆-inch nylon is not too much anchor rode for your dinghy. Smaller line is strong enough, but ⁵⁄₁₆-inch provides more chafe protection. With 4 to 6 feet of chain, a 50-foot rode should let you anchor securely in 8 to 10 feet of water.

Anchor rode shock cord | 349

When using an anchor to hold their dinghy away from a dock or bulkhead, Tom and Cheryl Whitaker on *Sun Shine* put a length of ³⁄₁₆-inch shock cord in their anchor rode. The shock cord holds their dinghy safely off the dock, but stretches enough for them to pull it up to the dock to climb on or off. We've tried it, and found it quite handy.

Recommended anchor | 350

The dinghy anchor of choice is a small Danforth or similar design. Although you must be careful with the flukes around the tubes of an inflatable, the holding power is just what's needed to keep your dinghy safely away from a dock or off the beach—even when the wind picks up. Other small anchors just don't have enough holding power in any but calm conditions.

Carrying an Inflatable

Davit alternative | 351

On *Westerner IV*, Tony and Brenda Collins installed a U-shaped stainless steel tube hinged on deck at the stern as an alternative to dinghy davits. Two block-and-tackle rigs hang from the tube for use in hoisting the dinghy. With the U-shaped tube held out from the stern at an angle of about 45 degrees above deck level, the dinghy can be raised just as if you were using davits. At this point, however, all similarity between this system and davits ends. With the motor and other gear removed from the dinghy, the U-tube itself can be pulled up until it rests vertically against the stern rail with the dinghy turned up on edge so that it lies flat against the transom and stern rail. The dinghy is then lashed securely in place. Tony says they've used this system safely offshore running before the seas in winds up to 60 knots.

Deflated on deck | 352

When daysailing on inland or coastal waters, carry the deflated dinghy either flat or rolled-up on the foredeck or cabinhouse and lashed securely. However, when sailing offshore on an overnight or longer passage, stow the dinghy in a locker or down below. If the weather deteriorates offshore, an inflatable—even deflated—on the foredeck or cabinhouse can be a serious obstacle to working the deck safely.

Inflated on deck | 353

Carry your dinghy inflated on the foredeck or cabintop only for day trips and only if it can be secured where it does not obstruct vision from the helm. Do not carry an inflated dinghy on the

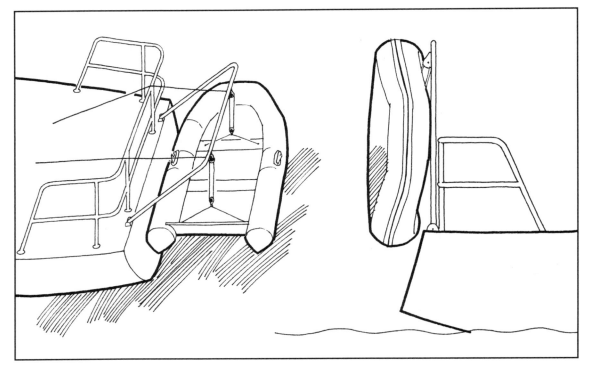

An alternative to dinghy davits for inflatables (Tip 351).

foredeck or cabinhouse for overnight or longer passages on large bodies of water. If the weather deteriorates in waters where deck-sweeping waves can develop, an inflated dinghy on deck risks unnecessary problems.

Fitting Out Your Dinghy

Dinghy painters
354

Robin and Pat Bowden on *Tournel of St. Mawes* recommend putting a snap hook or carabiner on your dinghy painter; you can then simply put the painter around a stanchion and hook it back on itself instead of taking time to tie a knot. You should, however, always make certain the painter is hooked securely.

Registration numbers
355

Use a black magic marker with permanent ink to "paint" state registration numbers on your dinghy—

Robin and Pat Bowden on *Tournel of St. Mawes*

Five years before we met them in Beaufort, North Carolina, Robin and Pat Bowden on the 40-foot cutter *Tournel of St. Mawes* left their home in England with a goal of sailing around the world. Three years later, their circumnavigation completed, they were back in England and living ashore—but only for a year before heading off once again, this time to spend two years cruising in the Caribbean and along the U.S. East Coast.

inflatable or hard. You can print them freehand as long as you make them the correct height and with the required spacing. The ink will last well over six months in the tropics. When it fades, it's an easy job to trace over the numbers again.

State registration decals 356

Decals were not made for use on the tubes of inflatable dinghies. Instead, mount the decals on the inside of the transom, port and starboard, where they are in plain sight. Putting registration decals on the transom may not meet the letter of the law, but it certainly satisfies the spirit of the law. Moreover, unlike the plastic registration number placards sold in marine stores to be hung from your dinghy, they can't be stolen.

Transom cleats 357

Jam cleats large enough to accommodate ⅜-inch line and mounted port and starboard on the inside of your dinghy transom are handy for fastening a stern anchor, towing, taking out a second anchor from your big boat, and other jobs. In fact, once you install transom cleats on your dinghy, you'll wonder how you ever got along without them.

Transom handles 358

If your dinghy does not have something you can grab handily to lift the stern, a set of transom handles makes life much easier. Sturdy brass handles big enough to accommodate your hand can be purchased inexpensively at any hardware store. Using machine screws with flat washers and locknuts, install the handles on the outside of the transom about 30 inches apart for comfortable lifting.

Maintenance and Repair

Keeping your bottom clean 359

When cruising in waters where algae, grass, and barnacles grow on boat bottoms, you can prevent fouling by lifting your dinghy out of the water once a week, giving the bottom a quick once-over with a plastic scrubber and a good rinse, and then sunning the bottom for a couple of hours.

Protecting your inflatable's fabric I 360

Do not use Armor All or any other product containing silicones on your inflatable dinghy. The silicones in these products remain on the fabric long after the wax has gone and may make repairs difficult. Glued patches won't adhere properly to dinghy fabric contaminated with silicones. Silicone reportedly can also cause seam failures when used on PVC inflatables.

Protecting your inflatable's fabric II 361

Use white Hypalon paint on the sides and top of your Hypalon inflatable to protect the fabric from solar UV and keep the tubes from heating up in the summer or tropical sun.

Removing marine growths 362

If you leave your dinghy in the water long enough for barnacles and weeds to start growing on the bottom, Karl and Carol Jensen on *Lorelei* report that a bit of chlorine bleach can save you a lot of work if your dinghy is made of wood, fiberglass, or Hypalon-coated fabric. Turn the dinghy upside down on your foredeck, and spray undiluted chlorine bleach on the marine growth. After a few minutes, when the grass has turned brown, it and any algae will just wipe off. Small barnacles will also wipe off easily with a plastic spatula and can be flushed away with water. *Note: Do not use chlorine bleach on a teak deck or a concrete dock.*

Security

(See also Tips 1,178–1,182, "Outboard Motors: Security.")

Locking your dinghy I 363

Dinghies—as are cars on land—are attractive items for theft. The villains may be locals, transients, or other boaters. As a result, it's usually impossible to determine whether it's safe to leave your dinghy unlocked in any given harbor. For that reason, lock the dinghy every time you leave it unattended.

Locking your dinghy II 364

A 20- to 25-foot length of plastic-covered lifeline wire with an eye on each end plus two rustproof padlocks is all you need to lock your dinghy. Combination locks have an advantage: you can't lose the key. Lock one end of the wire to a stainless eyebolt (see Tip 367, "Transom eyebolt") or a cleat (see Tip 357, "Transom cleats") installed on the dinghy transom. When going ashore, loop the other end of the wire around or through anything you can find to make it secure, and lock it. *Note:* Some people forgo a transom eyebolt (or cleat) and lock the security wire to their outboard motor. Only one problem: you can't lock the dinghy unless the motor is on it. With a transom eyebolt, you can use the dinghy without the motor and still lock it.

Locking your dinghy III 365

When the dinghy is alongside your boat or hanging astern, lock your security wire to a cleat or stanchion, through the toerail, or to the lifelines—always. Not only is locking the dinghy in this way a theft deterrent, it also serves as backup to the painter.

Nighttime security 366

In areas where dinghy theft is a problem, hoist your dinghy and motor out of the water at night. If you have dinghy davits, the job is easy. If not, use a halyard to lift the dinghy to deck level, running lines forward and aft to hold it in place. If your halyard winch doesn't like the weight, hang a four-part block and tackle from the halyard and use that to lift the dinghy, running the line to a sheet winch or anchor windlass. *Note:* Even though the dinghy is hanging in midair, you'll still need to lock your security wire to the boat.

Transom eyebolt 367

For attaching your security wire, a stainless steel eyebolt of ³⁄₁₆-inch minimum thickness is recommended. Two flat washers, a locknut, and bedding compound also will be needed. The eyebolt should be positioned in the middle of the transom an inch or two below the plate for the motor clamps. After installation, cut off excess bolt length and hammer out the cut end of the bolt so that the nut cannot be backed off.

Towing

Preparing the dinghy for towing 368

Remove the outboard and take all gear from the dinghy, including oars, gas tank, and anchor. If the wind picks up and you need to get the dinghy on deck while underway, gear left in the dinghy makes the job more difficult. Moreover, if the dinghy does get flipped, anything in it may be lost or damaged.

Towlines I 369

Use ³⁄₈-inch or larger polypropylene rope for towing your dinghy. It floats, and you won't have to worry about it getting caught around your propeller if you forget to pull your dinghy up close before going into reverse. For the record, conventional wisdom says to use nylon line as a tow rope because it stretches, thereby absorbing towing shock loads. However, unless your dinghy is quite heavy and you are moving quite fast, the loads on your towline normally will not be enough to stretch the nylon. So, you might as well use a line that floats. One word of caution, however: It is difficult to tie secure knots using polypropylene rope. We solved that problem by splicing the towlines to our dinghies' towing eyes and *securing* the splices

Fred Zeller on *Escort*

When we met him in the British Virgin Islands, Fred Zeller had been cruising on his 42-foot trawler *Escort* for just over a year. He started out from Lake Ontario and followed the New York State Barge Canal System, the Hudson River, and the Intracoastal Waterway to Florida before crossing to the Bahamas and island-hopping to the British Virgin Islands.

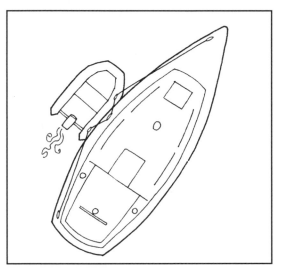

Your dinghy as a tugboat (Tip 372).

with multiple wraps of whipping twine. When making polypropylene line fast to a cleat, we use several hitches on the cleat. So far, this system has worked well.

Towlines II | 370

After having his dinghy towline chafe through, Fred Zeller on *Escort* believes in using two lines to tow your dinghy, one line to each stern cleat. The second line is insurance—a backup to the primary towline. If possible, the second towline should have its own attachment point on the dinghy. That way, you won't lose the dinghy if a towing ring fails.

Towing in open water | 371

Do not tow your dinghy in open waters; that's the advice of Jim and Terry Cazer on *Mariah*. To back up their suggestion, they tell of leaving George-town, the Bahamas, with seven other boats—all towing dinghies—and a favorable weather forecast. Six hours later, with winds of 40 knots and 15-foot seas, all the boats towing dinghies had either lost them outright or been forced to cut them loose. On one of the boats, the dinghy painter fouled the propeller and spade rudder, breaking the rudder and knocking out the transmission; that boat drifted for two days before being taken under tow by a fishing boat. *Mariah's* dinghy was on deck through all of this; they had no problems.

Tugboat Dinghy

Engine failure | 372

If your boat's engine fails, use your dinghy with its outboard motor as a tug if there is insufficient wind or maneuvering space for sailing. Tie the dinghy alongside amidships; be certain to run a spring line aft from the dinghy's transom. With someone in the dinghy to control the throttle and gearshift, use the mother boat's rudder to steer. *Note:* Do not rely on the dinghy to stop your boat's forward motion; it won't.

Diving and Snorkeling

General Tips

Buying gear   373

Purchase your snorkeling and/or scuba diving equipment before leaving home waters. You will have a much better sense of when and where the best prices are available. Moreover, it's easier to return items if there's a problem. (See also Tip 375, "Snorkeling.")

Scuba tank holder   374

Art and Lynne Bourne on *Suits Us* used 8-inch-diameter PVC pipe to make inexpensive holders for their scuba tanks. Art began by cutting the pipe into lengths equal to the height of their tanks. He then cut off the front half of each piece of pipe for about two-thirds of its length, curving the corners and sanding the edges to make them smooth. The purpose of the cutout is to make it easy to put tanks into the holders and take them out again. To mount the tank holders on deck, he used stainless steel carriage bolts, flat washers, and locknuts to secure them top and bottom to 2 x 4s fastened across two stanchions. Dive belts held between the upper 2 x 4 and PVC pipe by the top bolt on each holder serve as straps to secure the tanks.

Snorkeling   375

Learn to snorkel in a swimming pool or at a local beach before you go cruising. Not only will you learn to use the equipment in a more controlled

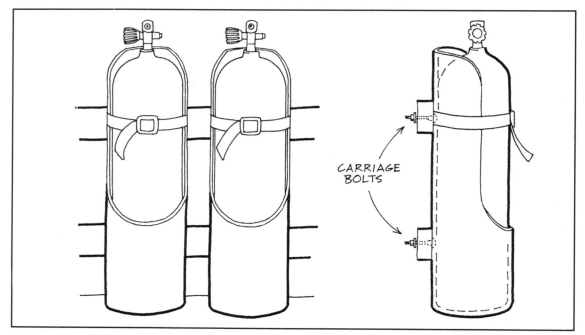

Scuba tank holder (Tip 374).

Art and Lynne Bourne on *Suits Us*

Art and Lynne Bourne were living aboard their 28-foot cutter *Suits Us* and cruising most of the time when we met them in Vero Beach. They'd been cruising for six months from North Carolina to Florida and the Bahamas, but Art had one final three-month work obligation the next year before they could begin to cruise full-time.

environment, but you'll also be able to test your gear so that you can replace uncomfortable or poor-fitting equipment while still on your home turf.

Equipment

Diving gloves 376

If you are going to dive for lobsters or fish, Bill and Linda Mueller on *Wind Weaver* suggest wearing diving gloves to protect your hands.

Wetsuits I 377

Even in tropical waters, a wetsuit will enable you to snorkel or scuba dive for longer periods. You

Bill and Linda Mueller on *Wind Weaver*

Bill and Linda Mueller on the 29-foot sloop *Wind Weaver* were nearing the end of a one-year cruise that had taken them along the coast from Maine to Florida and over to the Bahamas, where we met them. Their cruising appetite whetted, however, they were already planning a future two-year cruise.

don't need full-length suits, however. A combination of shorts and short-sleeved top will serve well in warm waters.

Wetsuits II 378

If your body shape prevents you from buying a wetsuit off the rack, consider having one custom made. Depending upon where you're located, the added cost may not be great. The added comfort, however, will be significant.

Wetsuits III 379

For cruising in non-tropical waters, a wetsuit can make the difference between being able to clear away such underwater problems as a fouled propeller by yourself or having to call for assistance. The wetsuit enables you stay in the water long enough to get the job done without suffering from hypothermia.

Working on Your Boat Bottom

Diving without tanks 380

For working on your boat's bottom, insert 40 feet of air hose between the tank and regulator. You can then leave the tank secured on deck amidships while you breathe normally through the regulator, working on the bottom without the burden of a tank on your back. Be careful to avoid fouling the long air hose.

Docking and Marinas

General Tips, 381–385
Mediterranean Moor, 386

Most of us become quite proficient in docking around our local waters. When cruising away from your home base, however, every dock you approach offers a new challenge—particularly if you're sailing for the first time in waters with strong currents or tidal flows.

General Tips

Coming up to a marina   381

Do not hesitate to ask advice from the dockmaster if you have any question about the best way to approach a dock or slip when coming up to an unfamiliar marina.

Docking in strong currents   382

Unless you can head into the current to approach or leave a dock or slip, wait for the current to ease—or even until slack tide—before making your landing or departure. Reverse gear on most sailboats is no match for a significant current from astern. Moreover, with the current astern, you cannot steer unless you're moving faster than the current.

Docking in strong winds or currents   383

If you have any question about dealing with wind or current in approaching a dock in new waters, use your VHF radio to ask about the wind and current at the dock itself. Sometimes, conditions dockside are significantly different than they are 200 feet off.

Marina strategy I   384

If you want to visit someplace where you must be in a marina, anchor nearby (or as nearby as possible) the night before so that you can arrive at the marina early in the day. This way, your one night's fee gives you most of your arrival day and half of the next—maybe till midafternoon if you ask—to do your visiting.

Marina strategy II   385

When going into a marina, don't hesitate to ask for a different slip if the one assigned is not suitable. Be sure, however, to explain why you don't like the one they've assigned—the turning area is too small, you prefer a port-hand (starboard-hand) tie-up, etc.

Mediterranean Moor

The frontal approach   386

The standard Med moor involves setting an anchor from the bow and backing up to the dock. Dick McCurdie on *Pelagic Vagrant* points out, however, that there's no reason why you must go in that way. Singlehanders, particularly, may find it makes more sense to put down a stern anchor and go up to the dock bow-first. The anchor line is handled close to the helm. You have better steering control going in bow-first. And, once the boat is secured, you'll have more privacy.

Dick McCurdie on *Pelagic Vagrant*

Dick McCurdie had been sailing singlehanded for seven years on his 36-foot double-headsail sloop *Pelagic Vagrant* when we met him in Annapolis. In those years, he had cruised throughout Europe, to the Soviet Union, Iceland, and, at the opposite temperature extreme, the Caribbean, as well as, of course, the U.S. East Coast between Florida and Maine.

Fuel

General Tips

Conserving fuel

You can greatly reduce fuel consumption—particularly if you spend much time motoring or motorsailing—by staying longer in places on your initial visit and less time backtracking to visit them a second or third time.

Testing diesel tanks for water

BOAT/U.S., West Marine, and other marine outlets sell a paste called Water Probe Indicator that you can use to test your fuel tanks for water. For a dipstick, you'll need a plastic rod or wood dowel that will reach to the bottom of your tank. Wipe the paste on the bottom 6 inches or so of your dipstick and insert it into the tank. If there is water in the tank, the paste will change color to the depth of the water.

Transferring fuel

William and Edna Baert on *Liebchen* suggest using clear plastic hose with a squeeze bulb like those used in outboard motor fuel lines for transferring fuel. Do not stow the hose, however, until it has had a couple of days to air out. We adopted this tip for transferring kerosene from our jerry cans to the stove tank and found it works well—no spillage!

Clean Fuel

Algae in diesel fuel 390

Algae are not a problem in fuel in the northern parts of the United States or Europe. In semitropical and tropical waters, however, you must add a biocide to your tank every time you take on diesel fuel, or risk the equivalent of an algae bloom in your tank that will clog filters almost as fast as you can change them. One brand of biocide is Racor; another is Biobor, which is also compatible with Racor filters.

Baja Filter 391

A Baja Filter is a special funnel/filter which lets you pump or pour diesel fuel into your tanks while screening out debris and water. The only place we have seen them for sale is at West Marine.

Buying clean diesel fuel 392

Bill Hammond on *Crazy Lady* suggests buying diesel fuel only from a high-volume dealer, and then late in the day after a number of boats have taken on fuel. Fuel docks that cater to charter boats, sport fishermen, and commercial fishermen generally have clean fuel. They can't afford the ill will that would come from delivering dirty fuel.

Fuel system vacuum gauge 393

On *Sunrise,* John and Maureen La Vake installed a vacuum gauge with their Racor filter so that they can see how hard the fuel pump is working to pull fuel through the filter. As the filter becomes clogged, the pump must work harder and harder to pull fuel through the filter. By checking the gauge regularly, you can readily tell when the filter element needs changing.

Keeping outboard motor fuel clean   394

Install a small filter in the line from your outboard's portable fuel tank to help keep dirty fuel from fouling your outboard's carburetor. Otherwise, you may find your motor cutting out one day when the water is choppy and gasoline sloshes around in the tank, stirring up the dirt that accumulates in your tank so that it gets sucked into your engine.

Jerry Cans

Hauling diesel fuel   395

In places where there are no facilities for yachts or large workboats, you will need to carry fuel out to your boat in your dinghy using jerry cans. For that reason, you should carry one or, preferably, two five-gallon jerry cans used exclusively for diesel fuel.

Plastic jerry cans   396

Plastic is the material of choice today for jerry cans of all types. However, the plastic jugs have one drawback: the plastic deteriorates gradually from exposure to sunlight, and so the containers must be replaced periodically. Two boats we've met have had plastic jerry cans fail

suddenly because of solar UV degradation from being stored continuously on deck. (See also Tip 99, "Jerry can covers.")

Stowing jerry cans of gasoline   397

Dave and Phyllis Carroll stow jerry cans of gasoline in *Flyway's* anchor well. The anchor well opens from the foredeck, is sealed off from the rest of the boat, and has a good drain overboard in case of a leak—possibly a minor water pollution problem, but much preferable to having gasoline leak down into the bilge. The anchor well also protects the plastic jerricans from the degrading effects of sunlight and keeps them secure when underway. The anchor well is organized so that the jerry jugs are firmly secured and do not interfere with anchoring or the anchor rodes.

Dave and Phyllis Carroll on *Flyway*

When we met them in Mile Hammock Bay (Camp Lejeune), North Carolina, Dave and Phyllis Carroll were one month into their fifth year of spending eight months a year cruising on their 32-foot sloop *Flyway*. They sailed each year from Island Heights, New Jersey, to the Delaware and Chesapeake Bays and along the Intracoastal Waterway to the Gulf Coast of Florida, retracing their wake in the spring.

Navigation and Piloting

"It's silly nowadays not to use a GPS. So today, I consider celestial navigation a backup to the GPS."—Dick McCurdie on *Pelagic Vagrant*

General Tips

Electronic navigation   398

Always assume that your electronics will fail—from a lightning strike in a thunderstorm, if from no other cause. (See also Tips 1,150 - 1,158, "Lightning Protection.") This way, you will stay practiced and be prepared to use traditional navigation and piloting tools, including celestial navigation, should the need arise.

GPS waypoints   399

Use GPS waypoints provided by other people with caution—even if they are printed in your favorite publication or cruising guide. There's too much opportunity for error in passing waypoints from one person to another, or in getting them into print. For example, in one publication we found that the GPS position given for the sea buoy at the island of Providencia in the western Caribbean was, in fact, a spot in the middle of reefs on the wrong side of the island.

Leadlines   400

Be sure to carry a leadline on your boat, and to have it readily available. Denis Webster on *Tiger Lily*, for example, points out the convenience of using a leadline from the dinghy to find the deep water when you run aground. Even more convenient, he says, is using the leadline from your dinghy before you run aground to sound out a channel while the big boat remains safely in deep water. Of course, a leadline also makes a handy backup to the depthsounder should it fail for any reason.

When in doubt . . .   401

When in doubt about where you are, where to turn, the water's depth—almost anything—slow down, stop, or reverse your course. By doing so, you'll give yourself more time to figure things out. Moreover, if you do make a mistake, the consequences will likely be less severe than if you had charged ahead at full speed.

Making Landfalls

GPS landfall waypoints   402

Make your landfall waypoint three or more miles short of your desired landfall to allow for discrepancies between the chart and the GPS. And even then, do not sail blindly toward the waypoint. Remember, in many cases the GPS is considerably more accurate than your chart.

Known error   403

Building a known error into your course, even in short crossings, is a time-honored technique for making sure you know which way to turn after making your landfall. If fog or rain reduces visibility, your electronics fail, or there are no distinguishing features to help you know exactly where you are, you will still know which way to turn upon making your landfall.

Noon landfalls   404

When making an overnight passage, Craig and Denise Firth on *Symphony* suggest targeting your landfall for noon. In that way, you don't have to worry about making your landfall in the dark: Your boat probably can't go fast enough to get there before sunrise, and it takes something pretty serious to slow you down until after sunset.

Sailing high | 405

If conditions permit, sail high (aim for a point upwind of your destination) for your landfall. You'll thereby have a better chance of making it in without a lot of last-minute tacking, even if there are unfavorable wind shifts. In the words of one sailor, "Distance to windward is money in the bank!"

Offshore Navigation

Celestial navigation cheat sheet | 406

If, like us, you are an occasional celestial navigator, a cheat sheet makes it much easier to work those first few sights after picking up the sextant for the first time in several months. We've outlined the process on one page of step-by-step instructions that make working sights go almost "by the numbers."

Celestial navigation computer | 407

A celestial navigation computer based on a standard calculator can greatly simplify the process for working out a sight. The computer contains nautical almanac data for many years in the future and is programmed to work sights with a minimum of input data. We have a Celesticomp navigation computer (purchased from Blue Water Books in Fort Lauderdale, Florida) on *Sea Sparrow*, but we also carry a current nautical almanac and the tables necessary for working our sights manually if necessary. We've also seen celestial navigation computers in the Defender catalog.

Celestial navigation refresher | 408

Before starting a passage, work a few practice sights to refresh your memory before you get offshore. This will also force you to make sure you have a current nautical almanac.

Chart work | 409

Update your position on the chart every six hours when offshore, more frequently if nearing the coast or other hazards. The GPS and your sextant give you latitude and longitude, but you'll need to plot them on the chart to know where you are relative to land masses or other navigational hazards.

Using GPS | 410

Log your GPS position hourly so that you always have a fix that is no more than one hour old from which to run a DR plot should the GPS go down.

Piloting

Chart marker | 411

Use black electrical tape or 3M Blue masking tape to make a small arrow for your chart. When underway, move the arrow to each buoy, turn in the river, or island as you come to it. The arrow makes it easy to keep track of your position. The system works best if you have some kind of plastic cover for the chart.

Low-tech piloting　　　412

Buy a good hand-bearing compass or binoculars with a built-in compass. Plotting the bearings on shore features provides an effective backup to electronics.

Spotlights　　　413

A hand-held spotlight can be a big help in locating unlighted navigation aids, or in reading the numbers even on lighted aids to navigation. That same spotlight, however, is a threat to your own and everyone else's night vision. To protect your night vision, the person using the spotlight should stand all the way forward on the bow so that the light does not fall on any part of the boat. To protect other boaters' night vision, use the spotlight as little as possible and be doubly careful to avoid shining the light on or toward other boats.

Offshore Sailing

"There are times when we say, 'If we get through this, we're going to sell the boat and buy a cottage in the mountains.' But once we get there, that's all forgotten."—Peter Schulz on *Kwa-Heri*

General Tips

Anchors　　　414

If you leave your anchors on the bow rollers when sailing offshore, tie them together and lash them securely to a cleat or other sturdy fitting as insurance that they cannot come loose in heavy seas. We should note, however, that many authorities recommend stowing anchors in cockpit lockers when heading offshore.

Annoying noises　　　415

A bag of small pieces of foam is handy for wedging things in place so that they can't jiggle or roll around and make noise.

Deck cargo　　　416

Keep deck cargo—jerry jugs, windsurfers, inflated dinghies—to a minimum. The risk in heavy weather of damage to the boat from deck-sweeping waves is too great. To illustrate the potential for boat damage, circumnavigator Robin Bowden on *Tournel of St. Mawes* says they lost three stanchions when deck-sweeping seas tore lee cloths from their boat.

Emergency gear　　　417

Carry bolt cutters large enough to cut the thickest stay so that you can free your mast if it comes down. The bolt cutters, which should be easily accessible, may also be useful if you become tangled in large fishnets.

New equipment　　　418

Test new equipment thoroughly before heading offshore, particularly if its failure would be significant. Singlehander David Jenkins on *Ty-DeWi*, one of several cruisers who offered this tip, says the bronze pedestal on the new club boom system for his staysail broke the third time he used it and tore the staysail. Similarly, his GPS failed three months after purchase. Most electronics failures occur during the so-called "burn-in" time—the first fifty to one hundred hours of operation. In both instances, the suppliers replaced or repaired the failed gear, but that's small consolation if new gear fails at sea.

Pre-departure checklist 419

A pre-departure checklist offers insurance against forgetting something vital before heading offshore. The checklist can be divided into two parts—things to do in the days leading up to your planned departure, and those things best left till the last day. Broadly, the first part should include tracking the weather and checking all systems, gear, engine fluids, electronics, tanks, safety equipment, and stores. The second part should include a final weather check, preparing meals and snacks, clearing the holding tank and emptying trash, topping off water tanks, stowing all gear normally used in port but not at sea, closing seacocks, and getting clothing and gear used offshore out where it will be handy.

Preventing chafe 420

Check all lines and sails each morning and late afternoon for signs of chafe. In addition, when sailing on one tack for long periods, adjust your sheets a few inches at each change of watch to prevent chafe.

David Jenkins on *Ty-DeWi*

Singlehander David Jenkins's unusual boat name, *Ty-DeWi*, is Welsh, meaning "House of David." When we met David in the British Virgin Islands he had been cruising on his 43-foot cutter for eight months, having sailed down the Hudson River from upstate New York to spend the summer in New England before heading to Beaufort, North Carolina, where three crew joined him for the offshore passage to the Virgin Islands.

Through-hull fittings 421

Close the seacocks on all but necessary through-hull fittings when making long passages. In the event of an unexplained rush of water below, you'll have fewer seacocks to deal with.

Food and Meals

Bacon 422

Dorothy Greenlee on *Cymba* suggests precooking bacon to the point at which it begins to curl, then layering it in paper towels and packing it in foil or plastic. Not only will bacon precooked this way keep well in the icebox, but it can be cooked at sea without spattering grease.

Cooking ahead 423

Unfortunately, many of us don't feel much like cooking when heading offshore until after we've had a day or two to get our sea legs. So, even though you expect to feel great from the moment you leave the dock, it's still a good idea to cook a lot of basic food before departing—such as hard-boiled eggs, boiled potatoes, rice, beans.

Dinnerware 424

Flat-bottomed serving bowls make excellent "plates" when dining offshore.

Hot meals 425

As conditions permit, prepare at least one hot meal and, preferably, two hot meals per day. It's good for the spirit. In cold, wet, or foggy weather, hot drinks and soups are good energy-boosters.

Meal planning 426

Plan two menus—one for when conditions permit using the stove to cook, the other for when it is too rough to cook safely.

Smoked ham 427

On *Tarok*, Mark and Sonja Gilg suggest getting a smoked ham and hanging it out of the way, wrapped in a kitchen towel. You can then eat the ham across the ocean, slicing off what you want as you want it. In foul weather, put the ham on a berth where it will be secure.

Snack foods 428

Snack foods are particularly important offshore. Suggestions include granola bars, candy bars, pop-top canned fruits, puddings, pâté, and baby foods in addition to crackers, pretzels, and hot drinks.

Heavy Weather

Changing headsails downwind 429

If circumstances permit—and you have a preventer securing your boom against an accidental jibe—fall off till you're sailing downwind, sheet the jib in tight, and head off a bit more. (See Tip 84, "Boom vang/preventer.") As soon as the jib loses the wind and collapses over the deck, drop it. Continue sailing off the wind until the jib is secured. If you need to put up a smaller headsail, raise the new sail in the lee of the mainsail while continuing to sail off the wind, then resume your previous course.

Changing headsails upwind 430

Heave to. With the jib backed, you can bring it down in a reasonably controlled manner, particu-

Mark and Sonja Gilg on *Tarok*

Mark and Sonja Gilg on the 37-foot sloop *Tarok* had been alternating roughly equal periods of cruising and work for six years when we met them anchored behind the reefs at the Puerto Rican island of Culebra. In that time, they had sailed from England to the Mediterranean and Aegean Seas and across the Atlantic to the Caribbean. After six to twelve months of cruising, they would fly to their home in Switzerland to work.

larly if you have a two-headsail rig and can bring the jib down against the backed staysail.

Cockpit/cabin communications 431

Install an opening port to the cockpit in the after end of the cabinhouse so that you can talk or pass small items back and forth without opening the companionway. Alternatively, put a small opening door in one of the companionway hatch boards. *Note:* If you put an opening port in the cabinhouse by the galley, it will also enhance galley ventilation.

Companionway security I 432

To keep the companionway hatch from being knocked open by waves coming into the cockpit, or in case of a knockdown, put a barrel bolt on the top companionway hatch board that will latch up into the sliding hatch.

Companionway security II 433

You need a way to keep your companionway hatch boards from falling out in a knockdown. One approach is to drill a 5/32-inch hole through the center of each hatch board. Next, run a short length of 1/8-inch line through each hole and tie a small bowline in each end of the line so that there is a 1-inch eye hanging out on each side of each hatch board. Finally, install padeyes or eyebolts inside and out at the bottom of the companionway.

In heavy weather, run a line from the padeyes (eyebolts) at the bottom of the companionway through the bowline eyes in the hatch boards, securing the boards so they cannot fall out if the boat suffers a knockdown. With bowline eyes on each hatch board, you can secure them no matter how many boards you have in the companionway at any time. By having padeyes and bowlines both inside and outside the companionway, you can secure the boards from either the cockpit or the cabin.

Food 434

Plenty of food that does not need cooking is a necessity. It should also be food you can eat when crew stomachs are queasy: canned fruits, rice or wheat cakes, crackers, granola bars, hard-boiled eggs, canned chicken or ham, small containers of pudding. Plan enough food of this type to last for your entire passage.

Reefing 435

If you wonder whether it's time to reef, the answer is yes. In other words, as soon as you begin to think about reducing sail, do it. The longer you wait, the more difficult the operation will be.

Sleeping 436

In heavy seas, put cushions on the cabin sole and sleep on the floor, if necessary. It's the place of least motion, and you cannot fall out of bed.

Safety

(See also Tips 481–484, "Safety Harnesses.")

Head safety I 437

Put handholds in the head so that you have something to hang onto when sitting on the toilet in a seaway.

Head safety II 438

An emphatic suggestion from Gunnar Dahl and Marie Louise Sterno on *Sandra*: Either remove the toilet seat lid—the part that covers everything—or secure it in the open position before heading offshore. Otherwise, that lid is a weapon pointed at your back. This is a tip we were quick to adopt, using a length of shock cord to hold *Sea Sparrow*'s toilet seat lid securely open.

Life jackets 439

Keep life jackets under the dodger secured with a piece of shock cord. This way, they are always at hand.

Offshore safety guidelines 440

Ron and Kathy Trossbach on *Mooneshine* recommend that any boat used for ocean passages be equipped to Category 1 racing safety guidelines of the Offshore Racing Council. The guidelines are included in the booklet "Recommendations for Offshore Sailing." To obtain a copy, call the U.S. Sailing Association in Portsmouth, Rhode Island, at (401) 683-0800.

Warning flare 441

Carry white aerial flares for your flare gun. If you think a ship may not see you and a collision seems possible, firing a white aerial flare may alert the captain to your presence and is legal for this purpose. Do not use a white strobe light as a warning light, because a flashing white strobe is an international distress signal and should be used only if your boat is disabled.

Sailing Comfort

Choosing your weather 442

Trying to maintain a schedule can get you into trouble with the weather. So, forget the schedule and wait patiently for a good weather window for starting your passage. Favorable weather at the beginning of a passage allows you to slip into the rhythm of the sea and watch schedule before you need to deal with adverse conditions.

Speed versus comfort 443

We now sail *Sea Sparrow* for comfort on passages rather than for speed. In practice, this approach means that we reduce sail as needed to maintain an acceptable level of boat motion. We also wait to increase sail until we're sure a drop in wind speed is real, not ephemeral. Although some passages may take a little longer than they used to, this approach to passagemaking is easier on the boat and easier on us. We sleep better, are up and down changing sail less often, and—even though we may end up spending more days at sea—we are generally much less tired at the end of a passage than we were before adopting this approach.

The *John Martin* philosophy — 444

Pete Seddon on *John Martin* recommends sailing to be comfortable when out on the ocean. "You want to wander the ocean," he says, "keeping the wind aft of the beam. But you don't want to sail straight downwind because the boat will roll too much. Instead, keep the boat heeling a bit so it's stable and doesn't roll. It doesn't hurt if the passage takes a few days longer. Going to windward or rolling with the wind astern is hard work and wears everyone out."

Seasickness

Anti-nausea suppositories — 445

Carry suppositories that will combat nausea for use if vomiting becomes severe and the person is unable to hold down fluids (water). Consult your physician.

Half-pills — 446

If one tablet of an anti-seasickness pill seems to help but makes you drowsy, try breaking the tablet in half. Some people find that a half dose (a child's dose) gives them the beneficial effect without the drowsiness.

Singlehanding

Catnaps — 447

Bill Wittenfeld on *Runinfree* catches his sleep in fifteen-minute catnaps during the night. He uses an electronic timer with "a loud, obnoxious, and persistent alarm" to wake him up to check the horizon. During daylight hours, he takes longer naps.

Radar watch — 448

Evangeliste St. Georges on *L'Eau Berge* uses his radar to keep watch while he sleeps by setting up a 360-degree alarm zone. Evangeliste says the radar alarm goes off whenever another boat or a rain squall enters the alarm zone, giving him time to wake up, evaluate the situation, and take any action needed.

Watchstanding

Hand steering — 449

When hand steering and you cannot leave the wheel, tie a line to the lee cloth of the next person on watch. When it's time to change, shake him awake by pulling the line.

Length of watch — 450

Do not automatically accept any given watch system just because it works for someone else. Experiment. For example, we finally settled on six-hour watches on *Sea Sparrow* because three- or four-hour watches did not give us long enough blocks of sleep to meet our needs.

Evengeliste St. Georges on *L'Eau Berge*

Canadian Evangeliste St. Georges had been cruising on his 35-foot cutter *L'Eau Berge* for most of six years when we met him in Beaufort, North Carolina, and was just starting on what he hoped would be a circumnavigation. In the previous six years, he had crossed the Atlantic four times—twice singlehanding, twice with crew—and cruised in the canals of France, the Mediterranean, Caribbean, and along the east coast of North America from Florida to the Gulf of St. Lawrence.

We maintain the six-hour schedule around the clock so that there is no question as to who is responsible for the boat's safety at any time and so that the off-watch person feels free to relax even during daylight hours.

Use a Walkman on night watches to listen to music, old-time radio dramas, or books on tape to help pass the time and stay awake.

Safety

"People who fall overboard aren't the first-timers. They're the old-timers who get careless."
—Dave Bennett on *Blue Ribbon*

General Tips

Boat horn 452

Even if you have a canned air or electric horn, carry a horn that relies only on good old human lung power. As Eugene Henkel on *Sea Fever* points out, canned air runs out. Batteries run down. But as long as you can breathe, you can get noise from a horn that you put to your mouth to blow.

Climbing the mast 453

Tony Collingridge on *Stage Sea* recommends using a Jumar jam cleat (mountain climbers use them to keep from falling when going up or down ropes) to provide an extra measure of safety when going up

Gene Henkel and Bill Zeisler on *Sea Fever*

Gene Henkel had been sailing for sixty years and living aboard sailboats for fifteen years when we met him with his friend Bill Zeisler on the 38-foot ketch *Sea Fever* in Vero Beach. Gene, who was seventy-seven, said he cruised about four months a year, generally along the east and Gulf coasts of Florida.

the mast. First, tie either your main halyard or a spare halyard securely to a mast cleat. Next, secure the Jumar cleat to your safety harness lead and attach it to the secured halyard, sliding it up as you go aloft. Whether you are using mast steps or a bosun's chair on another halyard, the Jumar cleat on the secured halyard will break your descent if you fall.

Cockpit whistle 454

Keep a mouth whistle handy to the wheel or tiller. If the person at the helm needs help when other crewmembers are below, a blast on the whistle will bring them topside.

Emergency ladder 455

If you do not have a permanently mounted ladder, David and Kathy Rudich on *Katie James* recommend fastening a rope ladder made with sturdy wood rungs to a stern cleat and securing the ladder to the stern rail when underway. If needed in an emergency, the ladder can be released to hang over the stern quickly.

Heaving line 456

Keep a heaving line readily accessible in the cockpit. It may be needed if a crewmember falls overboard, or if you need to get a line ashore. A compact heaving line in a weighted bag is available in marine stores.

High-water alarm 457

A high-water alarm in your bilge or, in a shallow-bilged boat, in the cabin just above the sole can be worth several times its weight in gold. If your automatic bilge pump fails or a leak develops that's too much for your pump, the alarm will alert you to the problem before it becomes a crisis.

LifeSling 458

Double-check your LifeSling at the beginning of each season (or every six months) to be sure the polypropylene rope will run freely. The middle of an emergency is not the time to discover the line is tied, tangled, or fused from excessive heat.

Propeller shaft security 459

Put a zinc collar on the shaft inside the hull. This

way, the shaft cannot be lost out the stern tube or drop back to foul the rudder if it comes loose from the coupling. And yes, it does happen . . . and could sink the boat.

Radios 460

Post simple, step-by-step instructions for using your boat's VHF, single-sideband, and/or ham radio(s) in the event of an emergency so that anyone on the boat—including guests—would be able to use the radio if needed to summon help. Test the instructions on someone who does not know how to use the radio to be sure they are clear. Also, make sure everyone knows where the instructions are posted and why.

Reflective tape 461

Put reflective tape (commonly sold at marine discount stores) on PFDs, life rings, and abandon ship bags.

Yellow dye marker 462

If sailing in a large body of water, Chris Autom and Alex Simcox on *Foamfollower* suggest carrying several yellow dye markers in your emergency equipment bag. If an air/sea rescue aircraft is trying to find your boat, putting a yellow dye marker in the water makes it much easier for them to spot you. Large orange streamers are also effective, particularly in rough areas when yellow dye would be less effective.

Emergency Bags

Abandon-ship bag I   463

Put your wallets, passports, zarpe, a copy of the ship's papers, and other important papers in a waterproof bag that you can grab to take with you no matter how fast you have to get off your boat in an emergency. Being shipwrecked is bad enough; being shipwrecked without identification and money is worse.

Abandon-ship bag II   464

Apart from your life raft, have a waterproof abandon-ship bag containing extra food, fishing gear, first aid kit, and enough closed-cell foam to ensure that the bag will float. Keep this bag readily available during any passage over a large body of water.

Abandon-ship bag III   465

Keep a 30-foot length of polypropylene rope with a carabiner clip on the end attached to your abandon ship bag so that when you throw it into the water, you can clip its tether to your harness, PFD, or around your waist until you can get the bag into the life raft.

Fire Protection

Smoke detector   466

Mount a battery-operated household smoke detector on the overhead in each major cabin. Test regularly and change the battery as recommended.

Wool-blanket fire extinguisher   467

Carry a wool blanket and stow it to be accessible quickly in case of a fire. Wool does not support combustion, and the blanket can be used to smother a fire. Moreover, it might even help you keep warm in chilly weather.

Flares

Distress flares   468

Another safety tip from *Foamfollower:* If you ever have occasion to use distress flares, use them in pairs, setting off a second flare one or two minutes after the first one has burned out. The reason: people are often not sure what they've seen with the first flare, so you need the second one for them to recognize what they're seeing and to get a bearing on it.

Flares   469

Learn how your flares work before you need them. Before test firing any distress flares, however, notify the Coast Guard and local marine police of your intent.

Flare guns   470

If you will be boating on the ocean, the Great Lakes, or some of the larger bays or sounds, do not rely on flares shot from flare guns to attract attention in an emergency. Instead, use SOLAS parachute flares, which burn three times as brightly and more than six times as long as the typical twelve-gauge flare-gun flare. Save the flare gun for use when a rescuer is headed for you and needs an

Chris Autom and Alex Simcox on *Foamfollower*

Chris Autom and Alex Simcox began their cruise by sailing from Scotland to the Mediterranean. Subsequently, they sailed from Gibraltar to the Caribbean via the Canary Islands, then up to the Bahamas and the U.S. East Coast. When we met them in Annapolis on their 37-foot sloop *Foamfollower,* they had been cruising two-and-a-half years with a long-term goal of making their way back to the British Isles by taking the long way around.

occasional flare to confirm your position. SOLAS flares are available at BOAT/U.S., West Marine, and other marine stores.

Interior Handholds

Companionway 471

Sturdy, short vertical handrails on both sides of the companionway (interior) will make it easier to climb the companionway ladder in a lively sea.

Doors 472

On *L'Eau Berge*, Evangeliste St. Georges has installed foot-long vertical handrails on each side of every interior doorway—that is, four handrails per door jamb—so that there is something to hold onto even when the door is closed if the boat lurches in a seaway.

Overhead 473

If the construction of your boat permits, install sturdy handrails on the overhead in the main saloon where they can be grabbed securely when moving about the cabin.

Jacklines

Nylon webbing 474

One-inch nylon webbing, available from most sailmakers, makes a strong jackline that will not roll under your feet. However, even though the webbing may be treated against solar UV, the nylon will be degraded by continued exposure to sunlight. To prolong their life, stow nylon webbing jacklines out of the sun when they are not needed.

Temporary jacklines 475

If your sailing requires use of jacklines only occasionally, run ½-inch nylon line along your side decks from bow cleat to stern cleat. After securing

the lines to the cleats, use a ⅛- or ¼-inch line to lash the jackline knots onto the cleats so they cannot possibly come undone accidentally.

Life Rafts

Boarding a life raft 476

Again, from *Foamfollower:* To climb into a life raft, duck down into the water and use your buoyancy and kicking to help boost yourself into the raft—much in the way you would get out of the water at the deep end of a swimming pool. Similarly, if trying to help someone else into the raft, push him down into the water and then yank him up on the rebound as the buoyant PFD pushes him up.

Life raft size 477

Do not get an extra large life raft because you think it will be more comfortable. Most life raft designs (Givens is a notable exception) include the occupants as part of the ballast. For example, two people in an eight-man raft may provide inadequate ballast and make the raft more vulnerable to capsize in high winds and seas.

Servicing your life raft 478

When having your life raft serviced, go with it to see the raft inflated and refresh your memory about its design and features. Look over all of the gear and supplies packed with the raft to see how they are stowed.

Nonskid

Location 479

Apply nonskid materials to your companionway ladder steps, cockpit coamings, and any other spots where you commonly step and there is presently no nonskid.

Gangplank nonskid 480

To put a nonskid surface on your wood gangplank, cut ½-inch wide grooves across the plank every 3 to 4 inches. The grooves, which should be about ⅛ inch deep, will keep the board from becoming slick when wet.

Safety Harnesses

Safety harness attachment point I 481

Install an eyebolt or through-bolted padeye on the bridge deck immediately outside the companionway so that you can hook on with your safety harness before leaving the cabin and your partner can go safely below before unhooking his/her safety harness. Having your harness attached on the centerline of the cockpit will also help keep you in the boat in the event of a knockdown.

Safety harness attachment point II 482

Install one or more through-bolted padeyes or eyebolts close to the steering position for the helmsman's use.

Safety tethers 483

Consider using two tethers—one long enough to reach from the companionway attachment point back to the wheel, and another much shorter tether to hook onto an eye next to the helm.

Shifting your harness tether 484

Always look to windward to check oncoming seas before moving your safety harness attachment from one point to another—for example, from a companionway eyebolt to a jackline.

Security

General Tips, 485–495
"Rob Me" Flags, 496–498
Securing Your Boat, 499–502

General Tips

Air horn alarm 485

Art and Carole Prangley on *Somewhere* suggest keeping a canned-air horn by your berth. If you have a problem—particularly at night—use the horn to sound the distress signal (five blasts on the horn). Be sure to repeat the signal several times. It will probably scare off any intruder and may also alert nearby boats to your problem.

Art and Carole Prangley on *Somewhere*

When Art and Carole Prangley on the 44-foot ketch *Somewhere* took in their docklines to begin full-time cruising, they were realizing a dream that had been in the works for twenty years. When we met them in the British Virgin Islands, they had been cruising the waters between Maine and Venezuela for more than four years.

Anchoring I 486

Your position in the fleet often determines whether you're a target for robbery. With that in mind, Pete Seddon on *John Martin* suggests anchoring well away from shore (it's harder for a thief to swim to your boat) and in the midst of several other boats. If staying a few days, get to know your neighbors so that you can keep an eye on each other's boats. If you are anchored by yourself in an anchorage with lots of space and a stranger anchors close to you, Pete suggests giving serious consideration to moving. At the least, find out who the newcomer is and assess his motive for anchoring so close to you.

Anchoring II 487

Listen to your instincts! Do not hesitate to pick up your anchor and move if you begin to feel uncomfortable about your surroundings—human or otherwise.

Assisting other boats 488

If you are out of U.S. waters, do not go to the aid of a strange boat—that's the advice of Ralph and Dorothy Greenlee on *Cymba*. Stand off, and call the Coast Guard or other appropriate authorities to request aid for the vessel in apparent distress. If people are in the water, drift your dinghy back to them to use as a lifeboat and send food and water to them if necessary, but do not bring strangers onto your boat unless you are able to establish their credentials.

Dining out 489

If you make dinner reservations over the VHF radio, Dave and Jan Miller on *Jewell* suggest making the reservation initially for one more person than is in your party. Then call back later to change the reservation to the correct number, explaining that one of your crew will be staying on the boat. That way, a thief monitoring the radio will not know your boat is left unattended. Similarly, when tying up at the dinghy dock, you can say to each other something like, "It's too bad that John had to stay on the boat."

Firearms 490

Art and Kathy Halenbeck on *Mischief* point out that firearms are a tempting and dangerous target

Art and Kathy Halenbeck on *Mischief*

In the mid-1980s, Art and Kathy Halenbeck bought a sailboat to cruise for a year along the U.S. East Coast and in the Bahamas. When we met them eight years later in Elizabeth City, North Carolina, they were halfway through a similar cruise. They had bought the 35-foot sloop *Mischief* in Oriental, North Carolina, wintered in the Bahamas, and were now headed for Maine. At their year's end, they were returning home to California.

for any thief. For that reason, any firearms on your boat should be secured out of sight in a sturdy, locked locker whenever the boat is left unattended.

Hiding cash 491

Divide your cash among several envelopes and hide each envelope in a different place. However, to keep a thief from tearing the boat apart to find your money, Mike and Susan Carlson on *Ariadne* suggest keeping one envelope of your cash in a somewhat obvious place with the hope that a thief will be satisfied upon finding that and quit looking for more.

Hitchhikers 492

Do not give anyone a ride to another anchored boat unless you know he or she belongs on that boat, or the owner is aboard to vouch for your hitchhiker. And, if you do take someone out to a boat only to find there is no one aboard, take the person back to the dock; do not leave them on the boat "to wait for Bill to come back."

Mystery vessel at night 493

If you are being shadowed at night by an unknown vessel and cannot make radio contact with it, get on the radio, call the U.S. Coast Guard, tell them the situation, give them your position, and ask for assistance. Usually, the shadowing vessel will either identify itself or leave.

Padlocks

494

Any lock for use in a marine environment should be made of stainless steel or brass and bronze so that it cannot rust. Also, combination locks have a major advantage over key locks—it's much more difficult to lose the key.

Planning your itinerary

495

Bypass places that you know are likely to have significant security problems. There are plenty of problem-free areas, so why waste your time and emotional energy on the few in which security is questionable?

"Rob Me" Flags

Dinghy names

496

Do not put your boat's name on your dinghy. It's a flag to a potential thief that your boat may be unattended.

Electronic displays

497

Cockpit displays for electronic devices are not only convenience items for the crew, but advertisements to thieves. To the extent possible, therefore, it makes sense to stow cockpit displays below deck when at anchor or, at the least, to cover them up. Also, before installation of new equipment, consider the security aspects of any cockpit displays.

New equipment

498

Ron Trossbach on *Mooneshine* notes that new equipment is more likely to be stolen than old equipment. Additionally, labels on external antennae advertise the presence of electronic gear below deck. So Ron suggests removing brand labels and using sandpaper or paint to make such equipment as dinghies, outboard motors (see Tip 1,182, "Making your motor 'ugly'"), GPS external antennae, and radar antennae look older and well used so that they are less attractive to a thief.

Securing Your Boat

(See also Tips 363–367, "Dinghies: Security," and Tips 1,178–1,182, "Outboard Motors: Security.")

Anchor light

499

Tom and Cheryl Whitaker on *Sun Shine* were the first of many cruisers to recommend hanging your anchor light so that it lights the cockpit at night instead of the foredeck. Few thieves will want to climb into a lighted cockpit. It's a tip we were quick to adopt.

Dog alarms

500

Dogs living on boats are effective crime deterrents. As a result, boats with dogs—even small ones—are seldom burglarized. (For more information about dogs on boats, see Tips 958–965, "Pets: Dogs.") ☞

Sliding companionway hatch

501

To secure your sliding companionway hatch from inside the boat, cut a length of wood to jam between the inside of the sliding hatch frame and the cabin-

Tom and Cheryl Whitaker on *Sun Shine*

When Tom and Cheryl Whitaker left the Chesapeake Bay on their 32-foot cutter *Sun Shine,* they followed the wakes of many other cruisers down the Intracoastal Waterway to Florida and across to the Bahamas. There, however, they stopped following the fleet and instead headed east offshore to the Virgin Islands, southwest to Bonaire, east along the coast of Venezuela to Trinidad, north through the Windward and Leeward Islands, and west to the British Virgin Islands, where we met them fifteen months into their cruise.

Dogs make good burglar alarms (Tip 500).

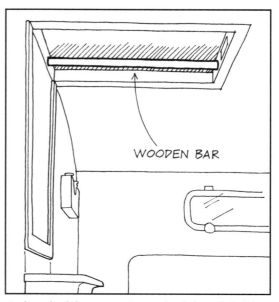

WOODEN BAR

Locking the sliding companionway hatch from the inside with a wooden bar (Tip 501).

house—much as you would use a bar to keep an intruder from opening a sliding glass door in a house or apartment. ☞

Velcro burglar alarms   502

Hatch screens held in place with Velcro make good burglar alarms whether the crew is awake or asleep,

because it's almost impossible to remove the screens surreptitiously. As the screen is removed, the Velcro will make its distinctive, loud tearing sound.

Travel Ashore

"You miss out on the best part of cruising if you don't travel away from the coast. You need to get off your boat and travel inland."
　　　　　—Jeff and Mary Ann Lawlor on *Passport*

General Tips

Public transportation   503

In the Caribbean and Central and South America, most local public transportation is in cars, vans, or even small buses that run specific routes with varying fares depending upon how far you travel. While it's a great way to travel and generally low-cost, the fare structure is sometimes confusing. For that reason, ask local people or the driver what the fare is before getting on the "bus" so that you can give the driver approximately the correct amount of money when paying your fare. *Note:* Nearly always, you pay the fare as you get off the "bus."

Taxis versus rental cars   504

Before hiring a local taxi to run errands, check the cost of renting a car. Renting a car for a day is frequently cheaper than paying multiple taxi fares, particularly if the cost is shared with one or two other couples. It is also usually more convenient for doing a lot of provisioning.

Tours versus public transportation   505

In many places, public transportation will take you within easy walking distance of major tourist attractions, providing you with the adventure of finding your way around and of experiencing the local flavor while sightseeing. A tour with a taxi driver or a tour bus, on the other hand, will cover ground faster and provide interesting commentary along the way. The tour, of course, is many times more expensive.

Tours versus rental cars   506

If you're comfortable with the idea of driving locally, check the cost of renting a car for a day before signing up for a tour to see local sights. The advantages of a rental car—particularly if shared with another couple—are significantly lower cost, the freedom to set your own schedule and itinerary, and the adventure of finding your way around in a new place. The major disadvantage of driving a rental car is that you miss the information and local insights a tour guide has to offer.

Visitor centers   507

Many communities—even in small island countries—have visitor centers. Bill and Lisa Hammond on *Crazy Lady* suggest making local visitor centers one of the first places you stop in a new port. The staff can provide all kinds of information about local attractions, directions to stores or other places of interest, public transportation, and more, making it almost always worth your while to stop in.

Bill and Lisa Hammond on *Crazy Lady*

Bill and Lisa Hammond were southbound for their second winter afloat on their 41-foot motorboat *Crazy Lady* when we met them in Annapolis. In their first year of cruising, they went north from the Chesapeake Bay to Cape Cod for the summer, then made their way south to Florida and the Bahamas before returning to the Chesapeake in the spring.

Bicycles

Bicycle choice   508

Jim and Maggie Smith on *Magic Carpet* suggest getting bicycles with large wheels and fat balloon tires. The larger wheels and fat tires provide better stability and handle potholes and rough roads better than small wheels and skinny tires. Jim and Maggie's folding bikes have 20-inch wheels.

Stowing bicycles   509

When sailing conditions are likely to result in spray on deck, stow your bicycles below if possible. They'll last much longer and require less maintenance. The V-berth, usually out of use in vigorous sailing conditions, can often be used as a garage, but be sure the bikes are well secured.

Inland Travel

Expanding your horizons   510

Plan your cruise so that you stop in harbors where you can leave your boat safely for inland travel. On a small island, a day trip may be all that's possible. In the Americas and other continental landmasses, however, opportunities for inland travel are limited only by your budget and imagination.

Visiting Other Countries

General Tips

Cruising guides   511

Next to navigational charts, a good cruising guide is the most valuable source of information you can have on your boat when cruising in another country. It will not only provide information about anchorages, but also about entry procedures, money matters, local customs, history, and sources of supplies. (See also Tips 522 and 523, "Travel guides.")

Dealing with cultural   512
differences

In Latin American countries, expect things to take longer than promised. One reason is that time is not as important in the Latin culture as it is to most North Americans and Northern Europeans. Another is that culturally it is very difficult for most Latinos to disappoint you by saying they cannot do what you want—even when asked directly. Instead, they are more likely to promise you something because they believe that's what you want to hear rather than disappoint you by saying they cannot deliver what you want when you want it.

Flying your flag   513

Always fly your ship's flag to show your nation-ality. That way, you can defend your rights as a foreign boat.

Honoring local customs   514

To ensure against offending local people when going ashore in a new country, Gordon and Nina Stuermer on *Starbound* recommend dressing conservatively until you've had opportunity to learn about local customs with regard to dress. Your obvious respect or disrespect for local customs can make a major difference in how you are received.

Horror stories   515

Listen to and learn from other cruisers' experience, but do not let their horror stories deter you from going places you have planned to visit. As Denis and Arleen Webster on *Tiger Lily* point out, not only are most horror stories exaggerated, but for every cruiser who has a bad experience in a particular country or port, there are usually many others whose experiences in the same place were delightful.

Language   516

If you will be visiting a country where the language is other than English, Dave and B. K. Bennett on *Blue Ribbon* suggest buying and using a phrase book and/or signing up for language lessons. They have found that the effort they've made to speak Spanish while cruising in Puerto Rico, the Dominican Republic,

The Stuermers on *Starbound*

In twenty-six years of cruising off and on, Gordon and Nina Stuermer had sailed around the world twice on their 50-foot ketch *Starbound*. After completing each of their circumnavigations, they'd had to resume their careers ashore, but when we met them in the Bahamas, they'd finally been able to retire from work and were cruising once again.

and Central and South America has enriched their cruising enormously. Remember, it's not your language skill that's important, it's the effort you make.

Money I   517

Although it is easy in many countries to make purchases with the U.S. dollar, you may find you get better prices by using the local currency. Moreover, using local currency is both a courtesy and a demonstration of respect for the country you are visiting. With a few notable exceptions, expecting local people to deal in U.S. dollars is rather arrogant.

Money II   518

In countries where dollars are difficult to obtain, using U.S. dollars to make purchases is tantamount to advertising that you have a cache of dollars on your boat.

Obtaining boat parts I   519

Before having parts shipped to you in another country, ask other cruisers and local residents whose businesses serve cruisers how best to have them sent, what the pitfalls are, and how to avoid those pitfalls. Then, provide clear, detailed, and preferably written instructions (by fax, if time is important) to the person shipping or bringing the parts to you.

Obtaining boat parts II   520

When having parts or equipment shipped to you, the declared value should represent only the actual cost of the part (excluding taxes, shipping, and other charges). Equally important, the insured value should be the same as the declared value. Some countries allow parts to enter freely to a "yacht in transit" if their value is below a certain threshold, but require complex and often costly clearance procedures requiring use of an agent for items of higher value. By including sales tax and shipping, insurance, and other costs as part of the declared and/or insured value, the shipper can trigger the more complex procedures even though the actual cost of the part alone is below the threshold.

Trading   521

In countries where people come to your boat to trade, Jeff and Donna Tousley on *Keramos* have found that any items that can be used for children—clothes, candy, powdered milk, pencils, crayons, coloring books—make good trade goods.

Travel guides I   522

Lonely Planet guidebooks are chock full of information that is useful and/or interesting—especially if you plan to travel at all in the country you are visiting—and are available in many bookstores. If you cannot find them, you can write for information from Embarcadero West, 155 Filbert St., Suite 251, Oakland, CA 94607. There are Lonely Planet guidebooks for most regions of the world, and we have found them a useful adjunct to our cruising guides.

Travel guides II   523

One area not covered by the Lonely Planet guidebooks at this writing is the Caribbean islands. For this area, we found *Fielding's Caribbean* travel book filled the gap quite well. It, too, should be available in most bookstores.

Courtesy Flags

Buying courtesy flags   524

Many courtesy flags can be purchased relatively inexpensively, and it's often worth spending the money to get them. Good sources include Bluewater Books & Charts at (800) 942-2583, Christine Davis Flags at (954) 527-1605, and Sea-Sun Greetings at (800) 927-8419. All three are located in Fort Lauderdale.

Making your own flags I   525

Get different-colored scraps of nylon spinnaker cloth from your sailmaker. Lay out the flag design on paper with a pencil or pen, labeling each design element for color. Use a hot knife to cut the fabric pieces, allowing about ½ inch for overlap where pieces join as well as for hems along the outer edges. Use contact cement to glue the pieces together where edges join, then stitch by hand or with a sewing machine. Fold, glue, and stitch hems. Cruising guides usually have drawings of the courtesy flags for the countries covered. There are also how-to books available that include patterns for making courtesy flags.

Making your own flags II   `526`

On *Impulse*, Mike and Pat Davidson suggest collecting scraps of white nylon spinnaker cloth to make your courtesy flags. Cut the cloth to flag size, allowing extra length for a hem at one end and a hem made up of three or four fabric thicknesses at the other end. Glue the hems using contact cement, then sew them securely. At this point, you have a flag "blank." Mark the design on both sides of the blank, label the colors on both sides, and fill in the colors using acrylic paints. Install grommets. *Note:* Consider making up a number of blanks ahead of time for use as needed.

Dealing with Officialdom

Aboard your boat   `527`

If local officials will be coming aboard, Tony and Brenda Collins on *Westerner IV* suggest that you make your boat look shipshape, dress yourselves properly, greet the officials in a friendly manner, offer them water, coffee, or tea—never alcoholic

Tony and Brenda Collins on *Westerner IV*

When we met Tony and Brenda Collins on their 44-foot ketch *Westerner IV* in St. Augustine, they'd been cruising for ten years since leaving their home in England. In that time, they'd spent six years exploring anchorages in the Mediterranean, four years in the Caribbean, and had only recently arrived in the United States to continue cruising new waters.

beverages—and seat them in the cockpit to go through the paperwork. If they want to search your boat, you cannot prevent it. Be as open and helpful as you can; make it easy for them to see that you have only your personal possessions and supplies. And insist upon accompanying them while they make their search.

Bribes   `528`

Rarely will you be asked to pay a bribe or give a gift to local officials. However, in countries such as Mexico where the practice is tolerated if not the accepted norm, Mike Hamilton and Barbara Davis on *Wild Duck* suggest that you will enjoy your visit more if you simply accept the practice as part of the experience and as one of the occasional expenses of cruising. Advice about this custom usually is provided in cruising guides. Other cruisers are also a good source of information about local practices.

General attitude   `529`

Always remember that you are a guest when visiting other countries, and behave accordingly when dealing with officials. Dress properly for that country. Behave courteously and respectfully. Expect your transactions to take a lot of time. If possible, greet local officials in their language. Even if "Good morning" or "Good afternoon" is the only thing you can say in their language, and even if you don't say it correctly, the fact that you made the effort will be appreciated and will help get your business off on a positive foot.

Truthfulness   `530`

Do not lie to local officials. If you came to anchor late, tell them so. If you have firearms aboard, acknowledge the fact. You may have to pay overtime charges or be inconvenienced by being truthful, but you can get in serious trouble by being caught in a lie—up to and including having your boat confiscated and being jailed. Moreover, once you have been caught lying about a minor thing like your arrival time, your credibility is zero when more important questions are being asked.

Entering and Clearing Ports

Dealing with regulations [531]

Holger and Christa Strauss on *Golem* point out that there often is no obvious logic to the rules or regulations involved in entering or clearing a port and that it does absolutely no good to fuss about them. To the contrary, challenging or questioning the validity of the local practices or regulations generally leads only to frustration and ill will.

Entering and clearing procedures [532]

Even if you have a cruising guide that spells out local entering procedures, check by radio or by dinghy with cruisers who have come in ahead of you to be sure the procedures haven't changed since the cruising guide was written. Then, when doing your paperwork upon entering, ask the officials you are working with about clearance procedures. And, be sure you have them straight.

Use of agents I [533]

In most Caribbean countries, you can do your own legwork for entering and clearing port. Two exceptions at this writing are Colombia and, to a limited extent, Venezuela. In Colombia, the system is set up so that you must use an agent. In Venezuela, you can go through the port captain and customs officials yourself, but must use an agent for immigrations.

Use of agents II [534]

If you must use or choose to use an agent for dealing with local officials, it often pays to shop around. Agents' fees can vary widely.

The "Ugly Cruiser" Syndrome

Making comparisons [535]

Dennis White on *Emma Goldman* specifically recommends against making comparisons between the country you are visiting and your home country. Or if you must, he says, keep them to yourself. Such comparisons are often offensive to the people whose country you are visiting, even though you may not intend them to be so.

VHF radio conversations [536]

Do not make negative comments about the country you are visiting, its customs, foods, culture, or people, when talking on the VHF radio. That radio is open to all listeners, including the many local tradesmen and women you must deal with on shore.

Watch your tongue [537]

When talking about local customs, foods, government officials, etc. where your comments may be heard by local people, follow this advice: "If you can't say something nice, don't say it." Critical or complaining comments can only generate ill will that will reverberate not only against you, but also against other cruisers.

Dennis White on *Emma Goldman*

Dennis White and Julie Robinson spent eight years cruising from California the long way around to Massachusetts. Along the way, Julie bore them two sons—Sasha, born in Australia, and Joshua, in Barbados. When we met Dennis in Beaufort, North Carolina, on their newly completed 41-foot wooden ketch *Emma Goldman*—Dennis, a ship's carpenter, had built her—Julie and the boys were still in Massachusetts winding up business before joining Dennis for their annual winter cruise.

Water Supply

General Tips

Electric pressure water 538

Turn off the potable-water pump at the circuit breaker panel when underway, switching it on only when you need it. Gunnar Dahl and Marie Louise Sterno on *Sandra* learned the hard way that you cannot hear the potable-water pump from the cockpit over engine noises. As a result, they pumped more than 100 gallons of their potable water supply into the bilge when a leak developed in their water system.

Extra potable-water storage I 539

To supplement built-in water tanks, use two-and-a-half-gallon jugs of water purchased in supermarkets. They can be refilled when taking on water. Some cruisers carry twenty or more such jugs on their V-berths, using that water only for drinking or cooking purposes.

Extra potable-water storage II 540

Use large, well-rinsed chlorine bleach bottles to carry extra water. You can collect them at laundromats. The bottles are sturdy, have good handles, and are easy to stow.

Hot water for drinks 541

When the stove is on at mealtime, fill a large thermos bottle with hot water to provide hot drinks throughout the day or night without having to light up the stove again.

Monitoring crew water consumption 542

Particularly in the tropics, it's important that the crew drink enough liquids. To keep track of how much water *Mooneshine*'s crew is drinking, Ron and Kathy Trossbach mounted a two-gallon plastic water bottle with a push-button spigot on a rack above the galley. They fill the bottle each morning and use this water only for drinking purposes (hot or cold drinks).

Rotating water tank use 543

Rotate the use of your water tanks. This way, you always have reasonably fresh water in all tanks. Also, regular use of the valves for switching from one tank to another keeps them in good working order.

Boat Baths and Showers

Boat baths 544

Personal hygiene does not necessarily require a bathtub or shower. Often, a mini-bath in the head is just as effective. A small SunShower works well for this purpose, as does a washcloth with a bit of water in the head sink.

Cockpit bathing 545

The cockpit well offers a comfortable place to bathe at anchor. Depending upon your boat's configuration and your need for privacy, you can sit on a cockpit seat or on the sole and bathe using a bucket and/or a shower arrangement. On most boats, the cockpit coamings and lee cloths will provide more than adequate privacy screens for bathing at anchor.

Cockpit showers I 546

Hang your SunShower from the boom to shower in the cockpit. Alternatively, buy a small plastic garden sprayer (one gallon) for showering: pump up the sprayer, and go at it. You can get one freshwater shower or, after washing and rinsing with seawater, two or more freshwater rinses from a gallon of water using the garden sprayer. (See also Tip 550, "Shower spray.")

Cockpit showers II 547

If you have a pressure water system and lots of water, you can make a wonderful cockpit shower by connecting a long hose with a shower head on the end to your galley sink faucet and turning on the water. If you have hot water in the galley, you can also have a hot-water shower.

Hot water for boat baths 548

In the tropics, your tank water will be warm enough for bathing without heating it. In colder areas, heat water on the stove or use solar energy to heat the water.

Inside showers 549

If you use a shower stall in the boat, plug the drain in the shower pan, put a gallon (or two gallons, however much you choose) of water in the pan, and mark the water level on the side of the pan. After draining the water, make a permanent line along that mark. Now, by plugging the drain when you shower, you can tell when you've used your allotment of shower water.

Shower spray 550

To get a better shower spray for a garden-sprayer shower (see Tip 546, "Cockpit showers I"), John Robinson on *Sheldro* suggests replacing the nozzle with the spray head from a hand-held shower or from an old SunShower. We tried it and found that he's right; it does make a better shower spray!

Collecting Rainwater

Collecting rainwater on deck 551

Do not collect rainwater from your deck or cabin-house when sailing offshore if there is any significant sea running. One wave or dose of heavy spray on deck during the rain, and you'll be putting seawater into the water tank.

Deck scuppers 552

If your boat has deck scuppers plumbed to a through-hull, insert a Y-valve between the scupper and the through-hull fitting. Next, connect a hose for filling your water tank or jerry jugs to the Y-valve. You can use the valve to direct rainwater runoff from the deck overboard until the deck has

John Robinson on *Sheldro*

When we met him in the British Virgin Islands on his 28-foot sloop *Sheldro,* John Robinson had been cruising from seven to nine months a year for about four years, mostly singlehanding but periodically joined by his wife Judy. After sailing from his home in England, John cruised along the coasts of France, Portugal, and Spain before heading off to the Canary and Cape Verde Islands en route to the Caribbean.

been washed off thoroughly by the rain, then flip the valve over to collect the rainwater.

Jerry jugs 553

As an alternative to putting rainwater into your main tanks, direct it into jerry jugs for storage. Use water from the jerry jugs for bathing and washing, thereby making your tank water last longer.

Rainwater filter 554

Rainwater collects dust, pollen, and other particles from the air as it falls. For that reason, it's a good idea to filter the water if possible before it goes into your tanks. The filter can be as simple as running the water through a linen handkerchief or paper coffee filter placed in a funnel. Alternatively, install an inexpensive in-line filter.

Rainwater tankage 555

If you have a choice, use only one tank for rainwater. The reason: If you collect a lot of rainwater, you will gradually find a buildup of sludge in your tank, simply because of the amount of dust the rain picks up from the air on its way down to Earth (see previous tip). It's nice to confine the sludge to one tank.

Treating rainwater 556

As a preventive measure, rainwater should be treated if stored in your water tanks. (See Tips 575 and 576, "Treating Potable Water.")

Conserving Potable Water

Cooking with a pressure cooker 557

Using a pressure cooker generally requires less water than conventional cooking. However, the water poured over the cooker to depressurize it often goes to waste. To conserve water you can either shorten cooking time (by about 20 percent) and allow the cooker to depressurize itself, or collect the depressurizing water in a basin so that you can use it later for dishwashing.

Foot pumps for potable water 558

If you have a pressure water system, install a parallel foot pump system for potable water. When water conservation is important, turn off the pressure water system and use only the foot pumps; you'll use a lot less water.

Hot water systems 559

When turning on the hot water, the first water out of the faucet usually is cold and goes down the drain. Depending upon the length of the pipe or hose between the faucet and hot-water heater, the cold water down the drain may be a lot or a little. To avoid wasting that water, keep a container handy to catch the cold water from the hot water faucet for use later.

Rinsing dishes with fresh water 560

A small hand-pump spray bottle (available in most drug stores) lets you rinse your dishes to remove seawater residues with a minimum of fresh water. Dinner dishes and cooking utensils for two people can be easily rinsed this way, using less than eight ounces of water.

Saltwater pumps 561

Install saltwater pumps in the galley and head so that you can use seawater for washing purposes and reserve fresh water for a final rinse.

Saltwater soap/detergent 562

Liquid Joy detergent works well in seawater for washing dishes, bathing, and shampooing. It is not satisfactory for doing laundry; it makes too much suds.

Shampooing your hair 563

If you shampoo with fresh water, you can save water by using a small hand-pump spray bottle with a fine mist spray to wet your hair.

Washing dishes in fresh water 564

If you must wash dishes in fresh water, use your rinsewater to make your dishwater. Here's how:

Start with a wet sponge, apply a bit of detergent, and wash your first dish, beginning with the least dirty dish. As you rinse that dish, collect the rinsewater. Continue, rewetting the sponge. As you collect the rinsewater, you'll accumulate more than enough water to wash even the dirtiest dishes.

Washing dishes in seawater   565

Clean seawater works fine for washing dishes, though a freshwater rinse is recommended. However, consider adding a teaspoon of chlorine bleach to your seawater dishwater if you're anchored near other boats and/or a village.

Potable-Water Filters

Activated carbon filters   566

Activated carbon filters let you have good-tasting water from your galley and/or head faucet. They are particularly effective at removing the chlorine taste often found with heavily treated municipal water supplies or after adding chlorine bleach to your water tanks.

Faucet-mounted potable water filter   567

An activated carbon filter mounted on the galley faucet lets you filter only the water used for drinking and cooking. A switch on the unit directs the water through the filter or not, as desired. Faucet-mounted units, however, generally require a pressure water system.

In-line water filters   568

Most activated carbon filters sold in marine stores and RV outlets are designed for pressure water systems and will not work satisfactorily with manual or foot pumps. However, Whale Pumps markets an activated carbon filter designed specifically for use with its manual or foot pumps. In the United States, the only way we've found to obtain this Whale filter is by special-ordering it through BOAT/U.S. or

West Marine. It is available at large chandleries in the Caribbean. We've used these filters for more than three years and have been well satisfied.

Potable water ashore   569

When traveling ashore in underdeveloped countries, carry a portable water filter/pump you can use to filter the water you drink if bottled water is not available. The best of these filters will remove bacteria and viruses as well as chemicals and organic material.

Taking on potable water   570

Do not use an activated carbon filter on the hose when putting water into your tanks. Robert and Carol Petterson on *Star Cruiser* were told by a state water quality engineer that filtering the water as it goes into your tanks will remove the chemicals put in the water to control bacteria. If you want to drink filtered water, he suggested filtering it as it comes out of your tanks.

Taking on Water

Jerry jugs I   571

Collapsible five-gallon jerry jugs will last several years if stored in lockers out of the sun when not in

Robert and Carol Petterson on *Star Cruiser*

Robert and Carol Petterson had been living aboard boats for fifteen years and cruising part-time and working part-time for five years when we met them on their 37-foot cutter *Star Cruiser* in Vero Beach. Their cruising had taken them as far south as the Caribbean and as far north as Maine. In each of the previous two years, they had spent about three months cruising in the Bahamas and worked the rest of the time.

use. (See also Tip 99, "Jerry can covers.") Their advantage is that they do not take up much space in storage. Their disadvantage is they are designed only for hauling water and not for keeping water on deck.

Jerry jugs II 572

Rigid jerry jugs made by Rubbermaid make convenient water carriers and can be used for extra water tankage when stored on deck or in lockers. They are rugged, and their suitcase shape with two built-in handles provides two carrying positions. Their shape also makes them easy to stow.

Special-purpose water tanks 573

Reserve one of your water tanks for "good" water only. What does that mean? If you cruise away from the United States, you will occasionally take on water from less-than-ideal sources. By refusing to put suspect water in your "good" water tank, you always know the water in that one tank is safe to drink.

The taste test 574

Unless you are familiar with the source of your water, Robin and Pat Bowden on *Tournel of St. Mawes* recommend tasting water before putting it into your tanks. Go about your taste test as if you were tasting wine. First, run some water into a clear glass to check it for sediment and clarity. Smell the water. Then—and only then—if the water looks and smells okay, taste it. If the taste is acceptable, put it in the tanks. If not, look for an alternate source of water.

LOOK

SNIFF

TASTE

The taste test: as if the water were a fine wine (Tip 574).

Treating Potable Water

Chlorine bleach `575`

The most widely recommended recipe for adding chlorine bleach to your water tanks is one *tablespoon* per ten gallons of water. In practice, many cruisers use less; a few use as much as twice that amount. Of course, the degree of suspicion you have about the source of your water will influence your decision as to how much chlorine to add.

Tincture of iodine `576`

As an alternative to chlorine bleach, you can treat your potable water using a 2-percent tincture of iodine solution, available at drug stores carrying surgical supplies. Purchase a pint container. Use two *teaspoons* per ten gallons, or twelve drops per gallon.

Watermakers

Changing prefilters `577`

Manufacturers generally recommend changing prefilters on a time schedule. As an alternative, Ralph DeGroodt on *Lyra* suggests changing them according to output. For example, with a new prefilter, measure the time required to produce a cup (or a quart) of water, and log that time. Then, every second or third time you use the watermaker, measure how long it takes to make the same amount of water. As long as the watermaker continues to produce water at the original rate, the prefilter is okay. When the production rate slows down a bit, it's time to change the filter.

Choosing a watermaker `578`

Get the largest watermaker you can afford and/or you have space to accommodate. The reason: Unless you plan to motor for long hours, you'll find yourself running the engine just to make water if you have a small unit. A larger unit lets you make a meaningful amount of water almost every time you start the engine.

Installation `579`

If you are planning a long cruise, install your watermaker well before you begin the cruise so that you have time to work bugs out of the system while you have easy access to the manufacturer for technical advice and to a plumbing or hardware store for items required to change the installation if necessary.

Manually powered watermakers `580`

Cindy Stein on *Island Bound* says the manually powered watermaker that you pump with your arms—like the PŪR Survivor 35—is easier to use and makes considerably more water with less apparent effort than the smaller Survivor 06 hand-pump model. This is one instance, Cindy says, in which bigger is definitely better.

Water intake `581`

If you have a choice of water intakes, choose the one closest to the keel. Otherwise, you may have trouble making water when the boat is heeled because water turbulence will interfere with the water flow.

Watermakers versus water tanks `582`

Do not cut back on water tank capacity just because you have a watermaker. Full tanks are your only

Cindy Stein on *Island Bound*

When we met singlehander Cindy Stein in the British Virgin Islands, she had been blending cruising with working for twelve years since learning to sail in Florida. One way she kept her cruising costs down was by doing her own maintenance and repair on her 35-foot sloop *Island Bound*. She had recently taken up refrigeration repair because "the refrigerator was the only thing on the boat that I couldn't fix."

backup to the watermaker. And when the watermaker fails, those water tanks will be very important.

Where to avoid using the watermaker
583

Jean Welin on *Soloky* cautions against using your watermaker in dirty or nutrient-rich water. It will work, but you will go through prefilters at a fast (and expensive) rate. Instead, shut down the watermaker and wait for cleaner water.

Jean Welin on *Soloky*

Jean Welin with crew Peter de Greef was just five months into her second cruise on the 41-foot sloop-rigged catamaran *Soloky* when we met her in Beaufort, North Carolina. Jean, her husband, and their two children had cruised between New York and the Bahamas for two years in the late 1980s before returning to land so the children could attend high school. With her daughter off to college and her son living with her now ex-husband, Jean had returned to cruising.

Weather

General Tips, 584–589
Weather Information Sources, 590–595

"Weather forecasts are so often wrong that we call NOAA 'Don't NOAA.' "
— Lauren and Fran Spinelli on *Club Cheer*

General Tips

All-band receivers
584

You do not need a single-sideband or ham radio to receive shortwave weather broadcasts. Ron and Jayne Demers on *Adelante* use a small all-band receiver to pull in these weather broadcasts.

Keeping dry
585

When leaving your boat, always assume it will rain, and close all hatches and ports—even if just visiting on another boat. If you close up, it will not rain. If, however, you leave your hatches open, it will rain—guaranteed!

Pre-trip preparations
586

Follow the weather patterns and conditions closely for seven to ten days before your planned departure on a vacation cruise or offshore passage to develop a feel for the weather systems and how they are moving.

Tape-recording weather forecasts
587

Because shortwave weather forecasts are sometimes difficult to understand the first time around, Pierre Angiel on *Defiance* recommends tape-recording shortwave forecasts so that you can replay them several times. We have found this tip particularly useful when listening to High Seas forecasts. (See Tip 592, "High Seas Operators," and Tip 594, "Portsmouth, Virginia.")

Weather forecast reliability
588

Do not rely solely on weather forecasts to make decisions in which the weather is an important element, particularly as your sailing takes you to more remote areas. Instead, supplement the forecasts with your own observations of local conditions and

Pierre Angiel on *Defiance*

Singlehander Pierre Angiel had been cruising off and on for fifteen years for periods of up to ten months when we met him on his 43-foot sloop *Defiance* in the British Virgin Islands. His cruises had taken him to the Caribbean three times, the Bahamas "several" times, the length of the Intracoastal Waterway "four or five times," and out to Bermuda on three different occasions.

weather patterns, and use all of this information to draw conclusions about the weather you can expect.

Weather windows | 589

Do not begin a passage or local cruise until you have a favorable weather forecast for at least the first forty-eight hours. Getting beaten up by strong winds and heavy seas is a poor way to start a trip.

Weather Information Sources

Caribbean weather | 590

David Jones on *Misstine* provides an excellent weather summary, as well as specific local forecasts in response to requests from cruisers in the Caribbean, on 4003 kHz from 0815 to 0830 Atlantic Standard Time (same as Eastern Caribbean Time) and 8104 kHz from 0830 to 0900 AST.

Cruising radio nets | 591

Most local VHF, ham, or single-sideband radio nets include a replay of weather forecasts, often from a variety of sources. Other cruisers in your anchorage usually can tell you about any radio nets serving the area.

High Seas operators | 592

Offshore weather forecasts are broadcast regularly by most High Seas Radio/Telephone stations. The schedules for these broadcasts are updated annually in *Reed's Nautical Almanac*. You can also call the High Seas Operator by shore line or with your radio to ask the times and frequencies for their weather broadcasts.

NOAA (National Oceanic and Atmospheric Administration | 593

Local weather forecasts are broadcast continuously on the VHF weather channels and are updated every three to six hours—more frequently at times of severe weather.

Portsmouth, Virginia | 594

On the U.S. East Coast, the Coast Guard broadcasts detailed weather summaries and forecasts for the northwest, west central, and south central Atlantic Ocean, the Caribbean Sea, and the Gulf of Mexico several times daily on a number of different shortwave frequencies from Portsmouth, Virginia. The frequencies and times of these broadcasts are updated annually in *Reed's Nautical Almanac*.

Your own observations | 595

Frequently the best weather forecasts are made from your own observations—particularly with respect to the conditions you can expect in the next twelve to twenty-four hours. For that reason, it's important that someone be responsible for keeping track of and logging wind direction and speed, changes in the barometer, and changes in cloud cover and sea state for the purpose of detecting and anticipating changes in weather.

Food

Cooking and Food Preparation

"You can do without a lot. I still marvel that at home I may use seven pots, when everything is cooked in one pot on the boat."

—Gerri Smith on *Yellow Bird*

General Tips

Cooking with seawater I   596

Use seawater in cooking only when you are well away from harbors and other sources of pollution.

Cooking with seawater II   597

Use half seawater and half potable water to cook veggies, including potatoes. Do not use seawater to cook pasta or rice; they soak up too much salt and become inedible.

Crunchiness   598

Dorothy Greenlee on *Cymba* recommends using canned water chestnuts as a convenient alternative for adding crunchiness to your salads, dips, or veggies when fresh, crunchy vegetables are unavailable. Just cut the water chestnuts into pieces sized for the "crunch factor" you want.

Double batches   599

Cook double batches of potatoes, rice, and meat, saving one half in the refrigerator or icebox to eat the next day. It cuts down on cooking in hot weather and saves fuel.

Flame tamer   600

Use a flame tamer with your propane or kerosene burner to spread the heat evenly over a pan bottom. Use it to cook with low heat, particularly when it's windy and the draft threatens to blow out a very low flame. Flame tamers—sometimes called flame spreaders—are found in the kitchen sections of most discount department stores.

Heating leftovers   601

Use a double boiler or steamer to heat leftovers, wrapping food in discrete packs with aluminum foil if needed. Cut larger items such as potatoes or meats into slices or bite-size pieces for faster heating. It uses only one pot, reduces dishwashing needs, and saves stove fuel.

Making toast   602

To make toast, use your flame tamer (see Tip 600) or an ungreased frying pan instead of carrying a separate stovetop toaster.

Meatloaf   603

Substitute instant rice for bread crumbs or cracker crumbs, using one-third cup instant rice per pound of ground meat.

One-pot meals   604

Make a concerted effort to develop and collect recipes for dinners that can be cooked in one pot, using your pressure cooker, steamer, or large frying pan. One-pot meals make cleanup easier, use less water in washing dishes, and save stove fuel.

Raw veggies for salads   605

When cruising in underdeveloped areas, Helen Connell on *Yeti* recommends soaking salad vegetables in a mixture of chlorine bleach and water (three tablespoons bleach to one quart water) for fifteen minutes. Rinse veggies in fresh water after soaking to remove the chlorine taste. The purpose is to kill bacteria without killing the taste of the vegetables. So, if you can taste the vegetables and don't get dysentery, Helen says that you've done it right.

White rice   606

Soak white rice from morning till dinnertime, and it will cook in half the time.

Ralph and Dorothy Greenlee on *Cymba*

Ralph and Dorothy Greenlee, both in their seventies, had been sailing part-time for forty years and cruising full-time for four years when we met them in the British Virgin Islands aboard *Cymba,* their 28-foot cutter. During those years, their cruising had taken them to Europe as well as to the Bahamas, Cuba, and the Caribbean islands south to St. Lucia.

Alternative Ovens

Barbecue oven | 607

Kim Larson and Kay St. Onge on *Blue Whale* use a heavy, cast-iron pot with lid (a Dutch oven) on their propane barbecue grill as an oven for baking bread and casseroles, and roasting meats. Of course, the grill's lid is left off to the side when cooking with the cast-iron pot.

Frying-pan oven | 608

A frying pan with a lid can be used to bake brownies. The burner should be turned as low as you can get it. Shift the pan around on the burner every four or five minutes to keep from burning the brownies in the center of the pan. If you have a flame tamer (Tip 600), you will not have to move the frying pan around on the burner, but you will need a slightly higher, although still low, flame.

Pizza oven | 609

A barbecue grill with lid makes a good pizza oven—assuming you have something for a pizza pan.

Baking Bread

Pan bread | 610

All you need to make this bread from William McAdams on *Double Deuce* are a frying pan with lid, self-rising flour, and a few drops of oil for the pan. We also added a bit of salt. Mix the flour and salt with enough water (approximately two parts water to three parts flour) to make the dough barely pourable—as thick as it can be and still able to be poured into an oiled 8-inch frying pan. Cook over a moderate heat with the lid cracked slightly for six minutes (the top should no longer be sticky), then flip it over. After another six minutes, test to see whether the bread is done by sticking a clean knife blade into the center (if nothing sticks to the blade, the bread is done).

One-quarter teaspoon of salt plus one-half cup of self-rising flour makes enough bread for one very large sandwich or bread for two people with dinner or breakfast.

Pressure-cooker bread I | 611

Put your bread dough into a greased stainless steel mixing bowl that fits into your pressure cooker. Put the trivet in the pressure cooker and place the mixing bowl on the rack. Remove the gasket and rubber safety button from the lid and put the lid on the cooker without the regulator. Bake as the recipe instructs with a moderately high burner.

Pressure-cooker bread II | 612

Put the bread dough directly into a greased pressure cooker. Put the lid on without the gasket, rubber safety button, and regulator. Use a flame tamer (Tip 600). Start out with a medium flame for five to ten minutes to get the cooker hot, then reduce the flame to a low level and bake for the allotted time. Some recipes call for flipping the bread to brown the top.

Yeast bread shortcut | 613

Use Fleischman's Rapid Rise Yeast to make once-rising bread. The bread may not rise quite as high as twice-rising bread, but Tim and Judy Gray on *Clarion* report that it's tasty and requires considerably less time to make.

William McAdams on *Double Deuce*

When we met him in the Bahamas, singlehander William McAdams on the 34-foot sloop *Double Deuce* had been cruising for about six years, mostly along the Gulf Coast from Beaumont, Texas, to Dry Tortugas (at the tip of the Florida Keys) and in the Bahamas. He was also taking time out to cruise in Europe—not on *Double Deuce,* but with his sister on her boat.

Beverages

Coffee I   614

The Melitta coffee filter cone with paper filters offers an easy way to make good coffee. The plastic cone is easy to stow, as are the filters. The paper filters are widely available. You can also make or buy reusable muslin filters, and eliminate trash—just grounds to dispose of.

Coffee II   615

In chilly weather, drip coffee into a thermos bottle so you can have coffee all day without relighting the stove.

Hot beverages   616

Fill one or more thermos bottles with boiling water in the morning to provide hot water for coffee, tea, hot chocolate, or instant soup all day. Glass-bottle thermoses keep the water hotter longer than those with stainless steel liners.

Solar tea   617

Put four or five tea bags into a two-liter plastic bottle of water out in the sun. You'll get good tea in just a few hours.

Cookware

Pots and pans I   618

Cuisinart stainless steel cookware has removable handles and stacks to stow compactly. Pan bottoms are a stainless/copper/stainless sandwich.

Pots and pans II   619

Heavy-duty cookware is helpful when preparing three- or four-pot meals on a two-burner stove. The heavy weight of the cookware retains heat and keeps foods hot while you are using the burners to cook the remaining foods. Cruisers who mentioned this kind of cookware felt it was worth the initial expense.

Stovetop grill   620

An inexpensive stovetop grill works well for cooking steaks and hamburgers. The most important trick in using the grill, according to Val and Eleni Rolan on *Delphini,* is cleaning it promptly after use.

Stovetop waffle iron   621

If you like waffles, Mike Karamargin on *Carrie Bennett* suggests looking in a gourmet kitchen shop for a stovetop waffle iron. The waffles are so good, Mike says, that he and Anne don't invite people for cocktails; they invite them for breakfast!

Dried Beans

Pressure-cooker beans   622

Soak two cups of beans overnight in an excess of water, ¼ cup cooking oil, and 1 tablespoon of salt (if using seawater, omit salt). Pour the soak-water into the head; the oil in the water will lubricate the head. (See Tip 169, "Vegetable oil.") Rinse the beans, and cook them in the pressure cooker following the instructions with your cooker.

Seawater soak   623

Use seawater to soak your dried beans, then rinse them as usual with potable water. The seawater

Mike and Anne Karamargin on *Carrie Bennett*

Mike and Anne Karamargin on their 36-foot Meadowlark ketch *Carrie Bennett* were enjoying their annual three- to four-month cruise when we met them in the Abacos. They use the boat, they said, as a "Florida condo," driving south from their Connecticut home for the winter months and cruising in the Florida Keys and the Bahamas—a lifestyle they'd been enjoying for four years.

soak works with navy beans, black beans, red beans, pinto beans, split peas, and lentils.

Pressure Cookers

(See also Tip 688, "Pressure-cooker leftovers.")

Cooking white rice 624

Put one cup of white rice in a stainless steel bowl on the trivet in the pressure cooker. Add one-and-a-half cups of water to the rice in the bowl and put one cup of water in the bottom of the cooker. Bring to pressure and cook five minutes. Then remove the cooker from the stove and let it cool down (depressurize) by itself. Open the cooker and let the rice set for another five minutes before serving.

Depressurizing the cooker 625

Rather than pouring water over the cooker to depressurize it, reduce your cooking time by about 20 percent, take the cooker off the hot burner, and let it cool down by itself. The food will finish cooking while the pressure cooker cools, and you will save both stove fuel and water.

Meatloaf 626

Form the meatloaf in a loaf pan that will fit on the rack in your pressure cooker. Alternatively, form the meatloaf on a double thickness of aluminum foil and put it on the rack, folding up the sides of the foil. Use one-and-a-quarter cups of water in a four-quart cooker. Once the pressure is up, cook fifteen minutes, remove from heat, and let the cooker cool by itself until depressurized. *Note:* You can put potatoes and carrots alongside the meatloaf and cook all at the same time; there is no change in the amount of water or cooking time.

Whole-grain brown rice 627

Put one cup of brown rice and one-and-a-half cups of water in a stainless steel bowl in the cooker. Put one-and-a-half cups of water in the bottom of the cooker, and cook at pressure for twelve minutes before removing from the burner to depressurize itself.

Fishing

General Tips, 628–630
Trolling Tips, 631–635

General Tips

Bag fishing 628

If you are anchored and fish are swarming around your boat, David Morand on *Ariel* claims that you can often catch a fish by holding a clear plastic bag open in the water and letting the fish swim into the bag. In fact, he says, "it's so easy, it almost seems unfair." A fish story? We don't know, but it sounds good.

Ciguatera poisoning 629

The ciguatera toxin is widespread, occurring in the coral reef areas of Florida, the Bahamas, the Caribbean Sea, the South Pacific, and Hawaii. The best way to avoid ciguatera poisoning is to avoid eating reef fish and fish that feed on reef fish, because you can't tell by looking at or tasting the fish whether it contains the toxin. One problem is that you can accumulate the toxin over time by eating several low-dose fish without being aware of it until the level of toxin in your body is high enough to cause symptoms of ciguatera poisoning. This means you could eat fish from a reef area for some time without symptoms, and then get sick. You could also eat just one fish with a high level of toxin and suffer an attack anywhere from ten min-

A fish tranquilizer that really works! (Tip 630).

utes to twenty-four hours later. Symptoms—particularly those affecting the nervous system—may persist for many weeks.

Fish tranquilizer | 630

When you bring a fish aboard and want to stop it from flopping around, Gordon and Nina Stuermer on *Starbound* suggest spitting or blowing a mouthful of whiskey into the fish's mouth or gills—a trick made easier if you lift the fish's head by picking up on the wire leader. It doesn't take much, and it'll knock him out immediately. Really. We've tried it!

Trolling Tips

Boarding a large fish | 631

When you get your large fish alongside, Earl Freeman on *Mowgli* suggests that you secure the leader and tow the fish alongside the boat for a few minutes. The towing will probably drown the fish, which can then be brought aboard safely. If there's still life in him when you get the fish aboard, a little whiskey in the mouth or gills as suggested in the previous tip will knock him out completely. For really large fish, you may need to heave-to in order to get them aboard.

Handline trolling | 632

Use an 80-pound or 100-pound-test monofilament line joined to a 12-foot wire leader by a good swivel. Secure a piece of ¼-inch shock cord to the boat end of the monofilament and drop your lure astern. Some people tie the end of the line to a cleat; others bring it to a cockpit winch. When you hook a fish, be sure to wear gloves when pulling in the line.

Hook size | 633

To some extent, the size of your hook determines the size of your fish. The adage is something like, "Big hook, big fish. Little hook, little fish."

Recommended lures | 634

Small fluorescent squid seemed to be the most popular lures among people we've interviewed. Some folks recommended pink squid, but Jim and Ann Toms on *Three Fishes B* have had particularly good success trolling for dorado and tuna with a small blue, pink, and white squid. The bottom line? Carry a variety of lures, and have spares for each.

Jim and Ann Toms on *Three Fishes B*

Jim and Ann Toms and their sixteen-year-old daughter Sarah had been cruising for two-and-a-half years on their 35-foot cutter *Three Fishes B* when we met them in Beaufort, North Carolina. They sailed from their home in England to Gibraltar before continuing on to the Caribbean via the Canary Islands. After cruising in Venezuela and the eastern Caribbean island chain, they sailed to the Bahamas and across to the U.S. East Coast.

Rod holders 635

A stainless steel rod holder can be clamped to the stern rail using stainless steel hose clamps. A piece of 1⅝ I.D. PVC pipe about 15 inches long also makes a good rod holder. Put your fishing pole in the rod holder with the brake eased slightly, the ratchet turned on, and your lure 100 to 150 feet or so astern. Then, wait for the action . . . but don't hold your breath!

Galley

General Tips

Cleaning pans 636

If your frying pan or griddle develops a cooked-on glaze, heat the pan, pour a tablespoon of wine onto the glazed area while the pan is hot, and wipe off the glaze. While cooking, or if food sticks to the pan after serving, add a tablespoon of wine (while the pan is hot) to "deglaze," and you'll find that stuck food easily becomes unstuck.

Coffee 637

Buy at least two cans of coffee, one for the can and the second for the extra plastic lid. Put the extra lid on the bottom of the first coffee can to prevent rust. Thereafter, buy coffee in foil bricks for easier stowing and use your coffee can to store the coffee once the foil pack is opened. On *Sea Sparrow*, we've used the same coffee can for nearly six years.

Electric appliances 638

A portable gasoline generator can be used to provide 110-volt electricity for such appliances as a toaster, electric frying pan, coffee pot, and microwave. Using these appliances conserves propane, which may be harder to get than gasoline for the generator.

Hot drinks 639

When serving hot coffee, tea, or soup in mugs to the cockpit crew, use a double-thick cap of aluminum foil on the mug so that wind doesn't cool the beverage so quickly. Save the foil caps; you can reuse them many times.

Paper towel holder 640

In many countries outside the United States, paper towels are available, but they come in different-length rolls. To accommodate these rolls in your plastic paper towel rack, cut a piece of PVC tube (pipe) that will fit your holder as if it were the core in a roll of paper towels. Then, simply slide the shorter towel roll onto the PVC tube and insert it in the holder.

Paper towels 641

Cut paper towel rolls in half using a sharp, smooth-bladed (not serrated) knife before removing the wrapping. You'll find the paper towels last much longer using half towels. You can use a PVC tube (see Tip 640) or shorten a standard paper towel holder to hold the half roll. You can also buy some paper towels perforated so that you have a choice of a half or whole sheet.

Salt and pepper shakers 642

Plastic film canisters for 35-mm film make good salt and pepper shakers. Camping stores sell shaker tops made specifically to fit them, with hinged caps that seal off the sprinkle holes.

Stovetop tray (Tip 643).

Stovetop tray   643

Frank and JulAnn Allen created gimbaled counter space in *Carpe Diem*'s galley by adapting a ready-made teak tray to fit the top of their gimbaled galley stove. First, they found a tray large enough to fit on top of the rail around their stove. Next, they fastened ¾ x ¾-inch strips of teak on the bottom of the tray, positioned so that they fit snugly inside the stove rail and the tray cannot slide in any direction. A nonskid mat such as Scoot-Gard on the tray helps keep things in place.

Dishes

Nonskid dishes   644

John and Maureen La Vake on *Sunrise* found that you can give your dishes nonskid bottoms using silicone caulk. Begin by marking a circle the size of the dish base on a piece of paper. Next, place a piece of waxed paper over the drawn outline and put a bead of silicone caulk on the waxed paper

about ½ inch inside the circle. Place the dish on the silicone bead and press lightly. Let cure overnight and remove the waxed paper. The flattened silicone forms an effective nonskid ring.

Plastic dishware alternative   645

Corelle and other china-like, break-resistant dishes can be used safely on boats by putting a nonskid ring on the bottom (see the previous tip).

Stains on melamine dishes   646

To remove stains from melamine, put denture cleaner in water, heat to boiling, and pour it into the cups or dishes. Let sit.

Handy Containers

Canister set   647

A Copco plastic canister set works well for keeping rice, flour, sugar, and other dry staples in a marine environment. The canisters, which have positive screw latch tops with rubber washers for an airtight seal, are easily found wherever kitchenware is sold.

Margarine squeeze bottles   648

Mike McGivern on *Decatur* reports that square-sided margarine squeeze bottles with the fold-down

Ed and Jean Baardsen on *Tropic Moon*

Fourteen years before we crossed paths with them in Fajardo at the east end of Puerto Rico, Ed and Jean Baardsen flew from Michigan to Grenada in the Windward Islands to move aboard their newly purchased 42-foot ketch, *Tropic Moon*. In the years that followed, the Baardsens cruised throughout the eastern Caribbean islands, the Bahamas, and up the U.S. East Coast to Maine before heading off to Europe and the Mediterranean Sea.

spouts make excellent storage containers and handy dispensers for mustard, ketchup, mayonnaise, and lemon or lime juice. You can also use them for oil and vinegar. Of course, good labels help!

Planter's snack cans 649

The foil-lined cardboard snack cans in which you buy Planter's corn chips and other snacks make excellent containers for keeping such foods as macaroni, dried beans, crackers, granola, and popcorn. Ed and Jean Baardsen on *Tropic Moon* cover the outside of the snack can with decorative plastic shelf paper (self-sticking) and put an extra plastic lid on the bottom to protect against rust. Jean said their first set of these containers lasted about ten years.

Heavy Weather

Coffee pot/thermos holder 650

If hot drinks are important to the crew, cut holes in a teak board that will fit over your thermos and coffee maker. Mount the board 4 or 5 inches above the counter so that it will hold the coffee maker and thermos securely even in very rough conditions.

Countertop fiddle boards 651

For use in heavy weather, make a set of 3-inch fiddle boards that form compartments on the countertop to hold eating bowls, mugs, and cereal bowls. Cut pieces of nonskid mat to fit in each compartment. Notch the fiddle boards where they cross so that they fit together like Lincoln logs.

Gimbaled counter space I 652

Cut a piece of ¼-inch plywood to fit on top of your gimbaled stove inside the guardrails. Use nonskid mat under the board to help keep it in place. (See also Tip 643, "Stovetop tray.")

Gimbaled counter space II 653

In severe weather, set a large loaf pan lined with a nonskid mat on top of your gimbaled stove and use it to hold the cups, bottles, and bowls involved in preparing food. If needed, a piece of nonskid mat under the loaf pan will keep it from sliding.

Stowage

Ceramic mugs 654

On *Runinfree,* ceramic mugs hang safely by their handles on brass cup hooks screwed into the underside of the deck about 5 inches apart. Skipper Bill Wittenfeld said the mugs stay secure even in rough seas. The key is placing the hooks far enough apart that the cups cannot bump into each other.

Cooking utensils 655

Spoons, spatulas, and other utensils can be held securely against a vertical surface using a nylon elastic strap fastened with panhead screws and washers at about 1-inch intervals. Just slide the utensil handles under the elastic.

Stowage for liquid soaps and cleaners 656

Use shock cord to hold dishwashing liquid, cleaners, and other such items securely against a bulkhead or cabinet side.

Cooking utensil stowage (Tip 655).

Wineglass rack

Wineglasses can be kept out of the way and secure in an overhead wineglass rack like those common in bars. In heavy weather, use corks, pieces of sponge, or rolled-up bubble wrap as spacers between glasses to keep them from migrating along the rack, banging into each other, and breaking.

Provisioning

General Tips

Bottle deposits

If you cruise coastwise, Bill and Joanne Weston on *Hummingbird* suggest stocking up on soft drinks and other beverages in states that do not have bottle and can deposit laws, so that you don't make cash deposits you won't be able to get back.

Karl and Carol Jensen on *Lorelei*

Karl and Carol Jensen had been cruising for about eighteen months on their 36-foot sloop *Lorelei* when we met them at the Puerto Rican island of Culebra. Originally, they had dreamed of sailing to the South Pacific, but after cruising from Florida's west coast to the Bahamas and down the Thorny Path to Puerto Rico and the Virgin Islands, Karl said they had decided "the Caribbean is a big enough bowl of water for us."

Carrying perishables 659

On *Lorelei*, Karl and Carol Jensen take a soft-sided insulated bag shopping with them to help keep meats and other perishables cold until they get back to the boat.

Carrying groceries 660

Net bags with sturdy handles, long-handled canvas ice bags, and nylon backpacks (see Tips 970 and 972) make great carryalls for toting your groceries from the store back to the boat. Alternatively, have groceries double-bagged in plastic bags, to protect against bag failure on the long walk back to the boat. (See also Tip 971, "Hand carts.")

Food record 661

Even on weekend cruises, keep track of how much of each food item is consumed. Over a period of several weekends, the record will help you plan how much food to take to the boat so that you don't have as much to carry back home at the end of the cruise.

Local transportation 662

If you need to do a major provisioning, try to find two or three other couples to share the cost of renting a car to do your shopping. If you can wait until the shopping is finished to pick up the car, you'll need to rent it for only one or two hours!

Planning for stowage 663

Before buying your stores, figure out where you will stow them. For example, large packages may save a few pennies per pound, but may be too big for your lockers.

Bahamas and Caribbean

Fresh fruits and veggies 664

Buy local fruits and veggies; they are much cheaper than produce flown in from the United States. Just use normal sanitation precautions, washing all produce well and peeling it as appropriate. Be sure to throw away the outside leaves of lettuce and cabbage. (See Tip 605, "Raw veggies for salads.")

Meats 665

Most meat in the Bahamas and Caribbean is sold frozen. Sometimes, however, the meat may have been thawed and refrozen several times because of the uncertain electricity supply. So, purchase meats carefully, preferably from larger stores with higher-volume business. And, eat your meat well done.

Shopping 666

Several cruisers offered this tip, but we heard it first from David and Valerie Wraight on *Dutch Maid:* If you see something you really like in a grocery store, stock up on it then and there. You may not see it again in another store—or even the same store—for a long time. We found it good advice indeed!

Canned Meats

Bacon 667

Canned bacon—available at discount department stores—keeps well without refrigeration. But, read the label to be sure refrigeration is not required.

Chicken and turkey 668

Excellent 12-ounce cans of chicken and turkey are available at discount department stores as well as at some supermarkets. Smaller cans of chicken and turkey are widely available in supermarkets.

Hal and Katie Ritenour on *Equinox*

Before they started full-time cruising, Hal and Katie Ritenour spent weekends and vacations for several years exploring the waters of the Chesapeake Bay on a trailer-sailer. Their cruising appetite growing, they bought the 33-foot cutter *Equinox,* lived aboard for three more years of work, and then took in their docklines to cruise full-time. When we met them in the Abacos, they'd been exploring anchorages along the U.S. East Coast, both coasts of Florida, and in the Bahamas for three years.

Canned fish 669

Canned tuna and salmon store well and can be used to make a variety of tasty meals.

Canned hams 670

Buy only canned hams that specifically say on the label that they do not require refrigeration until the can is opened.

Mail-order meats 671

Hal and Katie Ritenour on *Equinox* were the first to tell us about mail-ordering cans of beef, pork, chicken, and turkey. Three suppliers recommended by cruisers (we've tried all three) are Brinkman Turkey Farms in Findlay, Ohio, (419) 365-5127; Grabill Country Meats, Grabill, Indiana, (219) 627-3691; and Werling & Sons, Burkettsville, Ohio, (937) 338-3281. Cans range from 14½ to 32 ounces, but not all sizes are available from all vendors.

Nonperishable Foods

Dips 672

For snacking, choose dips that don't require refrigeration until after they are opened.

Milk 673

Powdered milk—whole or nonfat—works well on cereal or for cooking. Plus, it keeps almost indefinitely. An alternative is sterilized milk, sold in small boxes.

Powdered eggs 674

John and Carol Dingley on *Dessie Belle* introduced us to an excellent scrambled-egg mix made with powdered eggs. It is available from M. G. Waldbaum Company of Wakefield, Nebraska, (800) 344-5463.

Juices 675

To save stowage space and weight, purchase juice concentrates packaged in small boxes.

Nuts 676

Vacuum-packed nuts in cans or bottles keep almost indefinitely.

Spices I 677

If space is a problem on your boat's spice rack, try the half-bottles of spices sold by McCormick's.

Spices II 678

For fresher spices in the tropics, purchase spices whole and use a mortar and pestle or a grater to grind or grate them as needed.

Passages

(See also Tips 422–428, "Food and Meals.")

Refrigeration 679

Provision for long passages as if you will not have refrigeration, reserving the refrigerator only for a few special items. This way, Tim and Judy Gray on *Clarion* explain, you will not be faced with hardship if your refrigeration fails during the passage. (See also Tips 682–706, "Refrigeration: Doing Without.")

Meal planning 680

Stock up on foods you can eat without cooking so that the crew can eat well (if not gourmet quality) when sea conditions make cooking unsafe. Suggestions include canned chicken, turkey, tuna, meatballs, canned pasta dishes, hearty soups and chowders, stews, beans, fruits, and plenty of sandwich materials.

Seasickness 681

Plan for seasickness in your provisioning by including lots of bland canned fruits, crackers, rice cakes, hard-boiled eggs, puddings—foods that will appeal to people who don't feel well.

Refrigeration: Doing Without

General Tips

Beverages 682

Most of the beverages we're accustomed to drinking chilled are also good warm. They are somewhat different drinks when warm (or cool, if kept in the bilge), but you can get used to them quite quickly.

These include beer, soft drinks, mixed drinks, juices, and tea.

Condiments 683

When cruising along the U.S. coast, more than one cruiser has collected (with permission) extra plastic packets of mayonnaise, relish, ketchup, and mustard at mini-markets or fast-food restaurants when making other purchases. They keep a long time.

Easy meals I 684

Packaged noodle mixes combined with canned tuna, salmon, chicken, or chunk ham make tasty and easy meals.

Easy meals II 685

Take lots of dry pasta in different forms. Store with a bay leaf in each package to prevent weevils.

Meat substitute 686

Try adding chicken or beef bouillon cubes or powder when cooking pasta or rice.

Milk 687

Powdered and sterilized milk keep well without refrigeration. Mix up individual servings of powdered milk. Buy sterilized milk in small boxes that can be consumed in one meal.

Pressure-cooker leftovers 688

When cooking a meal in the pressure cooker, Jean and Angele Lerinckx-Parren on *Yorick* cook enough for two dinners and use a technique Angele picked up from a Lin Pardey article to save the leftovers without refrigeration: After serving the first half of the meal, replace the pressure cooker lid and regulator, bring the cooker back up to pressure, and set it aside with the lid and regulator in place until the next night. To prepare the second portion, remove the lid, stir (as appropriate) to be sure nothing sticks to the bottom of the cooker, add water if necessary, replace the lid, and bring the cooker up to pressure, letting the food cook under pressure for two to four minutes to reheat it thoroughly. When the cooker is depressurized, serve dinner.

Note: Pressure-cooking kills bacteria. Reclosing the lid and bringing the cooker up to pressure after serving the first meal should kill any bacteria that may have gotten onto the leftovers while the cooker was open. As a result, you are storing a sterilized meal for twenty-four hours in a closed pressure cooker, then sterilizing it again before serving dinner the second night.

Cheese

Canned cheese I 689

Dave and Vickie Johannes on *Westward* report that Washington State University Creamery produces and sells a variety of canned cheeses. For information, write to: WSU Creamery, Washington State University, Pullman, WA 99164-4410, telephone (509) 335-4014.

Canned cheese II 690

The WSU Creamery (address listed in previous tip) also offers instructions to sailors for keeping cheese with and without refrigeration. Hints include: Hard cheeses keep better than soft cheeses; store cheese below the waterline (the temperature is cooler and more constant); check cans regularly for integrity; once opened, do not store cheese in its can; and, if the cheese becomes moldy, throw it away.

Cheeses of choice 691

Buy hard cheddar cheese vacuum-packed in plastic. You may get a little oil separation, but the cheese keeps well. Also, individually wrapped cheese slices, Laughing Cow cheese wedges, and waxed cheeses such as Edam and Gouda keep well without refrigeration.

Storing cheese I 692

Store cheeses (and butter) in plastic containers on top of your water tanks—usually one of the coolest spots in the boat.

Storing cheese II 693

Your cheese will keep better if you coat it with paraffin or beeswax.

Storing cheese III   694

Put cheese (unwrapped) in a glass jar and cover with vegetable oil. Secure the lid and store upright so that the cheese is immersed in the oil.

Foods Not Requiring Refrigeration or Ice

Condiments   695

Despite popular misconception, condiments like mustard, ketchup, pickles, salsa, mayonnaise, and Miracle Whip will keep quite well without refrigeration so long as they are not contaminated in use. So, use only a clean utensil to remove the condiment from the jar or bottle, replace the lid promptly after use, and never put any excess back into the jar. Similarly, if making sandwiches, spoon into a bowl enough mayonnaise (or whatever) to make all of the sandwiches, then put the lid back on the jar so that it is opened only once for a brief time. Mary Ann Lawlor on *Passport,* the first of several cruisers to pass along this tip, said she's kept a jar of mayonnaise going for as long as a month by following these suggestions.

Dairy products   696

Dairy products not requiring refrigeration include butter, margarine in a squeeze bottle, and certain cheeses (See Tips 689–694, "Cheese.")

Drinks   697

Many of the drinks we commonly consume cold today were seldom chilled before the days of refrigeration—unless, of course, it happened to be winter. In any case, included among beverages not requiring refrigeration are boxed, canned, or bottled juices in containers that can be consumed in one day; soft drinks; beer; and powdered drink mixes.

Eggs   698

If they've never been refrigerated, eggs don't need refrigeration. Simply store them in a "cool" place and turn them over every day or two—easiest if you keep them in a plastic egg suitcase or egg carton.

Sandwich materials   699

The old standbys—jellies, jams, and peanut butter—do fine without refrigeration.

Sweet stuff   700

Since sugar in any form acts as a preservative, honey, syrup, and molasses do well without refrigeration.

Fresh Vegetables

Boat garden   701

You can grow your own fresh veggies by sprouting alfalfa seeds, lentils, mung beans, radish seeds, and others. The sprouting process requires little water, and the seeds take very little stowage space. You can buy them in health food stores. And, since you sprout your veggies as needed, no refrigeration is required.

Jeff and Mary Ann Lawlor on *Passport*

Jeff and Mary Ann Lawlor have combined cruising under sail with cruising ashore to explore the world around them. In the two years since leaving their Florida home base, they had sailed their 34-foot sloop *Passport* as far south as Venezuela, where they left the boat to travel by bus and train throughout Venezuela, Colombia, Ecuador, Bolivia, and Brazil. We met them in the British Virgin Islands.

Sprouting tip I 702

Marilyn Lange on *Kuan-yin* explains that all you need to sprout seeds are some glass jars (wide-mouth peanut butter jars are excellent), small pieces of nylon screening you can put over the top of the jar, and rubber bands to hold the screen in place. To start the seeds, soak them for six to eight hours, then drain off the water, rinse two or three times, and store the jar in a dark, warm place. Rinse the seeds each morning and night, and after three or four days you'll have a jar full of sprouts. Once the first tiny leaves appear you can set the jar in sunlight to let the sprouts "green up." If you collect the rinsewater, you can use it for drinking, cooking, or another purpose.

Sprouting tip II 703

Use good, potable water for the sprouts. Leave the screen-topped jars upside down so the water drains completely after each rinse. (If the seeds sit in water after the initial soak, they will rot.) By using more than one sprouting jar, you can provide fresh sprouts every day, if you want to.

Sprouting tip III 704

Because sprouts turn moldy easily in hot weather, one key to success is sprouting small amounts that can be used in one day.

Meat

(See also Tips 667–671, "Canned Meats.")

Cured sausages 705

Imported Italian pepperoni, hard summer sausage, and vacuum-sealed hard salami and hard sausage do not need refrigeration for storage. Moreover, they will keep for three or four days after opening—longer for the imported Italian pepperoni—even in the tropics.

Fresh meat 706

Cook fresh meat the same day you purchase it, using the pressure-cooker technique suggested in Tip 688 to save the leftovers for the next day.

Refrigeration: Electrical/ Mechanical

General Tips, 707–711
Electrical Systems, 712–715
Mechanical Systems, 716–718

General Tips

Defrosting the cold plates 707

Spray or pour salt water on frosted or frozen cold plates. It's much like putting salt on ice: the salt water promotes melting but without warming the cold plates significantly. Then, pump or sponge the salt water from the box and rinse with fresh water. The whole job will take less than five minutes, according to Bob and Sally Greymont on *Gypsy Spray.*

Increasing efficiency I 708

To increase the cooling efficiency and thereby reduce engine time required for their refrigerator, Christian and Marie Le Roye on *Blue Swanny* installed an oversized eutectic plate in the refrigerator.

Increasing efficiency II 709

To reduce the running time for your refrigerator, pack its bottom with refreezable ice packs or with

Christian and Marie Le Roye on *Blue Swanny*

When we met them in St. Augustine, Belgians Christian and Marie Le Roye had been cruising on their 40-foot cat-ketch *Blue Swanny* more than fourteen years. In that time, *Blue Swanny* had taken them throughout the British Isles, the Atlantic coast of Europe, and the Mediterranean as well as to the Caribbean islands, Venezuela, and the U.S. East Coast.

ice itself. When the refrigerator is running, the ice will refreeze and the box will stay cold longer than it would without the ice.

Reducing engine time 710

When you are on the move, run the refrigerator whenever you are running your engine to get underway in the morning and when going to anchor or to a dock in the evening.

Stowing frozen foods 711

Put frozen meats at the coldest part of the freezer—the bottom. Stow frozen vegetables directly against the cold plates.

Electrical Systems

Boat out of the water 712

Jack and Terry Roberts on *Packet Inn* suggest turning off the refrigeration and using ice to keep the refrigerator cold when the boat is out of the water in hot weather. Otherwise, Jack explains, your refrigeration unit will have to work overtime to dissipate heat from the refrigerator without the cooling effect of the water surrounding the hull.

Conserving power 713

Try turning your 12-volt refrigerator off at night so that it does not run. Depending upon local air and water temperatures, the refrigerator will often stay cold enough through the night to make the automatic cycling required to maintain a constant temperature an unnecessary luxury.

Electrical supply I 714

If you spend most of your time on the boat sailing or at anchor, generators and solar panels can help provide electricity for 12-volt refrigeration, significantly reducing engine time required to keep the batteries charged. (See also Tips 1,133–1,149, "Generators and Solar Panels.")

Electrical supply II 715

As an alternative to the boat's main engine to provide electricity for the refrigerator, use a portable gasoline generator that runs on deck. If you have a 12-volt refrigerator, use the generator to charge the batteries. If the unit runs on 110 volts, use the generator to power the refrigerator directly. Gasoline consumption will be a quart or less per hour.

Mechanical Systems

Maintenance I 716

A maintenance requirement that should be obvious but is frequently overlooked: Check the tension on the belt used to drive your compressor on a regular and frequent schedule, tightening the belt if needed.

Maintenance II 717

Engine-driven refrigerators are similar to automobile air conditioners in that they should not be left unused for long periods. So, if the boat will not be used for several months, try to run the refrigerator (that means running your engine) every four to six weeks to keep the seals from drying out and, eventually, leaking refrigerant.

Ship's engine alternative `718`

As an alternative to using the ship's engine to power their mechanical refrigeration, Peter and Valerie Schulz on *Kwa-Heri* added a 4-horsepower marine diesel to serve dual duty—run the refrigerator and drive a high-output alternator to charge the batteries. This way, *Kwa-Heri*'s main engine is saved for its primary function—moving the boat.

Peter and Valerie Schulz on *Kwa-Heri*

Canadians Peter and Valerie Schulz started their cruise on Lake Champlain more than six years before we met them in the British Virgin Islands. After motoring their 39-foot cutter *Kwa-Heri* down the New York State Barge Canal System and Hudson River, they headed out to Bermuda and on to the Caribbean, where they cruised throughout the Greater and Lesser Antilles.

Refrigeration: General

General Tips

Deodorizing the box `719`

Wash the icebox or refrigerator top, side walls, and bottom every four to six weeks with undiluted white vinegar. It kills mildew, deodorizes, freshens, and cleans.

Front-opening refrigerator `720`

Install sturdy padeyes on each side of your refrigerator door; then buy or fabricate a sturdy length of shock cord with hooks on each end that you can stretch from one padeye to the other. This will keep the door from opening accidentally and spilling the contents in a seaway.

Holding the lid open `721`

Install a strap on the underside of your top-opening refrigerator or icebox lid so that you can hook it to a fastener on the bulkhead or cabinets to hold the lid open while you are rummaging in the box.

Improved cooling `722`

Ron and Kathy Trossbach report that using a small, battery-operated fan to circulate the air in *Mooneshine*'s refrigerator reduces the overall temperature of the box by about 10 degrees F; it also keeps lettuce placed low in the box from freezing. One such unit is Fridge Mate, which is available from Defender Industries as well as at almost any RV store. Alkaline batteries last about two months, Ron says.

Temperature control `723`

Jim and Kay Stolte on *Siris IV* suggest buying an indoor/outdoor thermometer from Radio Shack for about fifteen dollars. With the temperature probe in the refrigerator or icebox and the display mounted on the outside where you can see it easily, the thermometer takes the guesswork out of controlling the box's temperature. Moreover, the thermometer operates on its own battery.

Insulation

Adding insulation   724

Most boatbuilders spray insulating foam onto the outside of the box liner before installation, leaving space between the liner's insulation and surrounding cabinetry, bulkheads, and other interior structure for additional insulating foam. To take advantage of this space, Rick Butler on *TranQuility* suggests drilling holes in cabinets or bulkheads surrounding the box and spraying insulating foam through the holes, working from bottom up. Inject small amounts at a time to avoid excessive pressures from overfoaming. The foam will expand to fill vacant space. Spray packs of foam are available at refrigeration supply stores.

Countertop insulation   725

By keeping a folded towel, a light throw rug, or a piece of closed-cell foam covered with terrycloth on the counter atop your refrigerator or icebox, you can reduce the cold loss from your box. In fact, you can tell that it's working because the counter will feel cold under the "insulation."

Exterior "insulation"   726

On *Lady Helen*, Al Roderick drapes a white sheet over the side deck and topsides above the galley when anchored or dockside to reduce the heat load on their refrigerator by preventing solar heating of the boat structure around the box. This is particularly helpful, he says, on boats with dark hulls and/or off-white decks and cabinhouses.

Space blankets   727

Use the aluminized bag from boxed wine or other food packages as an insulating "space blanket" in your refrigerator or icebox. Spread one bag over the freezer unit or ice and a second over the top of the food. John and Carol Dingley on *Dessie Belle* report significant power savings in running their refrigerator this way.

Stowage

Compartmentalizing the box   728

Use rectangular Rubbermaid bins or small plastic crates that you can lift out easily to organize your refrigerator or icebox foods and keep them from sliding around in a seaway.

Glass bottles   729

Save old socks and slip them over glass bottles in the refrigerator or icebox to help protect against breakage.

Refrigeration:
Iceboxes

"We have an icebox . . . and we haven't had to repair it yet."

—Hiram Connell on *Yeti*

General Tips

Icebox drain — 730

To help avoid smelly bilges, do not let your icebox drain into the bilge. Instead, run the drain to a one-gallon plastic milk bottle with a screw top, which you can empty morning and/or evening. Cut a hole in the screw top just large enough to fit the drain hose.

Ice melt — 731

When conserving potable water is a priority, use the water from your icebox drain to wash or rinse dishes, bathe, or shampoo your hair.

Ice supply — 732

When ice is difficult to find, Win Smith on *Rosinante* looks for a store or restaurant with a freezer. Often the owners are willing to put two or three large bottles of water in their freezer overnight to make ice if you supply the bottles. Depending upon the local water situation, you may also have to provide the water. Gallon milk jugs and two-liter soft drink bottles serve this purpose well. We had occasion to try this tip in the eastern Caribbean when ice was not available on one island because of drought, and it worked!

Pre-cruise chill-down — 733

To make his ice last as long as possible, Pierre Angiel on *Defiance* ices-down his box two days before starting a trip, then tops off the ice the last thing before raising anchor. He also starts out with all meats frozen and beverages and other icebox foods chilled before putting them in the box.

Win Smith on *Rosinante*

Singlehander Win Smith on *Rosinante,* a 34-foot sloop, was completing his first year of cruising when we met him in the anchorage at Cumberland Island, Georgia. In that year, he had cruised as far north as Newport, Rhode Island, as far south as Key West, and to the Bahamas.

Stoves

General Tips

Microwave oven

Roy Wilson on *Dreamer* finds that a small microwave oven serves well as an alternative to an alcohol, gas, or kerosene oven. All that's needed is a shore-power hookup or, when at anchor, either a portable generator on deck or an inverter and sufficient battery capacity to power the microwave through its relatively short cooking cycles.

Securing the oven door   735

To keep your oven door from being jolted open in a heavy seaway, secure it with a line running from the oven door handle to the burner guardrail.

Alcohol

Buying stove alcohol   736

You can save money by purchasing your stove alcohol at a hardware or home supply store rather than paying marine store prices. *Note:* In many Latin and South American countries, stove alcohol is difficult to find. (See also Tip 738, "Storing stove alcohol.")

Preheating burners   737

Use a Tilley wick, made for use with kerosene stoves, to preheat your pressurized alcohol burner.

It eliminates spilling, overfilling, or underfilling the preheating cup and subsequent flareups. For additional information about Tilley wicks, see Tips 741 and 742, "Kerosene: Preheating burners."

Storing stove alcohol   738

Whenever possible, purchase your stove alcohol in plastic containers (metal cans rust and may leak). However, do not throw away the old container until you have the new one in hand, in the event you have to buy your alcohol in a metal can. In that case, transfer the alcohol to the old plastic container right away—but do it ashore or in the cockpit, and only when all flames are out. Alcohol fumes are flammable.

CNG (Compressed Natural Gas)

Cruising with CNG   739

If you have a CNG stove, consider converting to propane before leaving U.S. waters. So far as we can determine, CNG is not available in the

Roy Wilson on *Dreamer*

Singlehander Roy Wilson had been cruising for a year when we met him in the British Virgin Islands. Roy, who said that cruising had been a lifelong dream, bought a 26-foot sloop to learn to sail, then traded up to the 38-foot double-headsail sloop he named *Dreamer* to sail from Florida to the Bahamas and down the Thorny Path to the Dominican Republic, Puerto Rico, and the Virgin Islands.

Bahamas, the Caribbean islands, or in Central or South America.

Kerosene

(See also Tip 1,166, "Deodorizing kerosene," and Tip 1,168, "Kerosene alternative.")

Kerosene fuel alternative `740`

For cleaner burning, use mineral spirits (yes, the same thing used to clean paintbrushes) in place of kerosene in your stove.

Preheating burners I `741`

Eliminate flareup problems by using a Tilley wick for preheating your kerosene burner. The Tilley wick consists of two kidney-shaped cups on a spring clip that fits around the bottom of your burner. The two cups are filled with a wick material. Soaked in alcohol and clipped to the burner, the wick will deliver enough alcohol to preheat your burner perfectly every time. When the flame on the wick dies (and not before), simply light

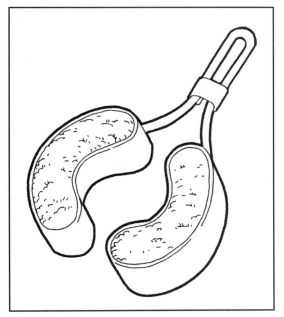

Use a Tilley wick for preheating pressurized kerosene or alcohol burners (Tip 741).

your burner. The preheating is so consistent that you can set a timer to alert you when the wick is about to go out. Tilley wicks—called "Tilley torches" in the U.K.—can be ordered by telephone directly from Tilley International, in Surrey, UK. From the United States, dial 011-44-127-669-1996. An alternative source is City Hardware in London. The telephone number from the United States is 011-44-171-253-4095. One wick per burner is recommended. They will last for years.

Preheating burners II `742`

Store your Tilley wicks (Tip 741) between uses in a small, round Rubbermaid food container filled halfway with alcohol. The wicks will be ready to go when needed.

Storing preheat alcohol in the galley `743`

The plastic 12-ounce bottles used to package saline solution for contact lenses or contact lens cleaning solutions make excellent stove alcohol containers for galley use. You can enlarge the hole in the tip with an awl for more efficient squirting, or cut off part of the tip for controlled pouring. To fill from a gallon container, use a table knife to pry the tip from the bottle and fill using a small funnel.

Propane

Bilge blower `744`

An ignition-proof bilge blower like those installed in boats having inboard gasoline engines can be used to remove safely any propane gas that may leak into your bilge. (Propane is heavier than air and will settle to the lowest part of the boat if not vented overboard.)

Propane safety I `745`

Never turn off your last burner at the stove. Instead, turn off the gas at the propane tank, usually by means of a remote solenoid switch, and allow the flame at the burner to burn itself out. Then, turn off the burner.

Propane safety II   746

Always check to be certain the burners are turned off before opening the propane tank valve and the in-line solenoid switch. If a burner is open and the gas turned on before you are ready to light the burner, the result could be explosive.

Propane storage I   747

If your wheel-steering boat does not have a built-in propane tank locker, or you want to store more tanks, John and Carol Dingley on *Dessie Belle* suggest building a propane locker in front of your steering pedestal. *Dessie Belle*'s propane box holds two 20-pound tanks and doubles as a cockpit table, with drop leaves to provide a larger table surface. You will, however, need to provide a drain from the propane locker overboard, emerging above the waterline.

Propane storage II   748

In an aft-cockpit boat, the space under the helmsman's seat at the after end of your cockpit may make an excellent spot to install a propane locker. The area is generally protected from the worst of the weather and seas, and usually is close enough to the transom to run a drain from the propane locker overboard (above the waterline).

John and Carol Dingley on *Dessie Belle*

John and Carol Dingley had been living aboard their 36-foot ketch *Dessie Belle* for seven years and cruising full-time for one year when we met them in the Bahamas. In that first year of cruising, they had sailed from the Chesapeake Bay to Maine, down the coast to Florida, and around to Florida's Gulf Coast before crossing over to the Bahamas. Their cruising plans at that time were open-ended.

Propane strategy   749

Carry two tanks of propane. When one runs out, you'll have another tank to use until you can get the first one refilled.

Propane system maintenance   750

Steve and Donna Thompson on *Donna Jean* recommend going over the entire propane system every two or three months to check hoses for chafe or cracking. Check all connections for leakage by opening the system between the tank and the burner, dabbing the connections with soapy water, and watching sharply for bubbles. It is especially important to check the hose on a gimbaled stove for chafe. Where the hose passes through a bulkhead, run it inside a short length of clear vinyl hose to protect it from chafe.

Propane tank shutoff   751

Alex Quintard on *Cetus* installed a top-quality ball valve, like those used on through-hull fittings, in place of the gate valve typically found on propane tanks. The ball valve makes it easy to close the tank by hand, and he can tell at a glance whether the valve is open or closed. Taking it one step farther, instead of using the usual solenoid valve, Alex has also rigged an accelerator cable with a handle so that he can close and open the valve from the galley.

Solenoid switch   752

Carry a spare solenoid switch—that's the advice of Skip and Gerri Smith on *Yellow Bird*. They had to jury-rig their propane line to bypass the solenoid switch in their system when it failed. Karl and Carol Jensen on *Lorelei* will second the Smiths' suggestion; when *Lorelei*'s solenoid switch failed, they were unable to cook anything for several days.

Solenoid switch failure   753

If the solenoid switch on your propane system fails, before assuming that the switch is bad, check the electrical circuit to be sure the switch is getting electricity. If the circuit is good, then replace the switch.

Stowage

General Tips

Chip bag closers 754

Use clothespins to close bags of chips or other snacks.

Dry-food containers 755

Mike Hamilton and Barbara Davis on *Wild Duck* strongly recommend spending the money for Tupperware containers and taking as many containers of various sizes as you have room for. Stick to square and rectangular shapes for optimal use of stowage space. The goal is to be able to match container sizes to both locker size and the requirements of the food being stowed (cereals, flour, sugar, pasta, snacks).

Food boxes 756

In tropical areas, either put cardboard or paper food containers into a Ziploc bag promptly or, better yet, repackage food from the box into a Ziploc and get rid of the box. Kathy and Conrad Johnson, Jr. on *Copasetic,* who offered this tip, report that they have found bugs trapped in their Ziploc bags containing food boxes. (See also Tip 107, "Prevention I.")

Fresh ginger 757

To keep fresh ginger, wash the root to remove any dirt, put it in a jar, and add gin, vodka, white rum—or even cheap white wine—until the root is completely immersed. The liquor or wine can be used later and will have a slight ginger flavor. The ginger will be unaffected by the liquor, but will remain fresh indefinitely.

Frozen food 758

Your boat freezer will not get as cold as a home freezer, making it particularly important to wrap freezer food well. Wrap foods in portions for one or two people with a good plastic wrap, then put them in Ziploc freezer bags with the air squeezed out. (See also Tip 711, "Stowing frozen foods.")

Locker organizers I 759

In deep lockers, use shallow trays to hold canned foods, then layer the trays. Distribute each specific food type among the trays from top to bottom so that you don't end up with all green beans in the bottom tray and all canned tomatoes in the top tray.

Locker organizers II 760

In settee bases or similar lockers, use plastic dishpans to contain canned food. The object is to keep cans from shifting around in the lockers.

Locker organizers III 761

Mesh bags with drawstrings make excellent organizers. Buy them in a variety of colors from an Army/Navy or camping supply store, and color-code them to keep different kinds of canned foods together and easy to find.

Preventing weevils 762

Hiram and Helen Connell on *Yeti* were the first to tell us about putting bay leaves in containers of flour, rice, grits, cornmeal, pasta, and other dry staples to prevent emergence of weevils. They also suggested putting unopened bags or boxes of flour and grains in large Ziploc bags with a couple of bay leaves. Although we did have trouble with weevils in our first two years of cruising, we have not seen another weevil aboard *Sea Sparrow*—knock on wood!—since we began using bay leaves.

Stowing glass jars and bottles I 763

Jean Baardsen on *Tropic Moon* says, "Dress your bottles in old knee socks—the thicker the better—to protect them from breakage." Many other cruisers have seconded that motion.

Stowing glass jars and bottles II 764

Also from several cruisers: If you like to knit or crochet, use leftover yarns to knit or crochet snuggies that fit over glass jars and bottles to protect them from breakage.

Hiram and Helen Connell on *Yeti*

When we met Hiram and Helen Connell in the British Virgin Islands on their 36-foot sloop *Yeti*, they had been out for about two-and-a-half years of a planned five-year cruise. After sailing from their New England home to the Caribbean, they cruised down-island to Venezuela and along the South American coast as far west as Bonaire before turning north to New England via the Bahamas for the summer and returning again to the Caribbean in the fall.

Wine cellar 765

Use the space beneath your bottom drawers for stowing wine. On *Alana,* for example, Dan Robbins and Pam Jeffreys simply removed the bottom drawers, laid wine bottles dressed in old socks on their sides under the drawer space, and replaced the drawers.

Alternative Use for the Icebox

Drinking-water stowage 766

Your icebox (or refrigerator, if it's not operable) makes an excellent stowage area for bottled water. Mike and Susan Carlson have used *Ariadne*'s icebox to keep as many as twenty one-liter bottles of potable water as a backup to their tanks and watermaker.

Dry-food stowage 767

If your icebox is poorly insulated and ineffective, forget the ice and use the box for dry storage. Use plastic containers to organize flour, rice, dried beans, even eggs. If the icebox is really large, stow paper towels and toilet paper in the bottom half and dry foods on top.

Canned Foods and Drinks

Bilge stowage of canned beverages 768

If you cruise in salt water, don't carry soft drinks or beer in aluminum cans in the bilge; they can be leaking from corrosion in a remarkably short time. We had a great party in Nassau, the Bahamas, with friends Richard and Dee Benedict on *Moon Dancer* trying to drink their beer before the bilge environment caused pin holes in all of the cans.

Bilge stowage of canned foods 769

There are five key points: (1) If you stow canned food in the bilge, use a waterproof marker to label the top of each can with the contents and date purchased. (2) Remove all paper or plastic labels so that you cannot possibly have can labels fouling your bilge pump. (3) Put cans in plastic tubs or crates, or secure them in sturdy plastic net bags (see Tip 761) so that you cannot possibly have loose cans rolling around in the bilge. (4) Install a high-water alarm in the bilge at a point lower than where your cans are stowed so that you are warned before bilgewater can get to them. (5) Regularly check each can stowed in the bilge for rust. They will rust, and much faster than you expect.

Canned-food safety 770

If you find any rust or corrosion on the inside of a can when you open it, chuck the food. Similarly, if you have any doubts about the food when you open a can, chuck it. Or, if either end of a can is at all puffed out (the end should be slightly concave) when you pick it up, chuck it. This is one time when you are better off safe than sorry.

Labeling cans 771

Use a waterproof marker to put the date and contents on the top (or bottom) of all cans. The date enables you to use the oldest cans first, while marking the contents on the top helps you find what you're looking for in a crowded locker. There is no need to remove the cans' paper or plastic labels unless you'll be stowing them in the bilge.

Eggs

Egg suitcases 772

Hard plastic egg "suitcases," sold in camping supply stores, are handy when cruising in areas where eggs are sold loose (not in egg cartons). Each suitcase holds a dozen eggs.

Maintaining eggs 773

Keep eggs in a suitcase or egg carton on a convenient shelf, and turn them every day simply by turning over the whole container. A piece of string tied around the egg carton or suitcase will keep it from falling open accidentally as you turn it over.

Fresh Fruits and Vegetables

Accelerating ripening 774

To ripen fruits like pears and plums, put an apple in with the bag of fruit overnight. Apples give off a substance that promotes ripening of other fruit.

Apples 775

Avoid stowing apples with any other fruit or vegetable—unless, of course, you want to speed up ripening (see the previous tip).

Bananas and plantains I 776

If you get a bunch (even a small bunch) of bananas or plantains, immerse them in a bucket of salt water (plain water if you're in a dirty harbor) for a few minutes to get rid of any roaches. Then, air-dry the fruit thoroughly before stowing them below deck.

Bananas and plantains II 777

When bananas or plantains reach the ripeness you want, put them in the icebox or refrigerator. The skin will turn black, but the fruit inside stays good for several more days.

Carrots 778

To keep them in a refrigerator or icebox, remove carrots from their plastic bag, air-dry, wrap them in a dry paper towel, and repack in a dry plastic bag. If the ends of individual carrots look suspicious or are sprouting, cut them off. Check each carrot every two or three days for soft spots or sprouts.

Lemons and limes

Don't throw away lemons or limes just because their rinds are dried out and hard. The fruit remains good for weeks after the rind becomes hard.

Potatoes and onions **780**

Do not store potatoes and onions in the same net or container. The onions will make the potatoes rot.

Heat-Sealed Bags

Seal-A-Meal **781**

Many hardware stores as well as discount department stores sell this inexpensive device for sealing food in plastic bags. The "bags" come in a 300- or 400-foot roll of an endless plastic sleeve; you make individual bags by sealing the ends. Freezer-weight plastic is recommended. The Seal-A-Meal unit runs on 110-volt power, but draws only 32 watts and can be used with a small inverter. The unit measures about 2 x 4 x 12 inches. A somewhat more expensive version of the same device enables you to vacuum-seal the bags. Dave and B. K. Bennett on *Blue Ribbon* suggest using the Seal-A-Meal unit to repackage flour, sugar, cereal, cornmeal, instant drink mixes, powdered coffee creamer, salt, baking mixes. Before

sealing, cut out labels and directions and put them in each bag along with a bay leaf to prevent weevils.

Inventory

File card inventory

Maintain a 3 x 5 card file box with a section for each basic food type—canned meats, canned vegetables, staples, snacks, canned fruits, beverages—and non-food items such as toothpaste, toiletries, paper products. In each section, you can keep track of your stores by listing the quantity, date purchased, and location of each specific item. As one of each item is consumed, delete it from the inventory. By noting how many of each item you started with, you can use your inventory to make shopping lists. As replacements are purchased, add them to the inventory. By keeping your tally in pencil, you can erase numbers to change the count.

Notebook inventory **783**

This is similar to the file card inventory above, but kept using a loose-leaf notebook. Organize either by food category as illustrated above or by locker, listing the contents of each locker on a separate page. The most important point is to keep the inventory current at all times.

Dave and B. K. Bennett on *Blue Ribbon*

Dave and B. K. Bennett began cruising in the early 1980s on their 32-foot cutter *Blue Ribbon*. By the time we anchored near them off the island of Culebra, they had cruised extensively along much of the U.S. East Coast, in the Bahamas, Europe, and the Caribbean and were studying Spanish in preparation for spending several months in Central America. They have since sailed to the South Pacific.

Life Afloat

Children

"One of the best things about cruising for the children was that it removed them from the peer-pressure value system of Reeboks and designer clothes. They wore T-shirts and learned to judge people on the basis of who they were, not the clothes they wore."

—Jean Welin on *Soloky*

General Tips

Establishing rules

Whether you are daysailing or cruising, Craig and Denise Firth on *Symphony* emphasize that there must be clear rules which everyone understands and are consistently enforced to describe limits for any children on the boat. Some rules may be absolute (for example, "no swimming after dark"); others may be conditional (for example, "ask permission first"). Some rules will be required for safety; others will be needed to enable the family to live harmoniously in a small space.

Getting children involved 785

From a very young age—two or three years—children can be involved in the care and operation of the boat. By delegating specific responsibilities to the children (and making sure they have the knowledge and skills required to carry out those responsibilities), the skipper enables the children to feel they are participants, not passengers. (See also Tip 819, "Getting teens involved.")

Keeping children entertained 786

John Russell and Mary Fellows on *Joint Venture* point out that children—even older children—are not entertained for long by sailing. As a result, they must be provided ways to keep their minds and bodies busy. Entertainment ideas include snorkeling, arts and crafts, bosun's chairs, sailing dinghies or windsurfers, rowing dinghies, books on tape, musicals on tape, videotapes, toys, knitting, crocheting, cross-stitch, and books, books, books. (See also Tips 791–793, "Curriculum enrichment.")

Private space 787

Children—like adults—need space that is theirs and theirs alone. It should be a place where they can keep their special things as well as one where they can be by themselves for needed private time. (See also Tips 820 and 821, "Teenagers: Private space.")

Adult Children

Selling your house 788

If your plans for cruising include selling your home, Karen Rettie on *Tarwathie* suggests you consider selling the house a year before you begin cruising and moving to a rental property so that your children have the opportunity to adjust to the loss of the family house before they need to deal with the reality of your cruising lifestyle. Often, parents discover when selling their home that the house was more important to their adult children than they or the children had realized.

Sharing your cruising lifestyle 789

Providing your adult children with some benefits from your cruising is one way to encourage their acceptance of your new lifestyle. Inviting them to join you for vacations is one level of sharing. Enabling them to join you by providing the airfare is another level of sharing.

Visiting your children 790

Leaving your boat to go visit your children is an effective way of demonstrating that you are still involved with them. In fact, visiting your children may also be important to your own continued comfort with the cruising lifestyle. For both reasons, regular visits to children are usually an important part of a cruising budget.

Education

Curriculum enrichment I 791

Museums in towns and cities where you stop provide an interesting and varied way to help children understand the history of the regions they are cruising.

Curriculum enrichment II 792

It is often possible to plan your cruise to visit places that are a part of the history lessons your children are studying. Similarly, the marine environment, piloting and navigation activities, and your involvement with the weather provide many opportunities for relating math and science lessons to your day-to-day environment and activities.

Curriculum enrichment III 793

One challenge is helping children absorb information about the places you visit and things learned. John Donnelly on *Marie Galante* developed a system of pop quizzes in which he asked the children questions about places they'd visited. The quizzes were meant to be fun as well as to reinforce learning experiences.

Curriculum sources I 794

If you will be cruising for a limited time—up to one year—and returning the children to the same school, get schoolbooks and curriculum guides from the schools they would be attending if you were not going to cruise—even if it's necessary to purchase them. Your children will thereby cover the same material as their classmates.

Curriculum sources II 795

The Calvert School, which advertises its home-study program in cruising magazines, is highly recommended by cruisers we interviewed who had used it.

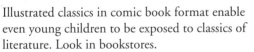

The Donnelly family on *Marie Galante*

When we met John and Mindy Donnelly and their children—Dorothy, sixteen; Annie, fourteen; Tom, twelve; and Sarah, ten—they were nearing the last leg of a one-year family adventure on the 37-foot double-headsail sloop *Marie Galante*. In the nine months since leaving their home on Lake Champlain, they had sailed across the Atlantic Ocean and into the Mediterranean as far as the Greek island of Rhodes, then back across the Atlantic to the Caribbean and up the island chain to our anchorage at Culebra.

Teaching materials— arithmetic 796

Math Bingo—a bingo game in which the squares on your bingo cards contain the answers to arithmetic problems (for example, 3 times 4)—is a fun way to teach and practice basic math facts. Math Bingo and math workbooks are available at teacher supply stores (look in the Yellow Pages under Educational Materials).

Teaching materials—art 797

Vickie Johannes on *Westward* found an art book recommended for home-school teachers very helpful. *Drawing with Children* by Mona Brookes is published by St. Martin's Press and is available at bookstores.

Teaching materials— general 798

Educational games that can be played by parents and children together make learning fun. A series of twelve IQ Games similar in format to Trivial Pursuit are based on history, geography, ecology, dinosaurs and prehistoric life, presidents, and so on. The IQ Games are produced by Educational Insights of Dominguez, California, (800) 995-4436, and may be found at teacher supply stores.

Teaching materials— geography 799

A set of flash cards filled with facts about the fifty United States and their capitals is published by Trend Enterprises, Inc., under the title "States & Capitals." The cards, for age nine and up, are available at teacher supply stores.

Teaching materials— reading I 800

Illustrated classics in comic book format enable even young children to be exposed to classics of literature. Look in bookstores.

Teaching materials— reading II 801

Carry a large number of children's books on the boat. In addition to making reading assignments from these books, encourage the children to pick out books on their own to read for pleasure.

Teaching system {802}

Many couples find it helpful to divide teaching responsibilities, with one parent teaching one set of subjects (say, science and math) while the other teaches another set (say, history, social studies, and language). With this system, each parent sets up in a different part of the boat. With more than one child, they also split up the children and then trade.

Teaching teenagers {803}

Teaching teenagers can pose special challenges because of the lure of many competing activities. One approach is to schedule schoolwork so that the teenagers see an identifiable benefit to themselves in the schedule. For example, while cruising in the Mediterranean, Ferdinand and Jeannine Cammaerts on *Eternity* squeezed the academic year into the five winter months when they were at a marina and outdoor activities were not so attractive. Mornings were spent in "class," afternoons with studying, and evenings with homework—six days a week. But, as a reward, their boys had seven months of "summer vacation" each year.

Ferdinand and Jeannine Cammaerts on *Eternity*

Belgians Ferdinand and Jeannine Cammaerts began cruising with their two teenage sons on a 41-footer, first exploring the Mediterranean for four years, then crossing to the Caribbean to sail up to the Bahamas and along the U.S. coast to the Chesapeake Bay. When we met them in Beaufort, North Carolina, their sons had both gone off to the university and Ferdinand and Jeannine were heading back to the Caribbean on a new-to-them 44-foot cutter, *Eternity*.

Infants and Toddlers

Diapers {804}

When sailing offshore, stream cloth diapers in a net bag to clean them, and rinse with fresh water. When water is scarce, disposable diapers are handy but expensive.

Food {805}

A baby-food mill lets you feed your infant or toddler the same food that you eat by making your own baby food.

Play areas for infants {806}

Babies requires constant vigilance on a boat. By creating play places you know the baby cannot fall, roll, or climb out of, you enable yourself to relax when the baby is in one of those places. But don't forget, (a) babies grow, and (b) what is a safe play place today may not be safe tomorrow.

Play areas for toddlers {807}

Depending upon the weather, toddlers can play safely with supervision in the cockpit or on deck (with netted lifelines) if they are wearing a safety harness with its leash attached inboard.

Sailing {808}

A car seat that can be lashed securely in the cockpit provides a safe place for an infant or toddler when underway. His berth, with special lee cloths, should also be a secure spot when underway.

Security {809}

A fold-away seat that can be lashed securely in different places on the boat becomes a seat for eating, a safety seat, and a potty seat. The infant or toddler can be strapped into the seat so that he can't fall out. When not in use, it can be folded and stowed.

Toys I {810}

Infants and toddlers require a great number and variety of toys because their short attention span makes them tire quickly of any given toy. However, toys need not be fancy or expensive; anything you can make that is brightly colored and safe will do. Also, you can recycle the toys by putting them away for a few days or weeks and reintroducing them to your child.

Toys II 811

Candia Fischer on *Moonshadow* recommends the book *Partners In Play—Homemade Toys for Toddlers* by Rita Anderson and Linda C. Neumann, to help supply toys for your child that you can make from odds and ends. Order it from any bookstore.

Safety

Dinghy safety 812

Children who cannot swim fairly well should wear a Type I life jacket when in the dinghy. Even young children who can swim should wear at least a water-skiing-style flotation vest in the dinghy. Non-swimming adults should also wear a life jacket in the dinghy—leading by example.

Jacklines 813

Install jacklines in the cockpit as well as on deck for use by your toddlers at all times and by young

David and Candia Fischer on *Moonshadow*

David and Candia Fischer, with obvious help from one-year-old son Justin, were fitting out their 40-foot sloop *Moonshadow* for a planned cruise to Australia when we met them in Beaufort, North Carolina. David and Candia met in St. Thomas, U.S. Virgin Islands, after Hurricane Hugo destroyed her boat but spared David's. *Moonshadow*, the successor to David's boat, was purchased in Martha's Vineyard after Justin was born.

children when sailing in other than calm seas. You need to be able to focus on the boat, not be constantly watching the children.

Life jackets (PFDs) 814

A child who cannot swim should always wear a life jacket outside of the cockpit, even if he is wearing a safety harness. If he falls overboard, the harness will keep him attached to the boat. The life jacket is needed to keep him afloat.

Netting on lifelines 815

Some people argue against using netting on lifelines to keep children from falling overboard, saying that they won't learn where the side of the boat is. All we can say is that a child who drowns will also never learn where the side of the boat is. If you cruise with younger than teenage children, use netting in the lifelines and change it at least annually. The netting deteriorates rapidly in the tropics.

Safety harnesses 816

Have an appropriately sized safety harness for each child. The harness should include a crotch strap, and the crotch strap must be worn. A harness that you can put on or pull off over the child's head if he raises his arms is worthless.

Wearing safety harnesses I 817

A safety harness has no value unless it is worn. Even at anchor or alongside, a crawling baby or toddler should be harnessed and attached to the boat by a leash. Older small children also should wear harnesses attached to the boat if they are out of the cockpit and cannot swim well—even at anchor or dockside.

Wearing safety harnesses II 818

Consider having your young children wear safety harnesses with leashes attached while they are sleeping. Dennis White on *Emma Goldman* reports that they found their younger son walking on deck early one morning without his harness. He'd awakened, climbed out of bed, and gone out on deck while Mom and Dad were still sleeping.

Teenagers

Getting teens involved 819

Teenagers increasingly are able to be full-fledged crew members and need to be given responsibilities that they can handle and that they recognize as important. As young teens, they can stand watches offshore with Mom and Dad. As they learn and mature, they can stand their own watches. They can assist with the piloting and navigation. And, as their skills and judgment grow, they can and should have increasing responsibility for boat handling under a variety of circumstances. All of these responsibilities are necessary both for the teen's self-image and for her to feel she is an integral and valued part of the venture, as opposed to an appendage being dragged along.

Private space I 820

Even more than for younger children, private space is important for teenagers—a space where they can create their own nest, keep mementos, post pictures, and be alone when they need time away from other people.

Private space II 821

The cabin of a small boat can sometimes become too small, and teens may need a place above deck where they can be alone with themselves. Fourteen-year-old Bob Atkinson on *Ho Bo V*, for example, found his place to be alone at the top of the mast. A second dinghy can provide another means for teenagers to get away by themselves without inconveniencing other members of the crew.

Seagoing telephone 822

VHF, single-sideband, and ham radios can enable cruising teenagers to communicate with friends on other boats—particularly useful in a lifestyle in which friends generally see each other only periodically. The teens can't hold long talks, of course, but keeping in touch with friends is more important than the length of the conversation.

Clothing

General Tips, 823–826
Cold-Weather Clothes, 827
Foulweather Gear, 828–830
Women's Wardrobes, 831–835

"When you pack your clothes to go cruising, do it three weeks ahead of time. Then, two days before you leave, put half of the clothes back."
—Gerri Smith on *Yellow Bird*

General Tips

Clothing needs 823

Most people take far too many clothes with them when they cruise, whether for a week, a month, or a year. Since your clothing needs are based on what you'll be doing and where you'll be cruising, start your wardrobe planning with those basic facts. First, since most of your time will be spent on the boat, most of your needs will be for boat clothes. Second, 90 percent or more of the time you are ashore, appropriate dress will be casual. Third, since most of your cruising will probably be in warm weather, you'll need mostly warm-weather clothes.

Clothing type   824

Virtually all of your clothes should be washable. Depending upon where you cruise, getting clothes dry-cleaned varies between inconvenient and impossible. If you cruise away from the United States, clothes should be easy to line-dry on your boat. They should also not be bothered by overly hot dryers. When you do find laundromats in many smaller countries, the dryers often have only one operating temperature—very hot.

Dress-up clothes   825

Your need for dress-up clothes depends upon your cruising lifestyle. However, most cruisers rarely need to dress up. Typically, one or two skirts for women and one or two pairs of slacks for men is all that is needed.

Shoes   826

If they are not worn often enough, shoes—particularly leather ones—have a tendency to grow mold in tropical and subtropical climates. To help protect leather shoes against mold when they will not be worn for several weeks or longer, seal them in Ziploc bags after cleaning and polishing them thoroughly. (See also Tip 206, "Leather Goods.")

Cold-Weather Clothes

Cold weather is a relative term. For example, after spending a winter in the Caribbean, we found springtime temperatures in the Bahamas and north Florida, and summertime temperatures in Maine, cold. We also ran into snow and ice in north central Florida during our first winter of cruising.

What to carry   827

Instead of carrying heavy clothes that are bulky to store, tend to mildew in hot, humid weather, and are difficult to dry if they get wet, pack lighter-weight clothes that can be layered as needed to keep you warm in colder weather. These might include thermal long underwear, long pants, poly-ester/cotton turtleneck, long-sleeved shirt, light- to medium-weight acrylic sweater, wool sweater, water-repellent, fleece-lined windbreaker, wool watch cap, and gloves. Combined with foulweather gear, these clothes will keep you warm through a wide range of cold weather and, with the single exception of the wool sweater, they are easy to wash and dry.

Foulweather Gear

Bright color   828

Have only yellow, orange, or red foulweather gear on your boat. If anyone wearing foulweather gear falls overboard, you want that person to be as visible as possible. Unfortunately, blue- or white-topped foulweather jackets (and the people wearing them) will simply blend in with the water and whitecaps.

Dry and warm   829

In foul weather, keeping dry is synonymous with keeping warm. So, even though you may wear it only a few times a year, you will need foulweather gear that can keep you dry in heavy downpours and windblown spray and rain.

Practical oilskins   830

As an alternative to the expensive and often ineffective foulweather gear sold to yachtsmen in marine stores, find out where commercial fishermen or watermen get their oilskins. While these oilskins do not have many frills, they will keep you dry, are sturdy, and are often considerably less than half the cost of the foulweather gear sold to yachties.

Women's Wardrobes

Planning your wardrobe I `831`

For going ashore, choose colorful clothes that look good wrinkled. Colorful designs help hide smudges that won't wash out, and wrinkles are inevitable.

Planning your wardrobe II `832`

Rather than carrying a variety of different clothes, take duplicates of a smaller number of clothing items that you particularly like—in effect, spares for your favorite clothes. The reason: you will lose or ruin favorite garments and be unable to replace them.

Planning your wardrobe III `833`

Tank tops can serve double duty—as a comfortable top in hot weather or as an undershirt in cold weather.

Planning your wardrobe IV `834`

Most cruisers wind up walking a lot whenever they are on land. Any shoes you bring for use ashore should be comfortable for walking long distances (a couple of miles or more).

Planning your wardrobe V `835`

If cruising outside of the United States, be sure to take clothes that will enable you to dress modestly enough to avoid offending local residents of countries you visit.

Entertainment

General Tips, 836–838
AM/FM Radio, Stereo, 839–841
Books, 842–846
Television, 847–848

General Tips

Board games and cards `836`

Any board game you have enjoyed playing as an adult or child is a good candidate for your cruising game locker. Computer games and reading are fine for solo entertainment, but a good game of Scrabble or gin rummy will let the whole crew join the fun.

Crafts `837`

Many cruisers enjoy doing cross-stitch, knitting, or other needlework. Others have fun making their own birthday and holiday cards to send to family and friends. All that's required for making cards is a supply of paper and envelopes, good-quality colored pencils and a bit of imagination.

Crossword puzzles `838`

Take one or more books of crossword puzzles. Not only can all crew members share in solving the puzzles, but crosswords also are something you can pick up and put down as time and interest allow.

AM/FM Radio, Stereo

CD players `839`

A CD player may make more sense today than a tape deck on a cruising boat. The CDs are more damage resistant than cassette tapes, and CD players have become quite reliable. But you needn't try to replace your existing stereo system. A small CD player can probably be plugged into your existing radio/tape deck, enabling you to play all three—radio, tapes, and CDs.

Radio/tape deck alternative | 840

As an alternative to an installed boat stereo system, try a boom box that will operate on 12 volts, 110 volts or its own dry cell batteries. A good boom box will yield excellent sound quality and will probably be less expensive than a marine stereo of equivalent quality. Most also now include CD players. On *Decatur,* Mike McGivern hangs his boom box under the side deck in the main saloon with shock cord at each end. He says it's an easy trick to take the boom box ashore in the dinghy for some beach time.

Stereo speakers | 841

If you need stereo speakers, Robert and Carol Petterson on *Star Cruiser* report that Bose loudspeakers sold for use on home patios make a less expensive alternative to speakers sold for marine use. Except for the electrical components, the entire Bose speaker is made of plastic and is impervious to moisture.

Books

"Books Aboard" burgee | 842

Try flying the "Books Aboard" flag when you have books to trade. The green-and-white burgee features the library symbol seen on highway signs. It's available for fifteen dollars from the Broward Public Library Foundation, Florida Center for the Book, Broward County Main Library, 100 South Andrews Ave., Fort Lauderdale, FL 33301.

Books on tape | 843

For passages—even a single overnight—a book on tape will help time pass more quickly during slow night watches. All you need is a Walkman or other

Mike McGivern on *Decatur*

Singlehander Mike McGivern on the 27-foot sloop *Decatur* had been cruising for more than five years when we met him in Vero Beach. Mike generally migrated with the sun, following the seasons between the Chesapeake Bay and the Gulf Coast of Florida, including the Florida Keys.

small cassette player and a set of headphones. Our own view is that you can't have too many books on tape. A spare headset or two is also a good idea. If your cruise is a short one, you can borrow some books on tape from your public library.

Reading and seasickness | 844

If reading makes your stomach queasy when sailing in a seaway, try reading a large-print book. Some people find that their queasiness is related to the size of type on the printed page. While they cannot read a normal paperback without getting seasick, they can read a large-print book quite comfortably.

Reference books | 845

Cruisers often find that a dictionary, world atlas, and recent world almanac enhance their cruising pleasure. An English/Spanish (or French, Italian, etc.) dictionary is also useful when cruising in countries where languages other than English are spoken.

The ship's library | 846

If you enjoy reading, Tony and Jenny Collingridge on *Stage Sea* suggest taking lots of paperback books along with you. Even if you have not been a reader before cruising, take some books. Reading is contagious among cruisers, and trading the books you've read with other cruisers provides opportunity for socializing.

Television

Video player

847

If you have a television set on your boat, a 12-volt video player (as opposed to a VCR) is useful. In areas where broadcast television is not available, a video movie can lighten a rainy afternoon or help pass time in a bouncy anchorage.

Videotape trades

848

Increasingly, cruisers are trading videotapes in the same way that for years they have traded books. It's not unusual for cruisers who use videotapes for entertainment to have fifty or more movies in their ship's video library.

Guests

General Tips

Arranging a rendezvous

849

Jack and Margaret Eady on *Grand Marjac* are among several cruisers who recommend strongly that you fix either the date or the place ahead of time when scheduling guests, but not both. The reason: problems with weather, the boat, or your health make cruising to a schedule difficult. If the date is set, you can telephone your guests a few days in advance to tell them where you are and let them make arrangements to get there. Alternatively, if the place is fixed, you can call to tell them you have arrived and that they can now make travel plans.

Guest stowage

850

On *Mooneshine*, Ron and Kathy Trossbach assign bunk bags fastened to ceiling strips alongside the pilot berths to guests who are visiting for several days. (See Tip 249, "Bunk bags.") Bunk bags are also assigned to crew on overnight passages. This gives guests or overnight crew their own lockers for clothing and other personal items.

Guest tags

851

Try using color codes with towels, washcloths, coffee cups, and drinking glasses so that each person can identify his own items at a glance. Simply assign a color to each crewmember and guest.

Jack and Margaret Eady on *Grand Marjac*

Jack and Margaret Eady both were in their upper seventies when we met them aboard their 32-foot sloop *Grand Marjac* in Somes Sound, Mount Desert Island, Maine, after they had sailed there from their home in Virginia. In thirty-five years of part-time cruising—"usually three to four months a year"—the Eadys had sailed the waters from Nova Scotia and New Brunswick, Canada, to the Caribbean, including Bermuda, the Bahamas, and the U.S. coastline from the Florida panhandle to Maine.

Length of visit

852

Do not invite first-time guests to spend more than a week with you on your boat. Similarly, consider limiting others to two weeks. Living on a small boat forces a level of togetherness that can test the best of friendships. It's also a good idea to have guests visit you where a variety of off-the-boat activities are available.

Safety orientation

853

Whenever a guest comes aboard for a day sail or longer, the captain should provide a safety orientation which includes showing the guest(s) the location of PFDs (with instructions for putting one on), location of fire extinguishers, operation of the radio, location and operation of the bilge pump(s), location and use of flares, and location of the first aid kit.

Scheduling guests

854

Space out your guests. While sharing your cruise with family and friends can add to your cruising pleasure, it's also possible to ruin your own cruising experience by not giving yourself sufficient time to "smell the roses." In addition, having guests on your boat adds a significant level of responsibility—okay as long as you don't let it become burdensome.

David and Valerie Wraight on *Dutch Maid*

When David and Valerie Wraight set sail from their home in England on *Dutch Maid,* a 49-foot cutter, they had planned on a one-year cruise. We met them three years later in the British Virgin Islands, with no end to their cruising in sight. Their cruise so far had taken them to the Mediterranean, across to the Caribbean, up the U.S. East Coast to the Chesapeake Bay, and back to the Caribbean.

Sharing expenses

855

If you are having guests, David and Valerie Wraight on *Dutch Maid* suggest sorting out with your visitors who will be responsible for what expenses—unless you are willing to cover everything yourself. Discussing things like sharing grocery and beverage costs, going Dutch treat to restaurants, and other subjects ahead of time can prevent possible problems and attendant ill feelings.

Laundry

Drying Clothes on Board

Clothesline　　　856

Run your clothesline between the upper shrouds and the headstay and from the headstay to the mast. Also, use the lifelines—but only after you've wiped them clean with a damp rag.

Drying sheets　　　857

Sheets will dry rapidly when there's a breeze if you hang them vertically on the aft lower shrouds. First, however, wipe the shrouds with a damp rag. Use four clothespins at the top to keep the sheet from sliding down the shroud, and then one clothespin every couple of feet on down the shroud.　☞

Storing clothesline　　　858

Wrap your clothesline around a paper-towel core for stowage.

Laundromats

Coin holder　　　859

If you're saving quarters for coin-operated washers and dryers, hold onto your empty 35-mm film containers. They make handy holders for quarters.

Delicate clothes　　　860

If you have clothes you do not want to go through a hot dryer, put them in a net bag for the washing cycle. To separate them from the rest of the laundry after washing, you need only look for the net bag.

Detergent　　　861

Collect empty small liquid-detergent containers from the laundromat wastebasket, and use them to carry your detergent to the laundromat—instead of lugging (and possibly forgetting) a large bottle of detergent with your laundry.

Dryers　　　862

The dryers in many laundromats—particularly outside of the United States—operate at high temperatures that may be hard on some of your clothes. This is one reason given by many cruisers for drying their clothes on the boat.

Washing Clothes on Board

Clothes wringer and agitator　　　863

The most difficult part of doing laundry by hand is wringing out each item. Bob and Sally Greymont on *Gypsy Spray* found a good clothes wringer (a wringer that does the job and does not break down) at a car wash supply house (car washes use them to wring out their chamois cloths). Bob also came up with a simple clothes agitator for the wash cycle—a small bathroom plunger. His washing machine is a bucket.

Laundry water　　　864

Since water is sometimes in tight supply, cruisers have found various sources for laundry water. On

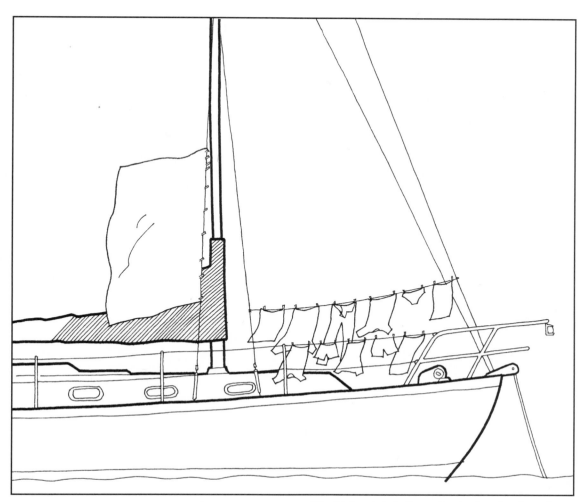

The shipboard clothesline, using the shrouds to hang sheets (Tip 857).

Blue Ribbon, Dave and B. K. Bennett use water collected in their shower footwell for laundry wash water, then rinse in fresh water. On *Sea Sparrow*, we've mostly used local water (it doesn't have to be potable) when anchored in places where we can jerry-jug the water to the boat. On *Blue Whale*, Kim Larson and Kay St. Onge use rainwater caught by stopping up their cockpit drains. Others report using rainwater caught in their dinghies.

Onboard washing machine 865

On *Yorick*, Jean and Angele Lerinckx-Parren have a small (about 18 inches in all dimensions) hand-operated washing machine called "The Easy Wash." The machine, sold in England, uses very little water

and requires only two minutes of hand cranking to do a load. Information is available by writing to W-4 Ltd./Ford Lane Industrial Estate/Arundel, West Sussex, BN 18 ODF, United Kingdom.

Rinsewater 866

If you must do laundry relying on the fresh water in your tanks, Dave Morand on *Ariel* suggests a system based on the principle of serial dilution that lets you wash and rinse in seawater, saving your fresh water for a final rinse. After rinsing all of the clothes thoroughly in seawater, wring well and rinse everything in a small amount of fresh water, lining up the items in the order they were rinsed. Assume the first one or two items are free of seawater, and hang them up. Rinse the remaining items in a new small amount of fresh water in the same order as before. Again, assume the first one or two items are rinsed completely and hang them up. Replenish the water, and repeat the process until all items have been rinsed in a fresh batch of water.

David Morand on *Ariel*

Singlehander David Morand on the 30-foot sloop *Ariel* had been cruising off and on for seven years when we met him in the British Virgin Islands. His first cruise, which lasted eighteen months, took him from Ontario to the Bahamas, before crossing to Florida to sell his boat. After returning to Canada to work for two years, he headed south again, this time on *Ariel*. When we met him, he was beginning his third cruise after working for two years in Puerto Rico.

Mail

(See also Tips 938–940, "Paying Bills.")
Receiving Mail, 867–873
Sending Mail, 874–881

Receiving Mail

American Express · 867

Many cruisers have found American Express offices a less-than-satisfactory place to receive packets of mail. AmEx offices will not accept packages and, unfortunately, local offices sometimes interpret a packet of mail as a package and refuse to accept delivery.

Fax mail · 868

Gunnar Dahl and Marie Louise Sterno on *Sandra* suggest using fax machines to receive mail from home. To get their mail, they find a public fax machine, send a fax home providing the number of the fax machine where they are, then return the next day to pick up their fifteen to twenty pages of

fax mail. This system can easily be set up with whomever is handling your mail.

Hand-carried mail · 869

In anchorages where cruisers tend to congregate, there is often a morning VHF cruisers' net. By asking

Gunnar Dahl and Marie Louise Sterno on *Sandra*

Gunnar Dahl and Marie Louise Sterno began their cruise by sailing from their home in Sweden through the rivers and canals of Europe to the Mediterranean before crossing the Atlantic to the West Indies. They then sailed to the Bahamas and to New York City to follow the Hudson River and the New York State Barge Canal System to the Great Lakes. When we met them aboard their 38-foot sloop *Sandra* at the North Carolina Visitors' Center in the Dismal Swamp Canal, they'd been cruising three-and-a-half years.

on the net whether anyone has visitors joining them from the United States, you may be able to find someone willing to hand-carry your mail to you.

Having mail sent to you   870

Upon arriving in a new country, ask other cruisers and local business people serving the cruising community what is the best way to receive mail. Sometimes, the postal service works well. Other times, United Parcel Service, DHL, and Federal Express offer the only reliable service, though it's expensive. In some popular cruising ports, local entrepreneurs have established mail services in which your mail is sent to an address in the United States, packaged with other mail, and shipped by air to the mail service office in your port. Usually the cost of these local services is reasonable.

Numbering envelopes   871

If you will be receiving more than one packet of mail, the person sending it should number the packets—"#1 of 3," "#2 of 3," "#3 of 3"—so that you know what you should be receiving. If you will be receiving mail several times in one port, each packet should be numbered consecutively— #1, #2, and so on. That way, you'll know whether a packet is missing because there will be a gap in the numbers.

Packages   872

Before having packages sent to you in another country—particularly if it includes boat parts— check with a knowledgeable local person about the local regulations and the best way to do it. You can save yourself much aggravation. Customs rules vary greatly from one country to another, and you cannot rely on people or courier services in your home country to understand nuances of the rules wherever you happen to be.

Record keeping   873

The person sending your mail should keep a list of the first-class mail enclosed. This way, if a packet does go astray, you have some hope of finding out what it contained.

Sending Mail

Audio-cassette mail   874

Voice mail by audiotape provides an alternative to letter writing for those who have a hard time putting pen to paper.

Hand-carried mail   875

In many anchorages, you will find cruisers who have guests visiting them. It's common practice to ask those guests—even though you don't know them—if they would take back flat, stamped mail for you and put it in a mailbox. Where there's a cruiser's net on the VHF radio, this subject usually is one of the routine agenda items.

Mail log   876

Keep a log of the letters and postcards you send out. Otherwise, you'll find it impossible to remember when you last wrote to someone. Also, noting the date gives you some idea of what you have written in your letters.

Postage stamps   877

If traveling out of the United States, take a good supply of U.S. postage stamps. You'll need them to put on letters that other people are hand-carrying back to the U.S. to mail for you.

Postal service alternatives   878

In some countries, alternatives to the local postal system have developed. The same mail services that you can use to receive mail can usually be used to send mail. In some Latin American countries, the local airlines handle mail, providing reliable and prompt service for a reasonable surcharge above local postage rates. You learn about these alternatives by asking questions of both other cruisers and local people.

Snapshot postcards   879

Use personal snapshots that you are not putting into the photo album as postcards. Simply draw a vertical line down the middle of the back to separate the message section from the address section, add lines for the address, and use it as you would any postcard.

Using local mail 880

Many cruisers—we among them—are reluctant to use local postal systems in less developed countries to send important mail home, especially since there are usually alternatives available. However, we have sent postcards home to be saved for us from every country we've visited, using the local postal systems. While our experience is limited to the Bahamas and twenty or so different countries in the Caribbean and South and Central America, all of the postcards we have mailed to ourselves have eventually reached their U.S. destination.

Video mail 881

Video mail is an effective way for cruising parents and grandparents to keep up with their children and grandchildren ashore, or for parents and grandparents ashore to keep up with their cruising children and grandchildren. All you need is a video camera and video playback capability.

Medical

General Tips, 882–887
Medical Kit, 888–894

"We were prepared for any emergency except minor cuts and scrapes."
—Sharon Sommers on *Sea Wolf*

General Tips

Bee, jellyfish, and sea nettle stings 882

To soothe a bee sting, rub it with a piece of raw onion. For jellyfish and sea nettles, urine or Adolph's meat tenderizer is recommended.

Burns I 883

Here we are talking about burns from bumping against a hot cooking pot, or from spills of boiling water or scalding food. In these situations, immediately put the burned area under a moderate flow of cold water to begin cooling the skin and to wash away any hot substance causing the burn. Then, apply ice or a cold pack promptly. Keep the ice (cold pack) on the burned area for ten minutes or longer. The purpose of the ice is to stop the burn from penetrating farther into the skin; it will also reduce pain.

Burns II 884

Aloe is particularly effective in relieving the pain and promoting healing of first- and second-degree burns (skin red or blistered), including sunburn. As a handy source of aloe, John and Petra Kowalczyk on *Ragtime Duet* are among several cruisers who keep an aloe plant in a decorative pot in the cabin. In case of a burn, break off part of a leaf and squeeze the liquid from the leaf onto the burned area.

Coral scrapes 885

Use merthiolate or hydrogen peroxide as an antiseptic on coral scrapes. Iodine and products containing iodine are less likely to be effective because iodine is a natural component of seawater.

Medical/first aid books 886

Two books are particularly recommended: *Where There Is No Doctor* (1992 edition) by David Werner, published by The Hesperian Foundation, Palo Alto, California, and *Advanced First Aid Afloat*, third edition (or later), by Peter F. Eastman, M.D., published by Cornell Maritime Press, Centreville, Maryland. We cruise with both of these books aboard *Sea Sparrow* and have found them excellent. They are written so that ordinary mortals can understand them, and contain a wealth of practical information and advice.

Veterinary supplies 887

Jeff and Mary Ann Lawlor on *Passport* have had good luck stocking their first aid kits and medicine chests at least in part from veterinary supplies. Veterinarians use many of the same bandages, antiseptic ointments and liquids, and drug products that medical doctors and nurses use in caring for their human patients. However, some of these products may be less expensive when sold as veterinary supplies. Ask your doctor—or veterinarian—about it.

Medical Kit

Abandon-ship medical kit 888

Cruisers sailing offshore or in coastal waters should consider having two medical kits—a primary medical kit for their cruising home, and a smaller, more specialized kit for their abandon-ship bag. The abandon-ship first aid/medical kit would contain any personal drug products used by crewmembers routinely, each crewmember's preferred seasickness preventive, a fragrance-free sunscreen (perfume-like odors may be nauseating in the confines of a life raft), antibiotic ointments, an antiseptic liquid, and gauze pads—all in a waterproof container.

Cuts and scrapes 889

As Sharon Sommers's comment at the beginning of this section emphasizes, it is easy to underestimate your need for antiseptic ointments and liquids and simple bandages. So, take several times what you think you'll need. In more remote areas, you may find yourself, as we did, providing simple first aid to local village children.

Dehydration 890

If a person vomits repeatedly so that you have concern about dehydration, water consumed orally between bouts of vomiting will be absorbed to some extent and help reduce risk of dehydration—even if most of it is regurgitated. Even better, have them sip Gatorade instead of water. If you don't want to carry bottles of Gatorade, use the powdered mix.

Expiration dates 891

Explain to your pharmacist your need for drug products with the longest shelf life possible since you are storing them against possible future need. Many prescription drugs are routinely given expiration dates of one year from the date of the prescription. (See also Tip 903, "Medical Kit Maintenance.")

Labeling 892

Be sure that all prescription drugs, vials of serum, and any syringes are labeled with a crewmember's name and the purpose for which they are intended. If you have guests or crew who leave prescription drugs behind when they leave your boat, dispose of the drugs. Reportedly, some authorities consider prescription drugs or drug paraphernalia illegal if the person for whom they're prescribed is not among your crew.

Medical kit inventory 893

Val and Eleni Rolan on *Delphini* point out that when you need medical supplies in a hurry, it's no good pawing through your medical kit to find what you need. They've printed a clear inventory of their medical supplies, including their location, and taped it inside the lid of their large medical kit. Any smaller containers used to organize supplies, pills, or bottles, also have inventory cards taped inside the lid. By keeping the inventory up to date—including the expiration dates for medicines—you can also see at a glance when you need to replace

Val and Eleni Rolan on *Delphini*

When Val and Eleni Rolan moved aboard *Delphini*, a 35-foot cutter, it was the culmination of five years of dreaming and one-and-a-half years of serious planning. When we met them in the British Virgin Islands, their home base as full-time liveaboards was a marina on the east end of Puerto Rico. About 40 percent of the time, they were away from the marina cruising.

any items. We were quick to adopt this suggestion on *Sea Sparrow* and have found it useful indeed.

Prepackaged medical kits | 894

Many cruisers report they can put together a better medical kit for less money than can be bought prepackaged through a marine equipment outlet; moreover, it is customized to their particular needs. Plastic toolboxes or fishing tackle boxes make good containers for medical kits. Suggestions for their contents are found in virtually all medical/first aid books written for boaters. (See Tip 886, "Medical/first aid books.")

Money:
Costs and Budgets

"Cruising in a small boat is the most expensive way in the world to travel third class."
        —Gordon Stuermer on *Starbound*

When living ashore, it's difficult to anticipate expenses encountered in cruising. As a result, many people find they have underestimated what it costs them to cruise. One reason for underestimating costs is that cruising involves a variety of special expenses that we don't have when living ashore. Another is that we often don't have a standard against which to compare our budgets. A third reason, particularly when cruising away from home shores, is that costs are sometimes seductively low in other countries, and cruisers find themselves purchasing goods and services that were not budgeted.

Cost of Cruising

Budget survey (1992) | 895

Of the ninety-five cruisers who reported having budgets (see table), 65 percent said their budgets were between $601 and $1,300 per month. Just under 10 percent had budgets of $600 or less per month. Some 20 percent reported budgets ranging from $1,301 to $2,000 per month. Only 5 percent reported budgets of more than $2,000 monthly.

Monthly Budget	No. of Boats
<$501	4
$501–600	5
$601–700	10
$701–800	5
$801–900	5
$901–1,000	26*
$1,001–1,100	2
$1,101–1,200	5
$1,201–1,300	9
$1,301–1,400	0
$1,401–1,500	4
$1,501–1,600	1
$1,601–1,700	3
$1,701–1,800	2
$1,801–1,900	3
$1,901–2,000	6
>$2,000	5

* Of these 26 boats, 21 said their budgets were $1,000 per month.

Cruising costs of singlehanders

896

Of fourteen singlehanders included in the budget survey, eleven had budgets of $1,000 per month or less. Seven had budgets of $800 monthly or less. Only one had a budget of less than $501 per month.

Effect of boat size on cruising budgets

897

Boat size does not appear to be a major factor affecting budget size. For example, well over half of the cruisers surveyed on boats 35 feet long or larger had monthly budgets between $600 and $1,300. The fact that all of the budgets larger than $1,500 per month in our survey belonged to boats of 35 feet or longer probably results from the fact that people who can afford larger budgets often can also afford larger boats.

Factors affecting cruising costs

898

The dominant factor affecting the cost of cruising appears to be lifestyle. That is to say, it would appear from our survey that for most people, a minimum cost of cruising is from $600 to $800 per month. Costs above that amount are more likely to be related to lifestyle than any other single factor.

Cruising Expenses

Customs, immigrations, cruising permits, port fees, and departure taxes

899

Although these fees individually are usually not large unless you incur overtime charges, they can add up to hundreds of dollars per year, depending upon where you are cruising.

Ice

900

If you use an icebox, you will need to budget for ice. Moreover, you'll use ice faster in the tropics than in cooler climates. Block ice typically costs from two to five dollars for a ten-pound block in the Bahamas and eastern Caribbean islands. Cubes are from two to three dollars a bag.

Laundry

901

Away from the United States, doing laundry off the boat is often quite expensive. We've paid as much as six dollars to wash and dry a single load.

Long-distance telephone calls

902

Most cruisers maintain contact with children and parents via telephone. Although this expense is controllable if you limit the length of your calls, a family or personal crisis can generate large telephone bills—especially if you're cruising away from your own country.

Medical kit maintenance

903

Medical kits often include such prescription and nonprescription drugs as pain killers, antibiotics, and antihistamines. Those drug products have a limited shelf life, however, and must be replaced regularly.

Nautical charts

904

If you move around so that you have to buy charts for new areas each year, nautical charts can add up to a significant expense.

Publications and annual membership fees

905

Cruising guides, paperback books, magazines, a nautical almanac, tide tables, credit or debit card annual fees, association or club dues often add up to an impressive total.

Receiving mail

906

When cruising away from your home country, the cost of receiving mail can increase dramatically—particularly if you decide to use such companies as Federal Express or United Parcel Service for mail delivery. Those costs are in addition to the possible expense of a mail service.

Repairing or replacing equipment

907

Pressure water systems, refrigeration, and auto-pilots were most frequently mentioned as sources of unplanned-for maintenance expense. Close behind were engine repairs and sail and canvas work.

Sightseeing ashore

908

Many cruisers feel that exploring ashore is one of the best parts of cruising—a part often forfeited by cruisers on very tight budgets. These expenses include admission to local museums and other attractions as well as travel by local bus, rail, taxi, rental car, and, in some larger countries, airplane.

Trips home

909

In one sense, trips home are a controllable cost—you can plan for them. However, a family crisis or personal medical emergency can impose major travel expenses unexpectedly, ruining your cruising budget if you haven't allowed for such contingencies in your planning.

Water

910

You may have to purchase potable water in some parts of the world. In the eastern Caribbean, for example, water often costs between five and fifteen cents per gallon. In water-short areas of the Bahamas, the price is fifty cents or more per gallon.

Low-Budget Cruising

Bargain hunting

911

Pete and Yvonne Seddon on *John Martin* suggest waiting until you find a bargain before you buy something you want. For example, if you need a dinghy, look for someone with an old one he is willing to sell cheap—with emphasis on cheap.

Boat insurance

912

If cruising away from U.S. and Bahamian waters, consider discontinuing insurance on your boat. The high cost of insurance when sailing farther afield makes self-insurance more attractive.

Health insurance

913

If you need health insurance and you are generally healthy, David and Kathy Rudich on *Katie James* suggest looking for a policy designed for healthy people. Although such policies carry a hefty deductible, David and Kathy were able to cut their health insurance premium by 65 percent.

Living off the sea

914

If you plan to catch your own seafood, Ken MacKay on *Take Two* suggests doing it because you enjoy it, not as a way to save money. At best, he says, living off the sea is a full-time job. More likely, it won't work. Why? In popular areas, waters and reefs have been fished out and, where there are fish, they may not be safe to eat because of the ciguatera toxin (see Tip 629, "Ciguatera poisoning"). In many places, spearguns are illegal and trolling is spotty. Finally, keep in mind that you always hear about the fish and lobsters that people catch, not the ones they didn't find.

Personal travel

915

By being completely flexible, Kees Oudt and Margaretha Christoffersen on *Ahoy* have found they could save hundreds of dollars on trips home by using special fares offered off-season by airlines trying to fill their airplanes. Also, by checking with other cruisers or a friendly travel agent, you can look for the least expensive routes. You can literally save hundreds of dollars sometimes by sailing to a different departure point for your trip.

Sneaky Costs

Boat equipment

916

Cruisers from other countries coming to the United States often find that boating equipment is significantly less expensive in the United States than in their home countries. As a result, they tend to purchase equipment that was not planned for in their budgets.

Cosmetics

917

In countries with low wage rates, it is tempting to have cosmetic work done on your boat that you wouldn't have done at home. If you have not planned it, however, spending money because "it's so cheap we can't pass it up" is a good way to seriously bruise if not break a budget.

Entertaining

918

In popular anchorages, there is often a very active social life, with nightly mini- and informal cocktail parties on one boat or another. Hosting or contributing hors d'oeuvres to such gatherings can become a significant budget item if you join the circuit.

Marina fees

919

Many long-term cruisers spend as little time as possible in marinas because marina fees add up so quickly.

Restaurant and bar bills

920

Eating ashore in new places is one of the benefits of cruising. Moreover, shoreside watering holes are often gathering places for meeting other cruisers. However, restaurant and bar bills can put a big dent in the budget if you are not careful—even when prices are cheap compared to your home waters.

Kees Oudt and Margaretha Christoffersen on *Ahoy*

Kees Oudt and Margaretha Christoffersen had been cruising for three-and-a-half years on their 37-foot sloop *Ahoy* when we found them anchored in Virginia's Great Wicomico River. They had sailed from their home in Holland to the United Kingdom before heading south to Portugal and Spain. After crossing the Atlantic, they cruised the Caribbean from Venezuela to St. Martin, then north to the Chesapeake Bay.

Money:
Earning While Cruising

"When you are working in other countries, it is almost always illegal and the pay is low."
—Holger Strauss on *Golem*

Earning money while cruising is not an easy enterprise. Those who do it most successfully either have specialized skills and return to their home countries for several months where they can be paid well by working in their specialties, or they have skills and equipment needed by fellow cruisers in out-of-the-way places, such as engine mechanics, refrigeration mechanics, electronics, and canvaswork. There are also, however, many cruisers who find creative ways to supplement their cruising kitties along the way.

General Tips

Advertising   921

If you have a business on your boat—say, you do canvaswork or equipment repairs—and are in another country, do not advertise or display a banner advertising your business. Also, do not discuss payment for a job over the VHF radio. The entry permits given cruisers in most countries specifically forbid working. Moreover, the perception that cruisers take work from local people creates ill will for those who follow you. Instead, rely on word of mouth, or a line on your boat card such as "Retired diesel mechanic." These are sufficient to let other cruisers know of your capabilities.

Boat watching   922

In ports where cruisers leave their boats to fly home for visits, or to travel inland for several days at a time, it's sometimes possible to get jobs watching other cruisers' boats when they are left at anchor. There is some work involved and a great deal of responsibility. The work includes making sure the boat stays aired out, turning over the engine once a week, and keeping an eye on security. Pay can be as much as $150 per month for watching a boat.

Charter boat captain/crew   923

The crews of two different boats we interviewed were able to earn money in the Caribbean by working as paid skippers and crew on bareboat charters. While the pay isn't super, tips can be good. However, getting these jobs can be a sensitive issue if you are perceived as taking work from local sailors.

Freelance writing   924

You should not plan on supporting yourself by writing about your cruising—there are too few markets and too many people trying to do the same thing. That said, however, writing is a rewarding way to share your experience and insights with others, and it occasionally may bring in some extra cash.

Haircuts   925

Haircutting skills enable some cruisers to earn money, especially if they're good with women's hair styles.

Jobs in the United States   926

Unless they have specialized skills that attract higher pay rates, most of the work cruisers find in coastal U.S. communities, where they can live on their boats while working, is low-wage work. As a result, rebuilding a cruising kitty usually requires effort from all crewmembers.

Jobs outside the United States

When cruisers are able to find work outside the United States, they are usually paid on the basis of local wage scales. As a result, the pay is likely to be roughly equivalent to the U.S. minimum wage or less.

Yacht deliveries 928

With the right qualifications, you can earn money delivering other boats. However, the job is usually anything but a picnic, and, as with any service job, you work according to your customer's timetable, not your own convenience.

Money Management

Cash and Traveler's Checks

Automatic teller machines 929

Your VISA or MasterCard credit or debit card will enable you to obtain local currency from automatic teller machines (ATMs) in the cities of most larger countries. In Latin and South America, however, your card may be limited to the ATMs of certain banks.

Cash of convenience 930

Cruisers in the Caribbean—including those from Europe—report they are able to exchange U.S. dollars for the local currency virtually everywhere and, often, more easily than they can exchange other currencies.

Credit card cash advances 931

If you will need a cash advance using your credit card, send a check for the amount of the advance to your credit card company, noting on the check that it is payment for a cash advance. After allowing enough time for the check to arrive, use your credit card to obtain the cash advance. Since you've prepaid the cash advance, there should be no finance charges.

Getting U.S. dollars 932

It is not always an easy matter to obtain a large amount of U.S. dollars in some of the smaller and/or less developed countries, so when you can get dollars, get enough to last you for three or four months. (See also Tip 517, "Money I" and Tip 518, "Money II.")

Traveler's checks 933

In some countries, you will suffer a significant exchange rate penalty when cashing traveler's checks at a bank, particularly if you want some other currency, such as U.S. dollars. The bank will first convert the traveler's check into the local currency (that is one currency exchange) and then change the local currency into dollars (a second exchange).

Credit Cards

American Express

The American Express card is reportedly quite useful in Europe, but less so for obtaining money in the Caribbean and the United States.

MasterCard   935

European cruisers report that the MasterCard has been good for making purchases and getting cash in the United States.

VISA   936

Cruisers report that the VISA card has been good for making purchases and obtaining cash throughout Europe, Madeira, the Canary Islands, the Caribbean including Latin and South America, the Bahamas, and the United States.

Debit Cards

VISA or MasterCard   937

Obtain it through your bank or from a brokerage house where you keep a money market account. The store, bank, or ATM where you use the card treats it as a standard VISA card or MasterCard, but each charge comes straight out of your checking account. It saves bill paying.

Paying Bills

Automatic bill payment   938

If you have any routine payments, such as insurance and mortgage, you can arrange to have them deducted automatically from your checking account.

Consolidating accounts   939

By consolidating your credit cards and telephone bill into an AT&T Universal Card, you can combine several accounts into one. David and Kathy Rudich on *Katie James* then take this idea one step further by telephoning AT&T every month to obtain their account balance so that they can send a check to pay off the balance even though they haven't yet received the bill. This way, they don't have to worry about finance charges if their mail is slow catching up to them. Moreover, the telephone call to AT&T is toll-free within the United States, and you can call collect from anywhere else.

Family bill-paying service   940

If you have a reliable family member who would be willing to do it, have your bills sent to that person and arrange for him/her to write checks on your account to pay those bills. Remember, however, that you can't complain very much if your family member makes a mistake; after all, he or she is doing you a favor.

David and Kathy Rudich on *Katie James*

When we met them on their 38-foot cutter *Katie James* in Vero Beach, David and Kathy Rudich had developed the fine art of enjoying late spring, summer, and early fall at their West Virginia home and the late fall, winter, and early spring cruising in Florida and the Bahamas. They had been cruising this way for five years.

Pets

"Only take a pet on board if you love him—because you have to give your pet equal consideration on the boat . . . and, sometimes, extra consideration."
—Lynne Bourne on *Suits Us*

General Tips

Advantage I   941

A dog or cat can greatly enhance a cruiser's sense of security. Dogs—even small dogs—are an effective theft deterrent. Both dogs and cats may also warn a sleeping crew that something is amiss with the boat.

Advantage II   942

On a boat as well as ashore, a pet provides companionship, affection, and (sometimes) entertainment.

Limitation I   943

If you cruise with a pet, it makes it difficult to leave your boat for very long at a time unless you can take the pet with you. As a result, your ability to explore ashore may be limited. When cruising farther afield, visits home will be more difficult to arrange and, possibly, more costly.

Limitation II   944

If you cruise outside of the continental United States, your dog or cat will be unwelcome in some countries—particularly those where rabies is unknown—without a substantial and sometimes expensive quarantine period. So, check out the rules ahead of time if you want to take your dog or cat cruising with you. The state of Hawaii and many of the British Commonwealth countries in particular have strictly enforced quarantine rules. In any case, you should keep a current rabies certificate for your pet with your ship's papers.

Cats

Cat hairs   945

Pet hair can be a problem on any boat. Jim and Maggie Smith on *Magic Carpet* solved the potential problem by using a 12-volt vacuum cleaner to "vacuum" their cat regularly.   ☞

Cat house   946

Not a joke! A piece of indoor/outdoor carpet in a cockpit-coaming locker provides a secure and cozy corner for your feline companion. Rick and Carol Butler on *TranQuility* say their cat "lives in there" when they are underway.   ☞

Jim and Maggie Smith on *Magic Carpet*

Jim and Maggie Smith on their 31-foot, sloop-rigged catamaran *Magic Carpet* were nearing the end of their first year of cruising when we met them at Beaufort, South Carolina. After leaving the Chesapeake Bay in the fall, they had followed the Intracoastal Waterway to the Florida Keys and up the Gulf Coast before cutting across Florida through Lake Okeechobee to follow the ICW north for the summer.

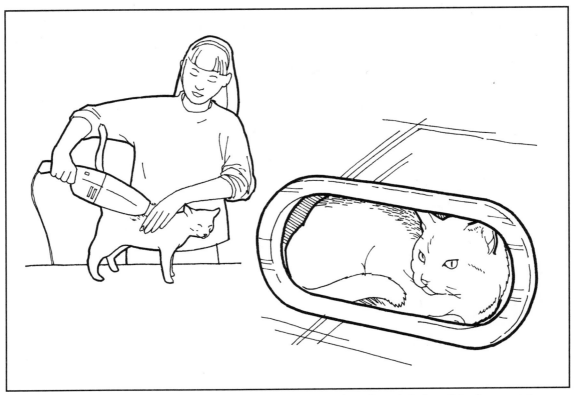

A 12-volt vac for cat hairs keeps flying fur to a minimum, and a cat house in the coaming locker provides luxurious living for your seagoing feline companion (Tips 945 and 946).

Fleas I
947

To avoid fleas, do not take the cat ashore. If he stays on the boat (the dog, too, if you have one), your cat will stay free of fleas.

Fleas II
948

To get rid of a cat's fleas, use a flea comb. The fleas and flea eggs come out with the cat's hair when you comb it. If you cannot throw the cat hair overboard, dip it in insecticide to kill the fleas and flea eggs.

Food
949

Cats can eat canned cat food, dry food, and table food. However, if you give your cat table food, set the cat's portion aside before you add spices.

Litter box I
950

Your kitty litter box should have the highest sides you can find and turn inward toward the top so that flying litter will ricochet back into the box instead of bouncing on out over the edge.

Litter box II
951

Another type of litter box has strips of heavy clear plastic hanging as a curtain over the entrance, keeping litter confined to the box. At first glance, it looks like a travel case for the cat. On *Ariel III,* where we saw it, this litter box is secured to the steering pedestal guard in the cockpit. A teak tray with a rail around it sits on top of the box to provide a cockpit table.

Litter box III 952

A different approach is offered by Kim Larson and Kay St. Onge on *Blue Whale*. Using a long Rubbermaid food storage container, they drilled two holes in one long side and tied it on deck to the shrouds. They use pebbles for the litter itself and a bucket of water to wash it out. Solid waste floats over the top. The water is poured out by putting the lid on loosely and tilting the box. The pebbles can be bleached periodically if they pick up an odor.

Safety 953

When anchored or dockside, hang knotted rags or a knotted towel over the rail into the water. If your cat falls overboard, he can use this to climb back onto the boat. Of course, this assumes you haven't had the cat declawed!

Safety harness 954

Several cruisers suggest fitting your cat or dog with a harness that fits around his chest and shoulders so that if he falls overboard, you have something you can grab or snag with the boathook to pull him out of the water.

Safety leash 955

On the boat, a leash attached to the cat's harness when he's in the cockpit or on deck will keep him attached to the boat if he falls overboard. Ashore, a retractable leash designed for small dogs will let him explore on a walk, but keep him attached to you if he's inclined to wander.

Scratching pad 956

As a scratching pad for your cat, try an old-fashioned sisal door mat under the navigation table. But keep the 12-volt vacuum handy!

Scratching post 957

To provide your cat with a scratching post, wrap ⅜-inch sisal rope around the pedestal for the helmsman's chair, the steering pedestal, the mast base in the main saloon, or the table pedestal in the main saloon. And again, keep the 12-volt vacuum handy.

Dogs

Dog food 958

If you will be cruising outside the United States and Canada, stock up on dog food before you leave and restock whenever you find dog food along the way. Dog food is not available in many less-developed countries.

Doghouses 959

One way to solve a housing shortage on your boat is to provide your dog with his own house somewhere on deck or the cabintop. Dave and B. K. Bennett, who cruise with two schipperkes on *Blue Ribbon*, took advantage of a propane storage box located between the mast and their cabintop turtle hatch by putting a small doghouse on each side of the propane box. The doghouses, which open aft, have drain holes at the bottom and air holes on both sides. They are made of plywood coated with two-part epoxy and painted white.

Passagemaking 960

On passages, heave-to for your dog to go up on the foredeck to do its business. Jim and Ann Toms on *Three Fishes B* say their dog learned quickly that "when we heave-to, that's her chance."

Kim Larson and Kay St. Onge on *Blue Whale*

Kim Larson and Kay St. Onge had spent twelve years on a farm fulfilling Kay's longtime ambition to try her hand at farming. When we met them in the Bahamas, they were seven months into a planned year-long cruise on their 24-foot cutter *Blue Whale* to fulfill Kim's longtime dream of cruising. They began their cruise in Gulfport, Mississippi, with plans to return to their Fayetteville, Arkansas, home at the year's end.

Poop deck 961

To provide for their standard poodle's needs, Sharon Sommers and Wolf Kuebler on *Sea Wolf* added a small deck structure to their canoe stern. They used stainless steel angle iron to square off the stern and put down a teak grate. The stern rail was changed to enclose the added deck space, which they quickly dubbed "the poop deck." The dog is trained to use that special deck area.

Portable poop deck 962

A piece of Astroturf about 2 by 3 feet kept on the side deck or foredeck provides a synthetic portable poop deck. With a piece of line from the Astroturf to a shroud or stanchion, you can drop the turf overboard to wash it off and put it right back in place. (See also the next tip.)

Toilet training I 963

It is easiest to train a puppy to the boat, using the same techniques you use to house-train him on shore. Once you have him trained to a newspaper in your house, teach him to use the newspaper on the deck of your boat. As he moves to the great outdoors for his toilet at the house, substitute Astroturf (see previous tip) for the newspaper on the boat. If, however, you have an Astroturf door mat at home, you may want to retire it to avoid confusing the poor puppy!

Toilet training II 964

Jack and Carly Dethorn on *Jacarde* trained their twelve-year-old black Lab to the boat by telling her it was "time to go for a walk" their first night at anchor. They then walked her around the deck a few times, until the dog jumped overboard and headed for shore. But they called her back to the boat, got her aboard, and resumed walking around the deck until the dog did her business to the accompaniment of lavish praise. "It took three days for her to be trained," Carly said.

Toilet training III 965

What happens if your dog simply refuses to use the poop deck? Ron and Kathy Trossbach on *Mooneshine* ran into that problem with their golden Lab. As a result, the dog cruises with them only part-time. When she is on the boat, they take her ashore three times daily.

Other Pets

Ceramic birds 966

Small ceramic birds make nice pets. They cost nothing to feed. There are no toilet-training problems. They are quiet. They cause no problems with government officials. And they cheer up the cabin. In addition to their dog, Jim and Ann Toms have a pet ceramic parrot "who hangs joyfully above the port pilot berth" on *Three Fishes B*. We have also had a pet ceramic bird for several years—a toucan named Tommy, who swings happily on his perch above *Sea Sparrow*'s starboard settee. These ceramic pets do need one bit of care, however. They must be moved to safer quarters when sailing offshore or in choppy waters to keep them from being jolted off their perches by rough seas.

Sharon Sommers and Wolf Kuebler on *Sea Wolf*

When we met Sharon Sommers and Wolf Kuebler on the 42-foot cutter *Sea Wolf,* they had reached Puerto Rico after a stormy offshore passage from Beaufort, North Carolina, in which they lost their engine to a failed raw-water pump and muffler meltdown. After making repairs in San Juan, they sailed to the Puerto Rican island of Culebra, where we met them. They had been cruising six months.

Useful Products

General Tips

Duvet 967

A duvet is a fabric envelope for blankets, quilts, and down comforters. It can serve as an upper sheet and a bedspread. More important, according to Frank and Karen Bastidas on *Karina II*, a duvet adds warmth, help keeps bedding from slipping off the berth, and keeps it clean. You can launder a duvet as you would a sheet—much easier than trying to wash blankets, quilts, and comforters.

Synthetic chamois 968

Spread the chamois on the countertop under the dish drainer to soak up drainage when washing dishes. In a seaway, wet the chamois, wring it out, and spread it on the counter or table as a nonskid surface.

Zipper lubricant 969

Use plain Chapstick as a lubricant for plastic zippers.

Carryalls

Backpacks 970

Sturdy backpacks made of Cordura nylon can be used to carry groceries when provisioning. Putting heavy items in the pack leaves your hands free for carrying bags of food.

Hand carts 971

A collapsible hand cart or dolly with large wheels makes toting laundry or groceries easier, especially if you carry two or three collapsible milk crates along with it. Large wheels are particularly helpful when there are no sidewalks.

Long-handled ice bags 972

Heavy canvas ice bags with handles 16 to 18 inches tall make sturdy shopping bags that can be carried by hand or slung over your shoulder. Of course, they're also useful for carrying ice.

Cleaning Agents

Ammonia 973

To clean your lifelines, put ammonia on a 3M ScotchBrite pad and scrub gently. The ammonia cleans the plastic lifeline surface without leaving it sticky.

Frank and Karen Bastidas on *Karina II*

When we met them at the North Carolina Dismal Swamp Canal Visitors' Center, Frank and Karen Bastidas had been cruising for about a year on their 38-foot sloop *Karina II*, visiting anchorages from the Florida Keys to Maine and in the Bahamas. Insofar as Karen—an artist— was still painting, teaching art, and showing her work at a Florida gallery, they planned to divide their time between cruising and life ashore.

Baking soda 974

Sprinkle baking soda in the bottom of your wet coffee or tea mug, let it sit for a few minutes, and use a damp sponge to wipe out the inside surfaces—tea and coffee stains disappear. Letting baking soda sit on a wet stovetop for a few minutes also makes cleaning your stovetop much easier.

Swimming pool shock 975

You can make your own chlorine bleach using granulated chlorine sold for treating swimming pools, also known as "pool shock." Mike and Pat Davidson on *Impulse* suggest using two to three tablespoons of granulated chlorine per gallon of water to make an approximate equivalent to liquid chlorine bleach. The chlorine crystals are safer to carry, less expensive, and take up much less stowage space than liquid bleach.

Tar remover 976

Use Avon's Skin-So-Soft oil to remove tar from your feet, shoes, hull, deck, dinghy.

Waterless hand cleaners 977

Waterless hand cleaners, sold for use by mechanics and painters, are good not only for cleaning dirty hands, but also as a spot and stain remover for laundry. Use them the same way you'd use any stain removal stick to pretreat the stain before washing.

White vinegar 978

Use white vinegar in the head as a cleaner, deodorant, and disinfectant and to dissolve calcium deposits. To clean brass, mix it with salt and flour to make a paste. Put the paste on the brass, let it sit for half an hour, and wipe it off to reveal a shiny brass finish. Use white vinegar also to clean epoxy (before it has cured) from your hands and tools.

Maintenance RUDDER PIN

Anhydrous lanolin 979

Anhydrous lanolin provides an effective moisture barrier and, in spray form, can displace water. Use in any joint of dissimilar metals and on battery terminals to prevent corrosion. You can order a one-pound jar of anhydrous lanolin (it has the consistency of axle grease) from any pharmacist, and the price is modest. Alternatively, Lanocote Corrosion Inhibitor, distributed by Forespar, is based on anhydrous lanolin and is available in both aerosol and jelly form at West Marine.

Bedding compound 980

If you need black bedding compound, Reade Tompson on *Sarasan* suggests using the mastic made for bedding automobile windshields. It does an excellent job and is easier to use than marine bedding compounds. *Note:* Diesel fuel, kerosene, and gasoline are windshield mastic solvents, so do not use the mastic where fuel might be spilled on it.

Boeshield T-9 981

This wax-like aerosol lubricant is particularly effective at protecting things from water. It's perfect for the clamp screws on your outboard motor, turnbuckle threads, and padlocks and is available at most marine stores.

Long Q-tips 982

Use long Q-tips for cleaning stereo heads, as swabs to apply small amounts of paint or epoxy (we've even used them for varnish repair), and as mini-mops to clean tight spots on the engine. Buy them at Radio Shack or other electronic supply stores.

Sportsman's GOOP 983

GOOP is an adhesive/sealant that works well on plastics and rubber. It is sold for repairing sneakers and a large variety of sports paraphernalia. You can also use it to reglue the soles of shoes and to repair foulweather gear, rubber boots, torn wetsuits, and other such items.

Syringes

984

Plastic syringes are useful for getting epoxy or liquid sealant into small places. After use, clean with white vinegar, then rinse thoroughly with water to remove vinegar residue.

Tongue depressors

985

A generous supply of tongue depressors will find many uses—such as stirring paint, mixing epoxy, cleaning in small places, shaping and cleaning up bedding compounds, making shims, etc.

Mike and Pat Davidson on *Impulse*

When we first met Mike and Pat Davidson, *Impulse* was a 30-foot sloop and, like us, they had just started cruising. By the time we caught up with them nearly three years later at Elizabeth City, North Carolina, *Impulse* had just become a 44-foot ketch. In the intervening years, Mike and Pat had been cruising the waters from Maine to Florida and throughout the Bahamas.

Maintenance

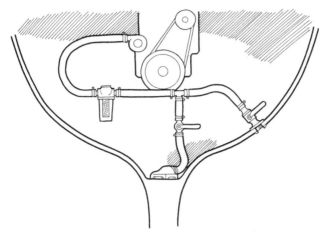

Backup Equipment

"Bilge pumps are one of those pieces of equipment that last forever—until they break."
—Dave Miller on *Jewell*

The amount of backup equipment cruisers carry on their boats depends in part on how far from home they'll be cruising. But even for a one-day outing, you need some backup equipment—for example, a spare anchor and anchor rode in case your engine fails and you need to anchor in adverse conditions. Depending on the size of your boat, you may want oars to back up your motor. Or, if not a spare bilge pump, as the comment from Dave Miller suggests, at least a bucket to bail with if the bilge pump (or battery) does fail.

General Tips

Deciding what backups to carry—Level I

986

List each piece of equipment on the boat and ask yourself seriously, "If this fails, can I do without it?" If the answer is "no," carry some form of backup.

Deciding what backups to carry—Level II

987

For each item on your equipment list, ask yourself seriously, "If this fails, do I want to do without it?" If the answer is "no," consider carrying some form of backup.

Bilge Pump Backups

Engine-cooling-water bilge pump

988

Rig the raw-water side of your engine's cooling-water system to pump the bilge in an emergency by putting a tee in the raw-water intake line ahead of the raw-water strainer. Run a hose with a shutoff valve from the tee to the bilge, mounting a strainer on the bilge end of the hose. To pump the bilge using the engine, *close the raw-water intake seacock before opening the valve to your bilge.*

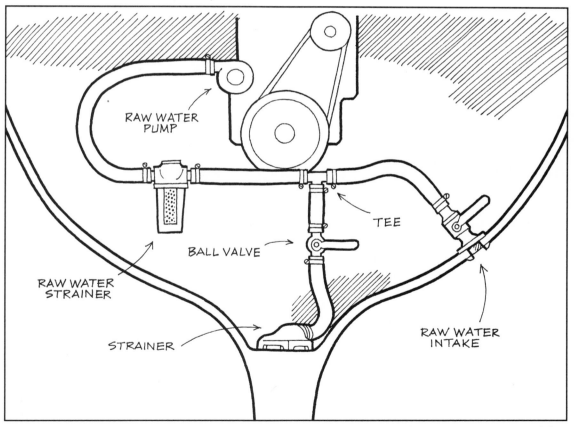

Using your engine raw-water pump as an emergency bilge pump (Tip 988).

Galley saltwater pump as bilge pump

989

If you have rigged your engine's raw-water system as an emergency bilge pump as suggested above, you can also use your galley saltwater pump in an emergency to help pump the bilge. Simply take the feed for your galley pump from the engine's raw-water system right after the water strainer—the most logical source for your galley saltwater intake anyway. If your engine is pumping water from the bilge, your galley saltwater pump will do likewise—if you turn it on.

Portable bilge pump

990

An old-fashioned Navy manual lift pump provides excellent backup to your fixed bilge pumps. Among a lift pump's virtues, Christian Le Roye on *Blue Swanny* lists the facts that there's almost nothing to go wrong with it, it's easy to stow, and it can move a lot of water.

Radio Antenna Backups

Ham radio emergency antennas

991

If you have a ham radio, Hustler whip antennas made for use on automobiles can provide emergency antennas if you lose your mast or backstay. Mike Hamilton on *Wild Duck* suggests carrying whip antennas for the 15-, 20-, and 40-meter wavelengths. Mount and test your backup antenna system.

Single-sideband emergency antenna

992

You can purchase a whip antenna called the Outbacker for your single-sideband radio for mounting on the stern rail. The antenna is adjustable for use on most single-sideband frequencies. West Marine carries this antenna, as do other marine single-sideband outlets. Mount and test your backup antenna system.

Mike Hamilton and Barbara Davis on *Wild Duck*

When we met them at the island of Culebra, Mike Hamilton and Barbara Davis on the 32-foot cutter *Wild Duck* had been cruising full-time for two years after several years of cruising six months on and six months off. Their cruises had taken them along the coast from Maine to Florida, throughout the Bahamas, and to most of the Caribbean islands from the Virgin Islands to Venezuela.

VHF antenna backup

993

Masthead VHF antennas are especially susceptible to lightning damage. A backup antenna mounted on the stern rail will keep you transmitting as long as you have a functioning radio. All you have to do is unplug the masthead antenna from the radio and plug in the backup. If your primary VHF radio is damaged by lightning, plug your handheld VHF into the backup antenna using the adapter wire described in the following tip. All backup systems should be tested to be sure they work. (See also Tips 1,155–1,157, "Protecting electronics.")

VHF Radio Backup

Handheld VHF radios

994

To make your handheld VHF a more effective backup to the primary radio, fabricate an antenna adapter wire so that you can connect your handheld radio to the masthead antenna. Required materials are 3 to 4 feet of antenna coax, a fitting on one end for connecting to the antenna lead, and a fitting on the other end for connecting to the handheld radio. The required materials are available at Radio Shack. Connections must be soldered, and the system should be tested.

Engines

"Don't buy a boat unless you can reach every part of the engine, or maintenance will be a bear."
—Jeff Lawlor on *Passport*

General Tips

Belts 995

Dwight and Karen Rettie on *Tarwathie* suggest using link belts rather than conventional "fan" belts on your engine and, if you have one, your prop shaft generator. One brand is the Brammer Nu-T-Link. An advantage of link belts is that you can replace an inside belt without removing the others because you can open and close the belt by removing a link. You can also carry a spare section of belt and add or take out links to adjust belt length.

Bleeding the fuel system 996

Acting on the advice of their mechanic, Art and Lynne Bourne on *Suits Us* installed a squeeze bulb in their diesel line between the fuel tank and fuel filter/water separator. They use that bulb to pump fuel through the system if they need to bleed it.

Disposing of dirty oil 997

Save the empty plastic containers your engine oil comes in, using a permanent Magic Marker to make large Xs all over the containers so that it's

clear they do not contain virgin oil. When you change your oil, put the dirty oil into these containers and save them until you are able to dispose of them properly. Always keep enough empty containers on hand to be able to change your oil. (See also Tip 1,012, "Spare oil.")

Engineroom light 998

Sooner or later you will need an engineroom light. If you don't want to install one permanently, carry a portable light with a long cord like that described in Tip 1,159, "Trouble light."

Cooling Systems

Freshwater cooling system 999

Remove and inspect the zincs in the raw-water side of your freshwater cooling system regularly, replacing them as needed. Also, inspect belts and hoses routinely. Belts must be removed and turned inside out to look for cracks. Check hoses for flexibility, cracking, and corrosion at the hose ends. If you see corrosion or any sign of leakage at a hose end,

Dan Robbins and Pam Jeffreys on *Alana*

When Dan Robbins and Pam Jeffreys on the 30-foot, sloop-rigged motorsailer *Alana* sailed away from their North Carolina home, they had planned to cruise for a year. When we met them in Vero Beach, they were well into their second year. Their cruise so far had taken them from North Carolina to Florida, throughout the Bahamas, and north to the Chesapeake Bay.

remove the hose and check the nipple carefully. As an example of what can happen: When Dan Robbins on *Alana* noticed corrosion where the cooling-water hose joined his transmission, the nipple broke off the transmission as he was removing the hose to investigate.

Heat exchangers   1000

On a regular basis—every three to six months—circulate a fifty-fifty vinegar-water solution through the raw-water side of your heat exchanger to remove salt or calcium deposits. Bill Hartge on *Alegria* also runs a stiff wire through each tube in the heat exchanger once a year to make certain of no blockage.

Engine Logs

Maintenance log   1001

A detailed engine maintenance and repair log provides a record of your engine's health that will help you spot potential problems before they arise. For example, you'll soon learn how often you can expect to change the zincs in your heat exchanger, or when to start looking for a water pump seal to begin leaking, so that you can anticipate maintenance needs and/or replacement of parts.

Operating log   1002

A detailed engine operating log will also help you spot potential problems and keep track of your fuel usage. In *Sea Sparrow*'s engine operating log, for example, we record the engine hour meter reading at the end of each day's run. We also keep a running total of the engine hours since the last oil change and since taking on fuel. In addition, we note each time we check the engine, transmission, and V-drive oil levels and the Racor fuel filter. Finally, we record when we change the oil, filters, etc. and note the engine hours and quantity whenever we add oil to the engine, transmission, or V-drive. This log provides us with an operating history of our engine, all in one fat spiral notebook. On three occasions, the log has enabled us to identify oil leaks from worn seals before they were visible to the eye or became a problem.

Fuel System

Fuel filter/water separator I   1003

Before opening your fuel filter/water separator for maintenance, close the fuel valve at the tank to prevent fuel in the line from draining backwards into the tank when the filter is opened. When finished with the filter, be sure to open the fuel line valve once again. *Note:* If you do not have a shutoff valve in the fuel line where it emerges from the tank, install one.

Fuel filter/water separator II   1004

Check your fuel filter/water separator on a regular basis. Visual checks should be made every time you open the engineroom. If there is water in the bottom of the glass bowl, drain it into a container. If you see a significant amount of dirt in the glass bowl, check the filter element for contamination. Algae or other dirt will be clearly visible on the filter element if present in significant amounts. If appropriate, flush the dirt from the glass bowl, replace the filter element, and refill the housing with clean fuel. *Note:* Put any dirty fuel drained from the filter/water separator into one of the plastic containers used for old engine oil. (See Tip 997, "Disposing of dirty oil.")

Lubrication

Additives   1005

If you buy a used boat, Win Smith on *Rosinante* recommends against using engine oil additives to clean the engine. If the engine is dirty, additives may break stuff loose and cause more problems than they will solve. Instead, change the oil more frequently than recommended and let the detergents in the oil clean the engine more gradually.

Changing the oil   1006

Follow the recommendations in your engine owner's manual religiously—with one exception.

If you are setting out on a passage of two days or longer, change your oil and oil filter before you go. If you must do a lot of motoring on that passage, it's much easier to change the oil and filter before you go than to discover halfway through your passage that you need to change them at sea.

Motoring long hours 1007

When motoring long hours, stop the engine at least every twelve hours to check the engine oil. Although your previous oil consumption history can give you some confidence about your engine's rate of oil consumption, prudence suggests monitoring the oil throughout long hours of operation.

Oil color 1008

Note the color of your oil whenever you change it and on the dipstick every time you check it. If cooling water is getting into your lubricating system, the oil will be white or gray.

Oil diapers 1009

Marine stores sell diapers for soaking up the oil in your engine oil drip pan, but Jim Cazer on *Mariah* recommends using disposable baby diapers as a less expensive and somewhat neater alternative. Jim also uses a disposable diaper to catch spills when he is changing the oil.

Jim and Terry Cazer on *Mariah*

In three years of cruising, Jim and Terry Cazer on the 32-foot cutter *Mariah* had explored much of the U.S. East Coast and the Bahamas and followed the Thorny Path to the Caribbean. There, they island-hopped east to the Leeward Islands and south down the Leeward and Windward Islands to Trinidad for hurricane season. We met them after they'd worked their way back north to the Puerto Rican island of Culebra.

Oil filters 1010

Many engine manufacturers recommend changing the oil filter every second oil change. Unanimously, cruisers who offered tips in this area said they change their filters with every oil change.

Oil level 1011

Pete Seddon on *John Martin* noted that if, when you check the oil, the oil level in your engine or transmission is higher than you would expect, you need to find out why. For example, a year or so after hearing this tip, the fact that we did not have to add oil to *Sea Sparrow*'s engine at normal intervals, but began adding oil to the transmission, helped us figure out that we were leaking oil from the transmission into the crankcase.

Spare oil 1012

If you will be cruising in remote areas, carry a minimum one-year supply of oil and replace the oil you use as soon as you can. That way you will always have oil when you need it. Even when cruising in local waters, carry at least enough oil for two complete oil changes.

Spare oil filters 1013

If you will be cruising in remote areas, you probably cannot carry too many spare filters. If you need engine oil, you may be able to get some in a pinch from another boat—even from a large ship—but oil filters that will fit your engine will be much more difficult to find.

Exterior

General Tips

Coaming access   1014

Install deck plates in the vertical surface of your coamings to provide access to the nuts on bolts fastening winches and other hardware to the coaming.

Epoxy cleanup   1015

Use white vinegar to clean up epoxy resin; be careful, however, not to get vinegar into places where you want epoxy to set up.

Teak   1016

Use oxalic acid to bleach teak. It is the primary active ingredient in many teak cleaners, but less expensive than the cleaners.

Boat Bottoms

Antifouling   1017

Conrad Johnson, Jr. on *Copasetic* is one of several cruisers we've met who recommend adding cayenne pepper to bottom paint to enhance its antifouling action. The formula Conrad suggests is four ounces of cayenne pepper powder to a gallon of bottom paint, mixed with an electric mixer to distribute it evenly. The pepper makes the paint surface a bit rough (like sandpaper), but Conrad swears by its effectiveness. Ever hopeful, we put cayenne pepper in our bottom paint and found that, indeed, it's a great

help! After twelve months in south Florida waters, there was only minor scum and a scattering of small barnacles on *Sea Sparrow*'s peppered bottom—a sharp contrast to earlier years when we had to scrub the bottom every couple of months to keep it clean.

Bottom paint   1018

If you'll be cruising in remote areas, carry enough bottom paint for at least one haulout. Paint the can bottoms to protect against rust. If, when it's time to haul, you find you can purchase the kind of paint you want, use the paint from your stores and save the new paint for future use—again, painting the can bottoms.

Prop and shaft   1019

Mike Karamargin on *Carrie Bennett* says that smearing anhydrous lanolin on the prop and shaft prevents barnacle growth. The prop and shaft must be clean, dry, and dust free for the lanolin to adhere properly. Anhydrous lanolin, which Mike describes as "awful stuff," is a thick, sticky grease obtained from wool. It is impervious to water and difficult, even, to wash off your hands. Ask a pharmacist to order Anhydrous Lanolin USP for you. A one-pound jar will go a long way. (See also Tip 979, "Anhydrous lanolin.")

Kathy and Conrad Johnson, Jr. on *Copasetic*

When we met them in Vero Beach, Kathy and Conrad Johnson, Jr. had been cruising the waters from Rhode Island to the Florida Keys and the Bahamas for more than four years on their 38-foot cutter *Copasetic*, and were planning to extend their cruising into the Caribbean.

Scrubbing the bottom I — 1020

When you're cruising in warm waters, scrub the boat's bottom every four to six weeks, swimming with a mask and snorkel. This frequency keeps growth to a minimum so that the job is relatively easy. However, you'll need a hard bottom paint to withstand the scrubbing.

Scrubbing the bottom II — 1021

Break the job into small parts—say, half of one side at a time—so that you do it over a few days rather than trying to do it all at once.

Scrubbing the bottom III — 1022

A scrub brush with a handle you can wrap your fingers around works well. Usually, you can knock barnacles off with the plastic frame of the brush. To remove seaweed growths that would otherwise clog the brush, use a flexible plastic spreader blade as a scraper. The plastic blade, commonly used to spread fairing compound or thick mastics, is also effective in removing baby barnacles.

Hull Stains

Cleaning dark topsides — 1023

Dark topsides that develop a white salt film can be cleaned using OSPHO, a phosphoric acid solution sold in marine and hardware stores. Dilute the OSPHO with water, wipe it onto the hull, and watch the white film disappear. Then, rinse thoroughly. Diluted OSPHO can be used safely in this manner on gelcoat and, we are told, such two-part polyurethane coatings as Awlgrip. On any surface, however, we suggest testing the OSPHO/water mixture on a small area before using it on the entire hull.

Removing hull stains I — 1024

Toilet bowl cleaners can be used to remove brown stains from gelcoat. Use a rag or small sprayer to apply, watch the stains dissolve away, and rinse the area thoroughly with water. *Caution:* Be sure to wear rubber gloves and goggles when using these cleaners on your hull. They are dangerous to your eyes and are hard on skin.

Removing hull stains II — 1025

Commercial jellied stain removers such as Y-10 or SLX will remove brown gelcoat stains effectively. Apply with a damp cloth and rinse thoroughly with water after the stain has disappeared. For some stains, a second application may be needed. Of the two products, we've found SLX much more economical to use; a quart bottle cleaned our entire 36-foot hull from waterline to toerail twice. Rubber gloves are advisable.

Removing hull stains III — 1026

A dilute phosphoric acid solution (OSPHO, see Tip 1,023) is another effective stain remover for use on gelcoat. Wipe on with a rag, wait five minutes, and flush off with lots of water. Use rubber gloves.

Paint and Varnish

Exterior teak — 1027

Paint your rubrail, caprail, outboard motor mount, and other hard-wear pieces of exterior teak. It may not be quite as pretty, but it greatly reduces maintenance—particularly in the tropics. If you take the trim down to bare wood and apply a single coat of varnish before painting, you can easily restore the original finish when you are no longer cruising and have more time for brightwork.

Name/home port lettering — 1028

For lettering that endures and is not affected by hull cleaners or waxes, paint your boat name and home port with the same two-part polyurethane used for your bootstripe and covestripe, applying the polyurethane coating right over the existing paint. First, sand the painted letters with fine sandpaper to remove the oxidized surface. Wash thoroughly with water and let it dry completely. Next, outline each letter with 3M Fineline masking tape, pressing the tape securely against the hull. When the lettering is completely taped, apply two coats of the two-part polyurethane on successive days. Don't worry about getting paint on the masking tape. Remove the tape carefully after the second coat has become tack free. If any paint has seeped under the tape, scrape it off gently with a knife.

Removing painted lettering from the hull   1029

Al and Helen Roderick on *Lady Helen* have good news for anyone faced with changing the registration number, name, or home port painted on their fiberglass boat. Easy Off oven cleaner provides an easy and effective way to remove the old lettering (unless it's painted with two-part polyurethane). Just spray it on, let it sit for a while, and wipe it off. Several applications will be required. When you're finished, there will be a faint image of the lettering remaining, but that fades away after a few weeks.

Silicone contamination   1030

Use fisheye eliminator, sold at automotive paint stores, to enable paint or varnish to adhere properly to silicone-contaminated surfaces. The most likely sources of silicone contamination of painted or var-nished surfaces are boat waxes and spray cleaners or polishes for plastic windows.

Plastics

Cleaning plastic windows I   1031

Davies Klear-to-Sea is recommended by Mike and Pat Davidson on *Impulse* for cleaning and repairing scratches in Plexiglas, Lexan, and soft vinyl windows.

Cleaning plastic windows II   1032

Use only window cleaners containing vinegar to clean plastic windows. Ammonia products will damage the plastic.

Dodger windows I   1033

Use plain Pledge spray wax to keep your dodger windows clear and supple. Note, however, that Pledge contains silicones that can complicate varnishing and painting. (See Tip 1,030, "Silicone contamination.")

Dodger windows II   1034

As an alternative to Pledge, Terry Cazer on *Mariah* suggests rubbing dodger windows monthly with baby oil to keep the plastic soft.

Scratch remover   1035

Sarah Tompson on *Sarasan* recommends using Plastic Scratch Remover to remove scratches in Lexan. It is a mild abrasive and requires a lot of rubbing, she says, but it works well. We have used this product on *Sea Sparrow* with success. It is available at BOAT/U.S.

Al and Helen Roderick on *Lady Helen*

Al and Helen Roderick sailed away from Massachusetts on a 35-foot wooden sailboat shortly after their marriage in 1974 to begin cruising. When we met them aboard the 36-foot fiberglass sloop *Lady Helen* in Oriental, North Carolina, they had been cruising continuously for eighteen years in a succession of boats, sailing throughout the Caribbean and Gulf of Mexico, along the U.S. East Coast from Maine to Florida, throughout the Bahamas, and up the Pacific coast of Central America to California.

Miscellaneous Maintenance

"Everything breaks sooner or later."
— Jeff Lawlor on *Passport*

"We're always fixing something."
— Dave Miller on *Jewell*

General Tips

(See also Tips 979–985.)

Canvas snaps · 1036

An occasional dab of petroleum jelly in the female half of a snap keeps the snaps on your canvaswork easy to fasten and unfasten.

Hose clamps · 1037

Check all hose clamps with a magnet before using them. Too often, even though the package says "all stainless steel," only the clamps are stainless steel; the screws are ferrous metal and will rust.

Moisture protection · 1038

To protect joints of dissimilar metals against moisture and corrosion, spray with Lanocote anhydrous lanolin spray. (See also Tip 979, "Anhydrous lanolin," and Tip 981, "Boeshield T-9.")

Padlocks · 1039

When padlocks become stiff from effects of the marine environment, soak them for 30 minutes in a weak vinegar solution of one part vinegar to four parts water. Use just enough in a small bowl to immerse one lock (open). You can soak several locks in succession without renewing the solution as long as the original solution seems to do the job. The locks will work like new, though the vinegar may affect the color of any brass. After letting the lock dry, spray inside and out with WD-40 or Boeshield T-9 (see Tip 981).

Toothbrushes · 1040

Save your old toothbrushes. They're handy for cleaning in tight places and can be used with most cleaners and solvents. Well-used, soft-bristled toothbrushes can also serve as paintbrushes for small jobs. We've even used toothbrushes to help clean our anchor chain (the inside of the links).

Vinyl overhead liner · 1041

When the soft vinyl overhead material begins to look old, clean it thoroughly and paint it with oil-based outdoor enamel house paint. Use a primer coat first.

Batteries

Adding water to batteries I 1042

A basting syringe (used for basting turkeys and roasts) is a handy tool for adding water to your batteries.

Adding water to batteries II 1043

Use an old battery acid bag that has been washed out thoroughly; alternatively, a small enema or douche bag works well. Whatever you use, rinse it thoroughly with distilled water before its first use for battery water and then dedicate it to your batteries to avoid future contamination.

Battery boxes 1044

Spread a layer of baking soda on the bottom of your battery boxes before installing the batteries. If the battery acid overflows into the bottom of the battery box during charging, the baking soda will neutralize the acid.

Cleaning battery terminals 1045

Sprinkle baking soda on the terminals and clean them off with a damp sponge. After cleaning, coat with anhydrous lanolin (see Tip 979).

Overfilling batteries 1046

When you charge a battery, the electrolyte (battery acid) expands and will overflow if you have added too much water. To avoid this problem, charge the batteries before topping off the water. If the battery water is extremely low, add enough water to cover the plates, charge the battery, and then bring the water up to ring level.

Brass and Stainless Steel

(See also Tip 978, "White Vinegar.")

Brass I 1047

Wipe the dust off interior brass fixtures regularly. If dust remains on the brass for a long time, it will absorb moisture and salt from the air and eat right through the protective lacquer coating.

Brass II 1048

A fine fiberglass rubbing compound works well as a brass polish and leaves a wax film to retard tarnishing.

Brass III 1049

Karen Rettie on *Tarwathie* recommends Bar Keeper's Friend brass polish, noting that she's found it in supermarkets in Florida.

Rust stains I 1050

Use a weak phosphoric acid solution (OSPHO, see Tip 1,023) to remove rust stains from stainless steel (or fiberglass). Wipe it on with a rag and wait five minutes before rubbing. If there's still rust, apply again and rub. Flush the stainless steel (or fiberglass) thoroughly with water when finished.

Rust stains II 1051

As an alternative to metal polishes or acids, use fiberglass rubbing compound to remove rust stains and polish your stainless steel. It does a nice job and leaves a thin coating of wax on the metal.

Routines and Record Keeping

Maintenance log   1052

Iain and Joan Lees on *Diura* are among a number of cruisers suggesting that you keep a detailed maintenance log—all in one book. They maintain logs for the engine (see Tip 1,001, "Engine Logs: Maintenance log"), the batteries and electrical system, fuel system, and water system, including seacocks. The log includes the date, a description of the problem or maintenance, who did the work, and a space for comments, including a description of symptoms and, if applicable, a summary of how the problem was diagnosed. Additional items worth logging are sail and canvas maintenance, and replacement or maintenance of running rigging.

Rituals   1053

A technique for ensuring that maintenance gets done in a timely manner is to develop rituals

Iain and Joan Lees on *Diura*

In just eighteen months after sailing from their home in Scotland, Iain and Joan Lees on the 31-foot sloop *Diura* had covered a lot of water when we met them in Annapolis. Their course had taken them to Ireland, the Iberian Peninsula, and Morocco before crossing the Atlantic to the West Indies. From the Caribbean, they sailed north to Maine via Bermuda, then worked their way south to the Chesapeake Bay.

around a maintenance schedule. For example, certain things are checked on a daily basis, others weekly, monthly, or whatever. If these rituals are formalized, it's a simple matter to lay out at the beginning of each week the maintenance items to be handled in the next seven days, and then to do them. The alternative is to do maintenance when you think of it, which too often will only be after a problem has drawn your attention to the need.

Sail Care

General Tips, 1,054–1,057
Repairing Your Sails, 1,058–1,061

General Tips

Bagged headsails   1054

To keep your bagged headsail off the deck, use a piece of ⅜-inch line to make a cradle for the sail by running it from port to starboard to port between the lower rail of the bow pulpit and the lower lifelines, securing the end with a clove hitch around the lower lifeline.

Roller-furling mainsails   1055

To prevent chafe of stitching on sails that furl into the mast, furl the sail either while heading directly into the wind or so that it rolls into the mast on the side opposite the sail (that is, the starboard side of the mast on the starboard tack). Otherwise, the upper panels of the sail will rub against the edge of the mast slot as the sail is furled, gradually wearing on the seam stitching.

Sail ties 1056

A 6- to 8-foot length of $\frac{3}{16}$-inch shock cord makes an excellent sail tie. Put a small loop in one end of the shock cord using a bowline, and pull the knot very tight. Run the end of the shock cord around the sail and through the loop, and secure the sail with a series of half hitches at 2- or 3-foot intervals.

Solar UV protection 1057

If the boat will be at anchor or dockside for a month or more in tropical or subtropical climates, strip the sails—including roller-furling jibs—from the rigging and stow them below or under an awning. Even though the sails may be under sail covers or have a sacrificial strip, the sun attacks the stitching and shortens the lives of the covers.

Repairing Your Sails

Resewing seams 1058

If a seam goes on a sail, stitch it up by hand using the old needle holes where possible.

Rick and Deanna Helms on *Themroc*

Rick and Deanna Helms set out from California on their 40-foot sloop *Themroc,* intending to sail in Mexico for six months to see how they liked cruising. Apparently they liked it. When we met them nearly five years later in Elizabeth City, North Carolina, they had cruised down the coast of Central America to Panama, transited the Canal, and crossed to Colombia before sailing up through the western Caribbean to Florida and along the U.S. East Coast to New York before turning around.

This avoids making new holes, which would weaken the fabric.

Sail repair kit 1059

In addition to awls, sail thread, and a sailmaker's palm, carry 20 feet or more of 2-inch-wide sailcloth tape with an adhesive backing. To make a simple patch by hand underway, first flush the area to be patched with fresh water to remove salt residue, if you sail in salt water. When the sail is dry, fit the torn portion together and apply the sailcloth tape to both sides of the sail. Stitch around the edge of the tape using continuous "zigzag" stitching. You may need a pair of pliers to pull the awl through the sailcloth if you are stitching through several layers, as along the leech tape.

Self-adhesive-tape alternative 1060

Rick and Deanna Helms on *Themroc* suggest using contact cement or Velcro adhesive to glue the sailcloth patch in place before sewing. Position the patch and mark the outline with pencil or pen. Apply cement to both the patch itself and the area to be patched. When the cement is tack-free, apply the patch and press firmly in place before stitching. It works. We've tried it!

Slides and jib hanks 1061

Sail slides and jib hanks can be an unexpected source of sail failure—particularly if your sail does much slatting in a windless, rolling sea. For that reason, you should carry spare slides and hanks as well as the waxed twine and webbing needed to attach them.

Sewing and Sewing Machines

General Tips

Buying a sewing machine 1062

Shop thrift stores (such as Goodwill and the Salvation Army) for your sewing machine: elderly but functioning sewing machines can be found for just a few dollars. For example, Larry and Elaine Quayle on *The Glass Lady* were able to combine parts from two thrift-store machines to get a foot-pedal-controlled, electric zigzag machine capable of sewing Sunbrella fabric for a total cost of sixteen dollars.

Hand-cranked sewing machines 1063

You can convert many electric sewing machines to use with a hand crank by purchasing a kit specifically designed for the purpose. A supplier recommended by Phil Jones and Anita Tomlin on *Sweet Pea* is SailRite Kits, 305 West VanBuren St., Columbia City, IN 46725, telephone (800) 348-2795, extension 5.

Larry and Elaine Quayle on *The Glass Lady*

When we met Larry and Elaine Quayle in Elizabeth City, they had been cruising for two years on their 34-foot sloop, *The Glass Lady*. Their cruise had taken them to anchorages up and down the coast from Maine to Florida and throughout the Bahamas.

Sewing machine needles 1064

If you want to use your sewing machine for sails or canvaswork, get industrial-quality needles made specifically for sewing sailcloth and canvas.

Sewing Velcro 1065

If you are going to sew Velcro, use Velcro without preglued backing. The glue gums up sewing machine needles quickly.

Sinking Prevention

(See also Tip 1,128,
   "Muffler warning.")

Definition: *Boat-sinking maintenance*—maintenance that can sink your boat if left undone.

Among the many maintenance needs on a boat, most are necessary only to keep the boat working well. There are some maintenance requirements, however, that are vital to keep the boat afloat, or to keep it from sinking.

General Tips

Chafe   1066

Chafe is not limited to sails, rope, and things outside of the boat. For example, Denis Webster on *Tiger Lily* found that his hoses were chafing where they went through bulkheads or rubbed against hard edges. To solve the problem, he put short

Denis and Arleen Webster on *Tiger Lily*

Canadians Denis and Arleen Webster on *Tiger Lily*, a 37-foot cutter, began their cruise in the Great Lakes nine months before we first met them in the Abacos. Their route took them down the New York State Barge Canal System and the Hudson River to New York City, then coastwise and along the Intracoastal Waterway to Florida before they crossed to the Bahamas. Two years later, we saw them again in Trinidad.

lengths of clear vinyl hose around his fuel and water hoses as chafe guards wherever he found evidence of chafe.

Hose clamps   1067

It's not enough to inspect hose clamps visually. Use a screwdriver to loosen and tighten the clamps every few months to be sure they are tight and to check for failure. On *Alana*, Dan Robbins and Pam Jeffreys report that a loose hose clamp resulted in their losing a tank of fresh water when the pressure water system kept on pumping as they motorsailed down the Intracoastal Waterway. On *Sea Sparrow*, a so-called stainless steel hose clamp on the raw-water strainer failed when we went to loosen the clamp. The second hose clamp was secure, and we were reminded why we have two hose clamps wherever the nipple is long enough to permit such doubling up. (See also Tip 1,037, "Hose clamps.")

Hoses   1068

Engine hoses on boats, like those on your car, will age from the effects of heat and vibration, and can fail. For that reason, you should check your engine hoses periodically. Be sure to remove hoses from their fittings to inspect the ends carefully; the most vulnerable section is the inch or two that slides over the metal nipple and is secured by hose clamps.

Seacocks   1069

Service seacocks at each haulout, lubricating them with water pump grease. Also, at least once a month, "exercise" your seacocks by closing and opening them several times to make sure they don't freeze in the open position. If they are hard to open and close, exercise them weekly.

Stuffing box hose   1070

At least once per year, carefully check the health of the hose connecting your stern tube to the stuffing box. On an older boat, consider replacing the hose. Jeff and Mary Ann Lawlor on *Passport* had their stuffing box hose fail while coming alongside a dock in Venezuela with a lot of shifting between reverse and forward. They felt lucky the boat didn't sink. Four pumps were needed to keep ahead of the water until they could get the leak stopped.

Spare Parts

(See also Tips 986–994, "Backup Equipment.")

"Always carry a spare part so that the first one won't break."

—Mike McGivern on *Decatur*

The boating literature is filled with recommendations for spare parts to carry if you are doing any long-distance cruising—such things as injectors for the diesel engine, and spare stays and shrouds. We've found greater need, however, for more mundane items like spare light bulbs, running lights to replace those damaged by lightning, zincs, two or three specific parts for the head, burner parts for the stove, and a variety of seals and gaskets for the engine.

spare parts bought in the U.S., rather than purchasing the same parts at the moment of need while cruising in the islands, can save a considerable amount of money. In fact, you don't have to use very many parts from your inventory to save enough money to cover the cost of your remaining spares.

Deciding what spares to carry I   1073

Denis and Arleen Webster on *Tiger Lily* suggest giving a lot of thought to spare parts. In their first year of cruising, they had to rebuild the head, used all of their spare engine and heat exchanger hoses, replaced the freshwater pressure pump, and replaced a propane hose when a fitting cracked and began leaking.

General Tips

A contrarian viewpoint   1071

Pete Seddon on *John Martin* follows a different philosophy than most cruisers when it comes to spare parts. "We don't carry many spares at all," Pete says. "You can buy them. And if the engine goes, you can always sail." Pete notes also that spare parts add weight to the boat, take up stowage space, and tie up money.

Cruising in "the islands"   1072

Most of the time, marine parts are much more expensive in small island countries than they are in the United States. As a result, inventorying

Pete and Yvonne Seddon on *John Martin*

Pete and Yvonne Seddon left their home in England to begin cruising fourteen years before we met them in the British Virgin Islands aboard *John Martin,* a 37½-foot sloop they had built themselves. In that time, they had cruised along the Atlantic coast of Europe from northern France to Gibraltar, into the Mediterranean, and back to the U.K. via the canals of France before crossing to the Caribbean.

Deciding what spares to carry II   1074

When a problem develops, get two of everything you need to repair it—within reason, of course. For example, when we had to replace the oil seal located where the shifter arm enters the transmission, we purchased two seals and two gaskets, under the assumption that we'll have to replace the seal again after a similar number of engine hours.

Deciding what spares to carry III   1075

When cruising away from the coastal U.S., load up on parts that you know need replacing regularly. Examples include water pump impellers, water pump shaft seals, head pump seals and snap rings, light bulbs, rebuild kits for heads and potable water pumps, and an excess of oil and fuel filters.

Engine parts   1076

At a minimum, carry spares needed to maintain your engine. This would include spare oil and fuel filters, belts, hoses, and a thermostat (unless your engine will run at the desired temperature without a thermostat). You should also carry enough oil to change the engine and transmission oil at least twice, and be sure to replace your spare oil as you use it.

Manufacturers' parts lists   1077

Carry the manufacturers' parts books or lists for your engine, transmission, and other equipment—the head, refrigeration unit, wind generator, stove. A parts list, complete with an exploded diagram of the unit, makes it easier to order replacement parts by telephone and will help you get all of the items you need to replace the critical part that failed—for example, gaskets or O-rings that should be replaced when you reassemble the unit. The exploded parts diagrams also will often illustrate how things go together (or come apart) better than a service manual.

Service manuals   1078

Carry service manuals for all of your mechanical equipment. Also, query the engine manufacturer to be sure you have the correct manuals to cover the engine, transmission, and, if applicable, the V-drive. Even if you don't want to make repairs yourself, the manuals may be helpful to the mechanic you hire to do the work for you.

Spares for major parts   1079

If a major part fails, buy a new one and rebuild the old part to keep for a spare. For example, when their starter motor burned out, Alex and Diane Allmayer-Beck on *Ariel III* purchased a new starter motor, but also had the old one rebuilt as a spare. Similarly, when we purchased a higher-output alternator, we kept the original alternator as a spare.

Spare parts inventory   1080

Spare parts are worthless if you can't find them, or forget that you have them. Maintain an accurate list of the spare parts carried and where each is stowed.

Tools

"You either need a lot of tools, or a lot of money."

—Jim Stolte on *Siris IV*

"You can't bring too many tools, no matter what the wife says."

—Kay Stolte on *Siris IV*

General Tips

Cordless electric tools   1081

Carry cordless tools that you can recharge on the boat using either an inverter or a 110-volt generator. If you have only one cordless electric tool, make it a drill. You can take it anywhere, even up the mast.

Soldering iron   1082

Brian and Pam Saffery Cooper on *Lucky Dragon* suggest including a butane soldering iron among your tools. This type is considerably easier to use than a 12-volt version. In addition to its obvious use for soldering, switching to a knife-like tip lets you use it as a hot knife to melt the ends of nylon and polyester line. Another tip functions as a miniature blowtorch and can be used to apply shrink-wrap insulation on wire joints. We took Brian and Pam's suggestion, and now wonder how we ever got along without it!

Special tools   1083

When cruising away from your home waters, take with you any special tools needed to disassemble your engine or transmission and put it back together—particularly for replacing oil seals. Although you can often find a mechanic capable of doing the work needed, he may not have the special tools required for your particular engine or transmission. Consult with your engine distributor.

Tool bag   1084

Apart from your toolbox, maintain a small ditty bag containing the tools you use most often—screwdrivers, pliers, wire cutters, box wrenches—for odd jobs around the boat and checking engine fluids. This way, you don't have to get out your heavy toolbox every time you need to tighten a screw.

Tool maintenance   1085

To prevent rust, spray your tools periodically with WD-40. If they are exposed to salt water, rinse them in fresh water, dry them thoroughly, and spray with WD-40.

Brian and Pam Saffery Cooper on *Lucky Dragon*

In the thirteen months since leaving their home in England, Brian and Pam Saffery Cooper on the 41½-foot cutter *Lucky Dragon* had sailed to the Caribbean, then followed the Windward and Leeward Islands north before hopping off to Bermuda and on to Maine and New Brunswick, Canada. When we met them in Beaufort, North Carolina, they were exploring their way south along the Intracoastal Waterway.

Major Equipment and Systems

Bilge Pumps

(See also Tips 988–990,
   "Bilge Pump Backups.")

Most boats with any kind of cabin come with a bilge pump as standard equipment; sailboats intended for cruising are frequently also equipped with a manual bilge pump located in the cockpit. As a result, bilge pumps are frequently taken for granted—until they are needed. Indeed, in a Florida anchorage it was a bucket brigade, not the failed electric bilge pump, that kept a nearby 35-foot sloop from sinking until the captain could find the leak and jam rags in the broken plastic through-hull fitting (with no seacock) at the bottom of a huge cockpit locker.

General Tips

Bilge pump float switch   1086

Place the float switch so that it does not have to get wet to float, by installing a remote trigger, as suggested by Wayne Koci on *Splinter*. Materials needed are a length of ½-inch PVC pipe, a cork or piece of closed-cell foam, and a ⅜-inch dowel. Begin by mounting the float switch amidships directly above the deepest part of the bilge. Next, measure the distance from the switch to about 3 inches above the bilge bottom, and cut the dowel to that length. Cut the PVC pipe about 4 inches shorter than the dowel. Glue the cork or foam securely to the end of the dowel. Insert the dowel into the PVC pipe, and secure the pipe/dowel system in the bilge with the cork/foam down so that the top of the pipe is an inch or less below the float switch. When the water level rises in the bilge, the cork/foam will float, lifting the dowel in the pipe until it pushes up on the float switch, triggering the bilge pump.

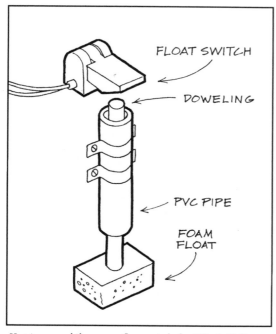

FLOAT SWITCH

DOWELING

PVC PIPE

FOAM FLOAT

Keeping your bilge pump float switch dry (Tip 1,086).

Wayne Koci on *Splinter*

Singlehander Wayne Koci had sailed from his home near Chicago a year and a half before we met him in the British Virgin Islands, taking his 36-foot double-headsail sloop *Splinter* from Lake Michigan to the Gulf of Mexico, around Florida, and up the coast to the Chesapeake Bay before returning south to cross over to the Bahamas and follow the islands to the Caribbean.

Bilge pump outlets   1087

Bilge pumps connected to through-hull fittings on the side of the boat are at risk of back-siphoning and flooding when the boat is heeled. For this reason, bilge pump through-hull fittings should be placed high in the middle of the transom whenever possible. An alternative is to run the bilge pump hose to the cockpit, with the hose plumbed to discharge directly into a cockpit drain.

Mounting a bilge pump in a deep sump   1088

To install an electric bilge pump in a deep sump, mount the pump on a length of teak ½ inch thick and long enough to reach the bottom of the sump. Secure both the hose and wiring from the pump to this piece of teak, ending the hose with an ell fitting and the wires with electrical connectors that can be sealed using Liquid Electrical Tape. Install the assembly in the bilge, securing the top of the teak board to a floor member. Complete the wiring and hose-to-outlet connections. *Note:* It's necessary to rig the hose and wires so they can be unplugged at the top of the assembly for pump maintenance or replacement.   ☞

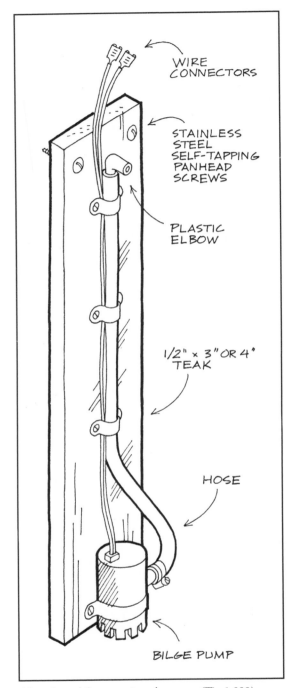

Mounting a bilge pump in a deep sump (Tip 1,088).

WIRE
CONNECTORS

STAINLESS
STEEL
SELF-TAPPING
PANHEAD
SCREWS

PLASTIC
ELBOW

1/2" × 3" OR 4"
TEAK

HOSE

BILGE PUMP

Diesel Engines

(See also Tips 995–1,013,
    "Engines.")
General Tips, 1,089–1,090
Troubleshooting, 1,091–1,092

General Tips

Battery charging   1089

Reduce to a minimum your need to run your ship's
engine solely to charge batteries—for at least three
reasons: Diesel engines do not like to be run without a load. Also, each hour of battery charging not
only consumes at least one hour of useful engine
life, but consumes fuel and oil—both of which may
be in short supply when cruising in remote areas.

Mechanics   1090

If a mechanic comes aboard your boat to repair
your engine (or anything else, for that matter), tells

Bob and Chesley Logcher on *Cygnet*

In the late 1980s, Bob and Chesley Logcher on
the 37-foot cutter *Cygnet* made a six-month sabbatical cruise from Boston to the Caribbean and
back to gain some long-distance cruising experience. After returning to work for four more
years, they moved aboard *Cygnet* to cruise full-
time and began making their way south. Six
months later, we met them in Vero Beach.

you he's found the problem, installs a new part, and the same problem recurs soon after, Bob and Chesley Logcher on *Cygnet* suggest that you not go back to him for a second try. Instead, find a better mechanic. The difficulty, Bob explains, is that some so-called mechanics (or servicemen) are, in effect, parts changers, and it can get very expensive as they replace first one part and then another in their efforts to solve your problem. What you need is a good diagnostician.

Troubleshooting

Engine stops running 1091

If your engine stops running, it is likely due to one of four reasons: the prop is fouled; the engine is overheated; the engine is not getting fuel; or, the air intake is blocked. Check each possibility in the following order.

1) Fouled prop: Put the transmission in neutral and attempt to turn the shaft by hand. If it turns freely for several rotations in both directions, that's probably not the problem.

2) Overheating: Do not try to turn over the engine with the starter until you have checked the cooling system and oil and let the engine cool for at least an hour. If the engine has seized, you may bend the crankshaft by trying to start it. First, check the water intake, the raw-water strainer, the freshwater coolant level, and the water pumps. If the raw-water intake is clogged, it has probably been fouled by a plastic bag and can be easily cleared. If no problem is apparent in the cooling system, check the oil level. *Note:* When the engine is hot, the engine oil will be so thin (because of the heat) that it may be difficult to get a dipstick reading until the engine has cooled somewhat.

3) Engine not getting fuel: The most likely fuel problems are an empty tank, a clogged filter, water in the fuel, or air in the fuel lines. Check the level of fuel in the tank first. If adequate, check the fuel filter/water separator(s), for water and/or a fouled filter. If the problem is not yet

found, check any other fuel filter and/or check fuel flow by opening one of the bleed screws and working the fuel pump manually to see whether fuel is being pumped through the system. If still no fuel, bleed the system for air in the fuel line.

4) Air blocked: Remove the air filters and try to start the engine. If it starts, shut it down, replace the air cleaners, and try again. If it won't start, you've found the problem.

5) If none of the above procedures identifies the problem, find a good mechanic.

Oil pressure 1092

If there is no oil pressure when you start your engine, stop the engine and do the following

1) Check the oil level. If excessively low, add oil and try again. If still no pressure, stop the engine.

2) Change the oil filter, and try again. If there is still no pressure after fifteen seconds, stop the engine.

3) If you have a remote (off the engine) oil filter, disconnect the hoses at the filter end and blow back through them to be sure the lines are not clogged. *Note:* You may have to disconnect the oil lines at both ends to blow them out. If so, put a container under the low end of the lines to catch oil blown from them. Reconnect the lines and start the engine. If there is still no pressure after about fifteen seconds, stop the engine.

4) Check the oil pressure sending unit to be sure it is clean and that any electrical connection is tight. Try again.

5) Change the oil. Try again.

6) If none of the above solves the problem, call a good mechanic.

Electrical Systems

"Many people look at electricity from a generating point of view— always increasing their generating capacity. We do the opposite. We go at it from a consumption viewpoint—trying to reduce our consumption of electricity. For example, our interior lights draw only 0.8 amp."

—Paul Wolter on *Economy*

General Tips

Cabin lights   1093

Fluorescent lights made for marine use can provide more light for less electricity. However, be sure to read the product specifications carefully to see that amps consumed multiplied by 12 volts equals or slightly exceeds the wattage output claimed (amps x volts = watts). Some fixtures designed for low electrical consumption do not provide sufficient power for the fluorescent tube to achieve its full lighting potential. (See also Tip 1,164, "Fluorescent lights.")

Choosing electrical   1094
equipment

All other considerations (except price) being equal, Tom Owen and Patricia Baily on *Licole* recommend choosing the product that uses the lowest amount of electricity when selecting electrical equipment. Paying a bit more for equipment that consumes less electricity is less expensive in the long run than buying larger alternators, bigger batteries, wind generators, and/or extra solar panels.

Electrical reference book   1095

Choose a good book about marine 12-volt systems. Study it, consult it, and keep it on the boat. The book won't make you an expert, but it will help you understand your boat's electrical system and troubleshoot it when problems arise—as they inevitably will. One such book is *Boatowner's Mechanical and Electrical Manual,* Second Edition, by Nigel Calder, published by International Marine.

Making electrical joints   1096
(mechanical)

Electrical supply houses (and many hardware stores) sell an antioxidant grease widely used in the housing industry to prevent corrosion when connecting aluminum wires to copper terminals. According to Eugene Henkel and Bill Zeisler on *Sea Fever*, the electrically conductive grease will also prevent corrosion on wiring in the marine environment. When making a mechanical (not soldered) electrical connection, simply dip the wire and/or connector in the compound before making the connection. If possible, wrap the connection with electrical tape.

Tom Owen and Patricia Baily on *Licole*

Tom Owen and Patricia Baily on the 38-foot wishbone ketch Licole had been cruising twelve years when we met them in the British Virgin Islands, pausing now and then to supplement their income. In that time, they had sailed to such diverse areas as Portugal, West Africa, South America from Argentina north, and the Caribbean.

OK

Plugs and sockets   `1097`

Mike and Susan Carlson on *Ariadne* suggest buying the quick-connect two-wire plugs sold for use with car trailer lights and using them as 12-volt plugs and sockets on your boat. Wire one of these into each cabin light, and you'll have a 12-volt socket with each light. You can also hook up one or more sockets to come out of your circuit breaker panel. *Note:* Always use the same end (the wires are color-coded to the male and female connectors) as the socket. ☞

Pumps   `1098`

Electric pump motors do not like to operate on low voltages. To help protect pump motors from voltage drops, run oversize wires to all electric pumps and make the run as short as practical. This will reduce voltage loss in the wiring.

Batteries

Battery location   `1099`

On some boats, the ship's batteries are located in what might be one of the best lockers on the boat for food stowage. It may be possible to relocate battery boxes and batteries to the engineroom or to other, less-accessible lockers. *Note:* Lead acid

Mike and Susan Carlson on *Ariadne*

In two years of cruising on their 35-foot cutter *Ariadne,* Mike and Susan Carlson had explored the coast from Massachusetts to Florida, crossed to the Bahamas, and followed the Thorny Path south. Once in the Caribbean, they sailed down-island to Venezuela, up to Jamaica, and across to the western Caribbean before returning to U.S. waters. We met them in Beaufort, North Carolina.

batteries require ventilation and must be accessible for periodic maintenance (checking electrolyte level and adding water as needed).

Plugs for 12-volt systems can easily be rigged to come out of light fixtures and the electrical panel (Tip 1,097).

Gel-cell batteries 1100

If you change from wet-cell acid to gel-cell batteries, check your alternator output. Gel-cells are particularly sensitive to damage if the charging voltage is too high. Typically, a gel-cell battery should not see a charging voltage above 14.1 volts. Marine voltage regulators, however, are often set to allow charging voltages of 14.4 volts, sometimes higher—okay for wet-cells, but not for gel-cells.

Golf cart batteries 1101

These are 6-volt deep-cycle batteries. Two connected in series (positive to negative) provide 12-volt power. One attraction to golf cart batteries is that it's much easier to lift two separate 6-volt batteries than the equivalent 12-volt battery. Another attraction is that if one cell goes bad, it's cheaper to replace one of the 6-volt batteries than a 12-volt battery. Still a third is that golf cart batteries often require less floor space for a given amp-hour capacity because they are taller than their 12-volt counterparts—a feature that can be a real advantage. For example, Skip and Gerri Smith on *Yellow Bird* were able to fit two taller 6-volt batteries into the snug battery box for their old 12-volt battery and gain a 50-percent increase in amp-hours from that old battery box.

Rechargeable flashlight batteries 1102

If you are going to use rechargeable NiCad batteries for flashlights, portable radios, voltmeters, and other devices, get the fastest charger available. If it takes fifteen hours to recharge batteries (as some chargers do), you may find you are consuming your batteries faster than you can charge the replacements. Chargers for NiCads in the 9-volt, D, C, and AA sizes are available for use in 12-volt or 110-volt systems.

Charging the Ship's Batteries

Adjustable voltage regulators 1103

Adjustable voltage regulators manufactured by Transpo, Inc. of Tampa, Florida, are available inexpensively for most alternators and can be ordered through almost any alternator service shop. The regulator is equipped with a small plastic screw that a technician can adjust while your alternator is running on the bench, setting it to the cutoff level you specify. Transpo is a major supplier of voltage regulators for Original Equipment Manufacturers, including Motorola. The Transpo adjustable regulator for *Sea Sparrow*'s alternator cost thirty dollars.

Alternator size 1104

Before buying a higher-output alternator, make sure you have enough battery capacity to handle the higher output. Rule of thumb: Battery capacity should be four times the maximum output of your alternator at the typical charging rpm (cruising speed). In general, maximum alternator output is about 80 percent of rated capacity. So, for example, a 100-amp alternator will have a maximum output at cruising rpm of about 80 amps. Minimum battery capacity required for that alternator is 320 amps.

Battery charge monitor 1105

Terry and Nancy Newton on *La Esmeralda* showed us an inexpensive system for monitoring our ship's batteries that consists of a digital voltmeter (about twenty dollars at Radio Shack) and a 12-volt plug we put on the voltmeter's red and black probe wires. The probe wires are simply plugged into a 12-volt socket anywhere in the electrical system and the voltmeter set to read the system voltage to hundredths of a volt—much better than the analog voltmeter on our electrical panel. By placing the voltmeter where your can glance at it routinely, you can easily monitor the voltage level of whatever batteries are in use, including the charging voltage if they are being charged.

Charging efficiency 1106

John Robinson on *Sheldro* reminds us that the inherent inefficiency of a battery means that for every amp you take out of your battery for running lights, radios, refrigerator, and so on, you need to put about 1.2 amps back into the battery to break even. So, don't assume that in ten hours of bright sunlight your solar panel rated at 2 amps will replace the 20 amps consumed by your masthead tricolor last night—because it won't. You will need either two more hours of bright sunlight or a larger solar panel output to do the job. (See also Tips 1,136–1,142, "Solar Panel Installations.")

Charging voltage 1107

Ask the manufacturer of your battery what is the recommended maximum charging voltage for your battery. Then, have your voltage regulator checked to be certain it does not allow a higher voltage. At worst, too high a charging voltage will ruin your batteries. At best, it will shorten their useful lifetime. Automotive batteries can generally tolerate a higher charging voltage than deep-cycle batteries.

Voltage-regulator bypass 1108

The Weems and Plath Automac lets you charge your batteries more efficiently by bypassing the voltage regulator so that you can adjust the amperage output of the alternator. When the charging voltage reaches a preset level, the Automac returns control to the voltage regulator automatically. *Note:* Weems and Plath will adjust the maximum charging voltage allowed by the Automac to the setting recommended by your battery's manufacturer. There is no charge for this service.

Inverters

Choosing an inverter 1109

To get the best balance between 12-volt power consumption and 110-volt power output from your inverter, choose an inverter large enough to meet your anticipated 110-volt requirements at 50 percent of its rated capacity. The reason: Inverters typically operate at about 95 percent efficiency at 50 percent of capacity. When they are used at 60, 70, 80, or 90 percent of their rated capacity, the efficiency is greatly reduced, and your DC power consumption is increased dramatically. You'll find an efficiency curve for each inverter in the product literature.

Electronic Equipment

General Tips, 1,110–1,115
GPS and Loran, 1,116–1,118
Radar, 1,119–1,124

"We consider electronics unnecessary conveniences. We've seen too many people spending their time in port waiting for parts to arrive for their electronics when otherwise they could have been out cruising around."
—Kirk Chamberlain on *Moxie*

General Tips

Backups 1110

Electronics fail. For that reason, Ralph and Sally Pendleton on *Peregrine* recommend maintaining non-electronic backups as important safety equipment. For example, a current DR plot will back up your GPS or loran; a leadline backs up the depthsounder; and if you sail offshore, a sextant, current nautical almanac, and the know-how to work a sight provide additional backup for your GPS.

Ralph and Sally Pendleton on *Peregrine*

Ralph and Sally Pendleton were two months into a planned six-month cruise on their 30-foot ketch *Peregrine* from Fort Meyers, Florida, to the Chesapeake Bay when we met them in Elizabeth City, North Carolina. Although they had been cruising weekends and vacations in Florida waters for some eighteen years and had spent two months in the Bahamas after Ralph's retirement four years earlier, this was their first cruise north from Florida.

Depthsounder 1111

Holger and Christa Strauss on *Golem* suggest using your depthsounder only for specific piloting purposes or when anchoring. Constantly monitoring the depthsounder often becomes a crutch, diverting attention from important skills involved in reading charts, relating what you see around you to what is shown on the chart, and learning to see and read the many visual cues on or in the water around you. It's a tip we heartily endorse.

Humidity protection 1112

If you are in a particularly damp or humid area, Chris Autom and Alex Simcox on *Foamfollower* suggest leaving your electronics on all of the time to keep them dry; it uses very little electricity. In more normal situations, turn on all electronics for several hours once a week to keep them dry and reduce the potential for corrosion.

Locating new equipment 1113

Before making a permanent installation of new electronics, connect the system temporarily and experiment by putting the display in different locations or positions. You may find that the most obvious place to locate equipment is not the best place.

Through-hull knotmeter 1114

If your through-hull knotmeter stops working, remove the through-hull assembly (inserting the plug, of course) and inspect to see that there is no apparent reason for malfunction (for example, the paddlewheel may be fouled). The next step is to open up the top of the through-hull unit (removing screws) and see if you can withdraw the wire splice that is under the cap. If so, the splice may be broken or corroded. Cut and resplice the wire, reassemble the unit, and test the knotmeter. If the problem is solved, withdraw the through-hull assembly once more, remove the cap, push the splice well down into the assembly, and pour epoxy resin into the unit until the splice is covered. Once the resin has set, replace the cap and reinstall the through-hull. *Note:* In most newer transducers, the wire splice is "potted" in epoxy at the factory.

Through-hull knotmeter preventive maintenance 1115

Pierre Angiel on *Defiance* offers this preventive maintenance tip—one he learned the hard way. Check your through-hull knotmeter assembly to see if there is a splice under the cap. If so, examine the splice to be certain there is no corrosion present (or redo it), then seal the splice with epoxy as described in Tip 1,114 above.

GPS and Loran

GPS antenna 1116

Before purchasing a remote antenna for your GPS, try using the unit with its integral antenna from different locations in the cockpit and cabin. The GPS will usually work quite well from the cockpit without a remote antenna. On many boats, it will also work well from a location inside the cabinhouse—again, without an outside antenna. A remote antenna can always be added later if needed.

GPS or loran mount I 1117

Use a swing bracket, available from marine stores, to mount your GPS or loran unit inside the companionway so that you can swing it out for viewing from the cockpit.

GPS or loran mount II   `1118`

Install a bracket and power lead on the cabinhouse under the dodger so that you can move your GPS or loran unit outside for visibility directly from the helm.

Radar

Learning to use radar   `1119`

John and Diane Rapp on *Runner* point out that by using your radar during good weather when you don't need it, you will learn to relate what is on the scope to what you see around you, and to relate scope distances to visual distances. That way, when you're fogged in or piloting in the dark, you will be able to interpret what you see on the scope in a meaningful manner.

Radar alarms   `1120`

At sea, your radar can be set to sound a warning if a ship comes within the distance you select; five miles is a good distance for ship warnings. Closer to shore, where you may encounter navigation buoys, a one-mile alarm semicircle forward will alert you to any buoy's presence.

Radar arch   `1121`

A stainless steel tube structure tied into the stern rail provides an alternative to mounting your radar unit on the mast. On *Pelagic Vagrant*, Dick Mc-Curdie's radar arch provides a radar platform about 6 feet above the coaming and gives a range of about ten miles.

Radarscope location I   `1122`

When piloting in tight quarters in limited visibility, either someone must sit by the radarscope and call steering directions to the helmsman or, preferably, the radarscope will be visible from the helm.

Radarscope location II   `1123`

Install an extra mounting bracket for the radarscope under the dodger so that you can have it in the cockpit when it's needed for active piloting.

Tim and Judy Gray on *Clarion*

In the three years before we met them in Baltimore's Inner Harbor, Tim and Judy Gray had been cruising on their 35-foot double-headsail sloop *Clarion* for periods ranging from a few weeks to several months in the British Isles, along the Atlantic coast of Europe, and from the Windward Islands north to the Chesapeake Bay. For long ocean passages, Tim and Judy or Tim alone were joined by family and friends as crew.

A small deck plate in the cabintop adjacent to the bracket will let you run cables to the scope without cluttering up the companionway.

Spinnaker-pole-track radar mount   `1124`

Tim and Judy Gray on *Clarion* had a bracket fabricated to mount the radar antenna on their spinnaker pole track. The bracket uses two cars. Most

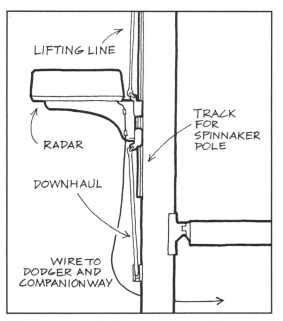

This spinnaker-track radar mount is removed for stowage below when not needed (Tip 1,124).

of the time, the radar is stowed below. When they want to use it, the antenna unit is mounted on the bracket and pulled to the top of the track. The wires run aft through the dodger and down the companionway hatch. The scope is mounted on a hinged bracket that swings out into the companionway for easy viewing. The key to the system, according to Tim, is the availability of small, lightweight radar antenna units.

Exhaust Systems

General Tips, 1,125–1,127
Mufflers, 1,128

General Tips

Anti-siphon valve 1125

If you have a raw-water-cooled engine, this valve sits atop the loop in your cooling-water line where it bypasses the engine's exhaust manifold. Its purpose is to prevent possible back-siphoning of cooling water into the engine through the exhaust system. In time, this valve will become clogged by salt and/or corrosion. To keep it clear, remove the valve at least twice a year and soak it for ten minutes in one part vinegar and four parts water. Test before reinstalling by blowing and sucking through the base of the valve. If necessary, soak longer.

Exhaust seacock 1126

If you will be sailing offshore or in the Great Lakes, give serious thought to installing a seacock at the exhaust through-hull fitting if your boat is not so equipped—even if the through-hull is above the waterline. When sailing in large following seas, closing that seacock may prevent engine damage from water siphoning back through the exhaust system.

Exhaust stains on hull 1127

To reduce problems of exhaust staining the stern of your boat, attach a short piece of wire-reinforced flexible plastic hose to the exhaust pipe, making it long enough to protrude a foot or more from the boat. If your exhaust outlet does not have a pipe protruding for the plastic hose to fit over, you can probably find a piece of thin-walled rigid PVC pipe about 4 inches long that you can fit tightly into the exhaust through-hull fitting to form a nipple for the plastic hose. A small line from the stern rail to the end of the exhaust extension will keep the hose from hanging in the water when the boat is at rest—a deterrent to back-siphoning.

Mufflers

Muffler warning 1128

Mufflers can fail. *Stainless steel mufflers* can fail from corrosion from the inside, where it is not visible to routine inspection. At the first sign of possible water leakage, your stainless steel muffler should be removed, pressure-tested, and repaired or replaced as appropriate.

Plastic mufflers are vulnerable to a meltdown if the engine cooling water fails. At the worst, such failure can flood the boat. At the best, it can put the engine out of commission. In our survey of 120 boats, one boat had its engineroom flooded when the stainless steel muffler failed; another boat lost its engine 600 miles offshore en route to the Caribbean from North Carolina when the engine's raw-water pump failed and the plastic muffler suffered a meltdown before the engine-overheating alarm sounded.

Fuel and Water Tanks

General Tips

Fuel tank preventive maintenance 1129

If you purchase an older boat or have had your present boat for several years, have your fuel tanks cleaned professionally. Otherwise, sediment that has accumulated in the bottom of the tank can be stirred up in rough seas, becoming suspended in your fuel and clogging your fuel filter in short order—possibly at a critical time.

Gravity-feed fuel tank 1130

When the combination of rough seas and a low level of fuel sloshing in the tank led to problems of air in his fuel system, Jean Lerinckx-Parren on *Yorick* installed a twelve-gallon gravity-feed fuel tank which he tops off daily from the main tank using a hand pump. The gravity-feed tank solved the problem.

Jean and Angèle Lerinckx-Parren on *Yorick*

Jean and Angèle Lerinckx-Parren on the 36-foot cutter *Yorick* sailed from their home in Belgium to the United Kingdom before heading south to Portugal, Spain, and on to Madeira and the Canary Islands en route to the Caribbean. After cruising in Venezuela, they island-hopped to the Bahamas and the United States, and followed the Intracoastal Waterway north to the Chesapeake Bay before heading south again. They had been cruising three-and-a-half years when we met them in Vero Beach.

Grounding aluminum tanks 1131

Mike Hamilton on *Wild Duck* suggests disconnecting the ground wires to any aluminum tanks that may sit in salty bilgewater (seawater). On *Wild Duck*, the aluminum diesel fuel tank failed after developing pin holes attributed to galvanic corrosion. Mike's belief is that grounding his aluminum tank in effect created a battery whenever the tank sat in seawater in the bilge, causing the corrosion that led to his tank's failure. Because of a similar concern, we deliberately have refrained from grounding *Sea Sparrow*'s aluminum fuel and water tanks. Those tanks are now more than sixteen years old. *Safety note: Gasoline tanks should always be grounded to prevent a buildup of static electricity that could otherwise spark a fire or explosion.*

Portable gasoline tanks 1132

For your dinghy, use two three-gallon tanks instead of one six-gallon tank. When filled, the smaller tanks weigh half as much, are easier to get on and off the dinghy, and are much easier to carry if you have to walk any distance to a filling station. When one tank gets low, switch to the second tank and fill the first one at your leisure. As an alternative to the second tank, use a two-and-a-half-gallon jerry jug for your reserve fuel.

Generators and Solar Panels

General Tips

Portable gasoline generators   1133

William Baert on *Liebchen* found they were getting exhaust fumes through open ports or hatches when running their portable gasoline generator on deck. The problem was solved by putting the generator all the way aft and adding a 3-foot extension to its exhaust pipe to direct fumes well overboard.

Power tools   1134

A 600-watt gasoline generator provides the power needed to operate basic power tools.

A 12-volt prop shaft generator   1135

Before purchasing a prop shaft generator, check the operating instructions for your engine's transmission to be sure you will not damage the transmission by allowing it to freewheel in neutral while under sail. *L'Eau Berge* skipper Evangeliste St. Georges reports that his 12-volt, belt-driven prop shaft generator develops from 6 to 8 amps at 6 knots. The unit is produced by Hamilton-Ferris in Ashland, Massachusetts; telephone (508) 881-4602.

Solar Panel Installations

(See also Tip 1,106, "Charging efficiency.")

Backstay mounts   1136

With a split backstay, one or more solar panels can be mounted on a platform rigged between the two backstay wires. A length of 1-inch stainless steel tube running between the split backstays provides the support for the platform.

Bimini mounts   1137

On *Foamfollower*, a simple platform is welded to the aft crosspiece of the bimini frame and holds a solar panel above the bimini.

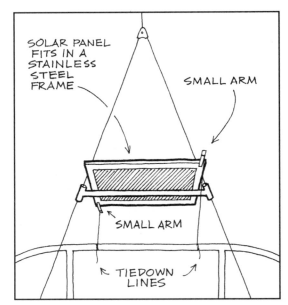

Solar panel mounted between split backstays (Tip 1,136).

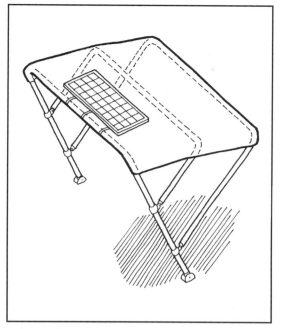

Solar panel mounted using the bimini frame (Tip 1,137).

Dinghy davit mounts `1138`

On boats with dinghy davits, it's a simple matter to fabricate a solar panel platform that fits across the davit arms.

Lifeline mounts `1139`

Using eye straps, a solar panel can be hung on the lifelines just forward of the stern rail. Alternatively, a stainless steel rail can be rigged for the solar panels between the stern rail and first lifeline stanchion on each side. The panel is attached to the rail using plastic antenna mounts, sold in marine stores. With either system, a lightweight wood leg from the solar panel frame to the toerail will hold the panel up to the sun. By swinging the leg alongside the panel frame, the solar panel can be dropped against the lifelines to get it out of the way for coming alongside. We have had solar panels mounted in this way port and starboard on *Sea Sparrow* for more than two years, in conditions ranging from calm to full gale offshore, without problems.

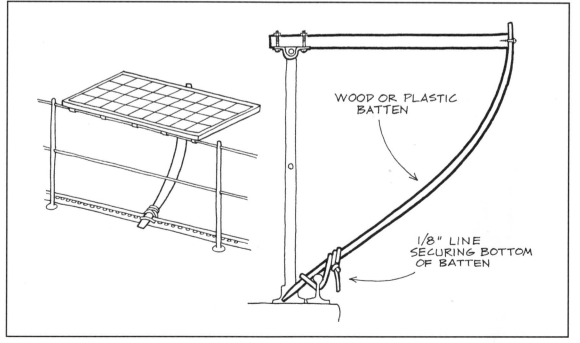

WOOD OR PLASTIC BATTEN

1/8" LINE SECURING BOTTOM OF BATTEN

Solar panel hung on the lifeline (Tip 1,139).

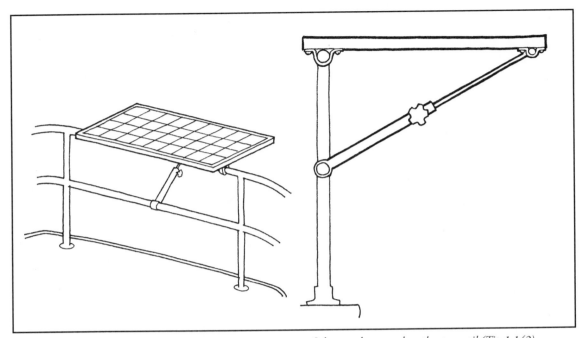

Solar panel mounted on the stern rail (Tip 1,142).

Mainsail mount 1140

At anchor, solar panels can be placed atop the furled (and covered) mainsail, held securely in place with shock cord. Adjustments to allow for the sun's elevation are made by shifting the panels to one side or the other of the furled sail.

No mounts 1141

Conditions permitting, Kirk Chamberlain lays their solar panel on *Moxie*'s deck where it's exposed to the sun. The panel is moved as needed to keep it in the sun. We've seen several other boats using the same system.

Stern-rail mount 1142

John and Diane Rapp use an adjustable platform on *Runner*'s stern rail to help keep their solar panels angled toward the sun. The platform rotates on brackets clamped to the stern rail. An adjustment arm for changing the platform angle runs to the lower crosspiece on the stern rail. ☝

Water Generators

Propeller line length 1143

Some water generators are designed for use with a 35- to 40-foot line between the generator and the propeller being towed behind the boat. Dick and Kay Torpin on *Thorfinn* found, however, that an 80-foot line works better in large seas.

Retrieving the generator propeller 1144

Slit a large funnel, slip it over the line to the propeller with the small end of the funnel pointing forward, and let the funnel slide back over the prop. It will stop the rotation and make it easier to pull in the line. *Note:* This will not work on units having a weight in front of the propeller for use with a short line.

Dick and Kay Torpin on *Thorfinn*

Four years after they set out from their home in Australia to sail around the world on their 45-foot cutter *Thorfinn,* Dick and Kay Torpin were about two-thirds of the way through their voyage when we met them in Beaufort, North Carolina. Their trip thus far had taken them to Bali, across the Indian Ocean to the Red Sea, through the Suez Canal to the Mediterranean, across the Atlantic to the Caribbean, and up the U.S. East Coast.

Universal joint | 1145

If the water generator does not have one, it is worthwhile installing a universal joint on the generator shaft to handle the different directional pulls from the propeller line caused by the boat's motion. The universal joint translates the varied angles of force into a straight-line pull.

Jack and Terry Roberts on *Packet Inn*

When we first met Jack and Terry Roberts on their 31-foot cutter *Packet Inn,* we'd been cruising only a few months. When we interviewed them two-and-a-half years later, they'd been cruising for five years, moving north and south with the seasons between the Chesapeake Bay and the cruising grounds of Florida's Keys and Gulf Coast, later extending their range to include the Bahamas.

Wind Generators

Hazards | 1146

If your wind generator is not designed for high winds, pay close attention to local weather forecasts so that you can shut down the generator if weather systems containing potentially strong winds are forecast. Winds in a cold front, squall, or thunderstorm can easily exceed the design limits of some wind generators, with potentially devastating results. Jack and Terry Roberts, for example, reported that the propeller blades of *Packet Inn*'s wind generator self-destructed in a squall, with one blade fragment slicing through their dodger window and another gouging a piece out of their cockpit sole. Several other cruisers have reported similar experiences.

Mounting height | 1147

Wind generators must be mounted high enough that a person standing beneath the generator cannot possibly be struck by the blade—even if he raises his arm.

Noise I | 1148

Some wind generators make a great deal of noise. If such noise would disturb you or your crew, try to find boats having the kind of wind generator you are considering so that you can learn firsthand just how noisy the generator will be—before you make your purchase. In general, the larger the propeller blades, the more noise they make.

Noise II | 1149

If your wind generator makes a significant amount of noise, anchor well away from other boats so that the noise of your wind generator does not intrude on your neighbors' peace and quiet.

Lightning Protection

General Tips

Be prepared 1150

Plan on being struck by lightning. Among the 120 cruisers we interviewed, 16 had been struck by lightning at least once on their present or an earlier boat. We have been struck twice on *Sea Sparrow*. Two other boats—*Dolly* and *Sea Fever*—each reported damage from direct or indirect lightning strikes on three different occasions.

Develop a lightning strategy 1151

Plan ahead so that all members of the crew will know what to do in a severe lightning storm. If any steps are needed to protect equipment, those responsibilities should be delegated. More important, each crewmember should know how to protect him- or herself. For example, if you're at anchor, everyone should go below and stay away from any metal components—such as the stove or sink. If you're underway, only the minimum crew needed for safe boat handling should stay on deck; all others should go below. On *Sea Sparrow*, we've even been known to heave-to and go below to wait out a severe thunderstorm.

Navigation lights 1152

Carry a spare for each of your boat's navigation lights. If you are hit by lightning, the odds are good that one or more of your navigation lights will be destroyed.

Protective Systems

Bonding your stays, shrouds, and major above-deck metal components 1153

The purpose of bonding above-deck metal components is to protect the crew from overvoltages which can otherwise occur in a lightning strike. Bonding consists of running a heavy-gauge wire (minimum, No. 8 AWG) horizontally through the boat to tie together all shrouds, stays, the mast, pedestal steering, metal handrails, and deck winches—any large metal parts that the crew might be touching when lightning strikes. The bonding system should also be connected to the ship's ground.

Grounding your mast 1154

If your mast itself and/or your upper shrouds are not grounded, ground them. Although a ground

Tony and Jenny Collingridge on *Stage Sea*

In the two years since sailing from their home in England, Tony and Jenny Collingridge on the 36-foot sloop *Stage Sea* had sailed to Madeira and across the Atlantic to the Caribbean. After cruising in Venezuela, they followed the Windward and Leeward Islands north, then sailed to the United States and up the coast to Nova Scotia. When we met them in St. Augustine, Florida, they were bound for the Caribbean coast of Central America.

plate or grounding to the ballast keel is best, even a heavy wire or chain clamped to an upper shroud and dropped overboard when thunderstorms approach can provide an effective ground. Tony and Jenny Collingridge on *Stage Sea*, for example, reported scorch marks on their hull showing where the lightning that struck their boat followed the grounding chain down to the water. The ground won't keep your boat from being struck by lightning, nor will it protect your electronic gear or other electrical equipment. It may, however, save your life. By grounding the mast, you make your masthead the most attractive target on your boat.

Protecting electronics I   1155

Install electronic equipment so that you can easily disconnect antenna and power leads in thunderstorms. While not guaranteed to prevent damage to electronics, disconnecting the equipment will prevent damage in most circumstances. Steve and Donna Thompson on *Donna Jean* were among several cruisers who reported that their disconnected equipment survived lightning strikes, whereas equipment not disconnected was damaged. We've had the same experience on *Sea Sparrow*.

Protecting electronics II   1156

Use twisted-pair wiring to provide power to your electronics. Failing that, twist the two power leads tightly around each other as far back from the equipment as you can reach. The twisted leads will help protect your equipment from overvoltages.

Protecting electronics III   1157

Install lightning arresters designed for cable TV in each of your antenna leads to protect radios from a lightning strike to the antenna. The lightning arrester should be grounded to your boat's grounding system.

VHF radio antenna   1158

Mount your VHF radio antenna on the stern rail; your only sacrifice is a few miles of range. Otherwise, unless you have a separate lightning rod at masthead that is taller than your antenna, your masthead antenna functions as a sacrificial lightning rod and will almost certainly be destroyed if your boat is struck by lightning. *Sea Sparrow*'s stern-rail-mounted VHF antenna has survived our two lightning strikes.

Steve and Donna Thompson on *Donna Jean*

Steve and Donna Thompson started out from San Francisco to cruise for two years on their 39-foot cutter *Donna Jean.* When we met them in Beaufort, North Carolina, they had been out for six years, including four-and-a-half years in Central America, while tracing the North American coast from San Francisco Bay down to Panama and up to Maine. They were then, however, making plans to wend their way back to California.

Lights and Lighting

General Tips

Trouble light | 1159

On *Cygnet,* Bob and Chesley Logcher carry a plastic 12-volt trouble light (also called a droplight) with a cigarette lighter plug on the wire for use in the engineroom. The plastic cage protects the bulb, and the hook lets you hang it where needed. You can find these lights in auto supply stores as well as in some marine stores. The same light also serves *Cygnet* as a cockpit light.

Waterproof flourescent light | 1160

West Marine sells a waterproof 12-volt fluorescent lightstick that can be used under water if necessary. This obviously waterproof light uses an easily replaceable standard fluorescent tube and makes a good all-weather cockpit light.

Flashlights

Flashlight holders | 1161

Keep flashlights in holders by the companionway and head so that you don't have to go looking for a flashlight when you need one.

Rechargeable flashlights | 1162

Marine stores sell rechargeable flashlights that can be kept fully charged when not in use. One style simply plugs into a cigarette lighter outlet. Another has a holder that is wired into the boat's electrical system and will keep the flashlight charged as long as it's in the holder. We keep a rechargeable flashlight plugged into an outlet in our sleeping cabin on *Sea Sparrow.* A small red light on the unit reminds us that it is there and waiting should it be needed.

OVERTON'S

Underwater flashlight | 1163

Bill and Joanne Weston on *Hummingbird* suggest carrying a flashlight designed for use by divers. While they bought theirs originally for snorkeling, they say it's proved to be an excellent foulweather flashlight.

Interior Lights

Fluorescent lights | 1164

By far the best interior cabin lights we've seen were recommended by several cruisers we interviewed, and we now have two on *Sea Sparrow.* They are high-efficiency fluorescent lights made and sold di-

Bill and Joanne Weston on *Hummingbird*

In their first year of cruising, Bill and Joanne Weston sailed their 37-foot sloop *Hummingbird* from the Chesapeake Bay, where they purchased her, to Lake Ontario and their upstate New York home for the summer before heading south to the Florida Keys and the Bahamas. When we met them in Beaufort, South Carolina, they were returning to Lake Ontario to sell their house and car, and planned to continue cruising.

rectly by Alpen Glow, P.O. Box 415, Eugene, MT 59917. On a low power setting the lights draw 0.4 amp; on a high setting, 0.8 amp. At the same time, they provide much brighter light than incandescent lights using much more electricity. Because they are more expensive than the lights they were replacing, we put the Alpen Glow fixtures only where the lights are used a lot—one each in the galley and main saloon. (See also Tip 1,093, "Cabin lights.")

Reading lights   1165

The so-called airplane lights sold in RV stores make excellent 12-volt reading lights. They use a bulb resembling an automotive sealed-beam headlight that can be pointed where you want the light to shine.

Kerosene Lamps

Deodorizing kerosene   1166

Add 4 ounces of isopropyl alcohol (rubbing alcohol) to one-and-a-half gallons of kerosene to reduce the odor and smoking. The alcohol puts any water contaminating the fuel into suspension and allows it to be burned off. The result is less odor and a brighter flame.

Hanging lamps   1167

If you use a brass shackle or hook to hang a trawler lamp, check regularly for wear from the swinging motion of the lamp. Otherwise, the brass hanger may fail, dropping the lamp with potentially disastrous results.

Kerosene alternative   1168

Dwight and Karen Rettie on *Tarwathie* suggest using mineral spirits (the same thing used to clean paintbrushes) as lamp oil. It burns brightly and cleanly with no odor. Mineral spirits also can substituted for kerosene in your kerosene stove, according to Reade and Sarah Tompson on *Sarasan*. The Tompsons routinely used mineral spirits to fuel their stove for years.

Kerosene lamps in hot weather   1169

By hanging your kerosene lamp below an open hatch, you can enjoy the light while the heat generated by the lamp is vented quickly through the hatch.

Navigation Lights

Masthead tricolor   1170

Gunnar Dahl and Marie Louise Sterno on *Sandra* suggest using your masthead tricolor only on open waters. In waterways where there is small-boat traffic, they point out that other boat operators are looking for lights near water level—not 50 or 60 feet in the air—and may not see your tricolor. We can confirm Gunnar's observation. We were roundly chewed out one night on Maryland's Sassafras River by the irate skipper of a motorboat who accused us of sailing without lights when, in fact, we had our masthead tricolor on. He hadn't seen the tricolor, however, because it was so high above the water. *Note:* Don't forget that the masthead tricolor is for use only when you are sailing. If motoring, you should also be showing a white steaming light.

Reflected glare   1171

On *Carpe Diem*, Frank and JulAnn Allen were bothered by reflected light from the running light mounted on their bow pulpit. They solved the problem by wrapping the sections of the bow rail involved with ⅛-inch line in a series of half hitches so that the hitches spiraled about the rail, making the surface nonreflective.

Outboard Motors

"Our outboard looks old because you have to make it look old so it won't be stolen."
—Jean and Angèle Lerinckx-Parren on *Yorick*

General Tips

Horsepower   1172

If you are inclined to get an outboard for your dinghy, consider the following: In general, most cruisers we've met who started out with very small engines wound up getting or wishing they had a larger motor. Conversely, those who started out with a 15-horsepower or larger motor frequently changed down to something smaller. The very small engines are a handicap because they limit what you can do with your dinghy. The large engines are hard to get on and off the dinghy, more attractive to thieves, and very expensive to replace if stolen. See the accompanying table for information about the sizes of outboard motors carried by the 112 boats in our survey with outboard-powered dinghies.

Outboard Motors Carried for Dinghies
(survey of 112 boats)

Motor size	No. of motors
0.5 to 3 hp	.49
3.1 to 5 hp	.21
5.1 to 8 hp	.22
8.1 to 10 hp	.19
10.1 to 15 hp	.14
15.1 to 25 hp	.4
	Total 129*

*The 17 boats carrying two outboards accounted for 15 of the 49 motors of 3 hp or less.

Lifting your outboard motor I   1173

Using 5/16-inch rope, make a lifting harness that fits snugly on your motor and can be left on at all times. Even if you lift the motor by hand to put it on or take it off your dinghy, attach a halyard or other line to the harness so that the motor remains attached to the boat if it is dropped accidentally.   ☞

Lifting your outboard motor II   1174

Use a four-part block and tackle with a cam cleat on the upper block to lift the motor. The block and tackle can be hung from a halyard to raise and lower the motor. Alternatively, use your boom as a cargo boom, hanging the block and tackle from the boom to lift the motor and swinging the boom as needed to shift the motor out over the dinghy or back aboard the big boat. (See also Tips 62 and 63, "Cargo Booms.")   ☞

Maintenance

Outboard motor's screw clamps   1175

The screw clamps used to fasten your outboard onto its mount often become stiff because salt, dirt, or corrosion fouls the threads. Use an old toothbrush dipped in vinegar to clean the threads, then spray them with Boeshield T-9 lubricant.

Running up the motor   1176

Sometimes when you're flushing out the fuel system or trying to diagnose a problem, you need to run the outboard motor at a higher rpm than

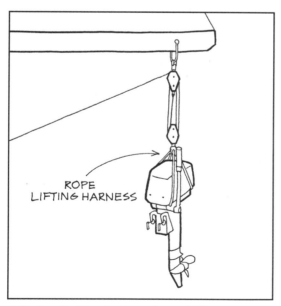

ROPE LIFTING HARNESS

A block and tackle takes the work out of lifting your outboard from the dinghy (Tips 1,173 and 1,174).

allowed in neutral. However, in forward gear, you'd be going too fast to do the job. So, on *Blue Ribbon*, Dave and B. K. Bennett solved the problem by running the outboard engine in reverse with the dinghy hanging off the stern. With the dinghy painter tied securely to a stern cleat, put the motor in reverse and go straight back slowly at idle speed until the painter is taut. Then open the throttle gradually—still in reverse—until the engine is running at the desired speed.

Motor Mounts

Stern rail mounts   1177

Bob and Sally Greymont on *Gypsy Spray* have found that plastic radio antenna mounts make simple and inexpensive motor mounts for small outboards. The rectangular plastic mounts clamp securely onto the stern rail and are easily spaced to fit your outboard. After lowering the motor onto the mounts, tighten the motor's screw clamps and lash the drive unit to the lower rail. These devices are sold as High-Strength Antenna Rail Mounts in marine discount stores. Use machine screws in place of the thumb screws to secure them on the stern rail.

Security

Locking the outboard   1178
motor I

Most small outboards can be locked to the dinghy or the motor mount on your stern rail by locking the handles used to tighten the motor's mounting clamps. Tighten the clamps so that the two handles point toward each other, thread the lock's shackle through the hole in the end of each handle, and lock the two handles together. If you use a combination lock, be sure to orient the lock so that you can see the dials to unlock it.   ☞

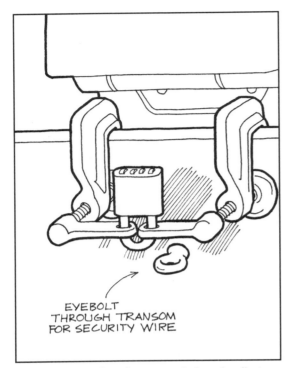

Threading a lock through your motor's clamp handles is an easy way to lock your outboard (Tip 1,178).

Locking the outboard motor II
1179

The plastic-coated locking bars for outboards sold by many marine stores should not be used in a saltwater environment. In our experience, the bars and locks both rust quickly.

Locking the outboard motor III
1180

Dwight and Karen Rettie on *Tarwathie* suggest an additional means for securing your dinghy's outboard. The Retties use a U-shaped bicycle lock large enough to fit around the shaft of their 7.5-horsepower outboard motor and through two holes in the dinghy transom, whereupon it is locked. The same lock is used to secure the motor shaft to the stern rail.

Locking the outboard motor IV
1181

If none of the suggestions above for locking the outboard motor are workable, a short length of light chain or stainless steel wire can be run through some part of the outboard frame—say, through the lifting handle—and both ends locked to the same transom eyebolt used for the security wire (see Tip 367, "Transom eyebolt"). *Note:* All outboards should always be locked to their dinghies; even very small motors are sometimes stolen.

Making your motor "ugly"
1182

As the comment at the beginning of this section suggests, shiny new outboards are particularly attractive to thieves. As a result, many cruisers—ourselves included—have tried to make their motors less attractive by aging them artificially. Coarse sandpaper will quickly take the shine from the plastic cowling of your outboard. Sanding off the decals makes people guess both about the make and size of your motor. To further age their motors, some cruisers paint the cowling, usually in a dull color. Some also spray parts of the shaft with green zinc oxide paint to suggest that the shaft has had corrosion problems.

Steering

Tiller extensions
1183

Many cruisers find that the tiller on their outboard is too short for comfortable steering. A tiller extension can be made cheaply and easily from a piece of PVC pipe 12 to 18 inches long and about 1½ inches in interior diameter. (Check the diameter of your motor's control handle.) If you need to open the end of the pipe a bit to fit your motor's tiller, use a hacksaw blade to cut five or six lengthwise slits about 4 inches long equally spaced around the circumference of the pipe. These slits will allow the pipe to open up a bit to fit over the tiller. Secure the handle with a hose clamp. If the pipe diameter is a bit too big for your tiller, cut five elongated vees (also about 4 inches long) evenly spaced around the circumference of the pipe. Slip the cut end of the pipe over the handle and secure it with a hose clamp.

Troubleshooting

Motor runs rough   1184

If the motor runs rough at low speed, check for dirt or water in the fuel. If it runs rough at high speed, try changing your spark plugs. *Note:* Some motors have a drain on the bottom of the carburetor bowl, making it easy to drain water from the carburetor.

Steering Devices

General Tips, 1,185
Autopilots, 1,186–1,190
Tillers, 1,191–1,193
Wind Vanes, 1,194–1,198

General Tips

Emergency steering   1185

If your wheel-steering boat is not equipped with an emergency tiller, develop a system for steering the boat if your wheel steering fails. Then, practice using the emergency steering system at least once each season. If you do have an emergency tiller, try it out at the beginning of each season to be sure you know where it is, how to connect it, and how to steer with it. Although modern wheel-steering systems are generally reliable, they can fail—even when sailing in local waters.

Autopilots

An autopilot is useful even if your boat is equipped with a wind vane. For example, when you are motoring in calm seas under a hot sun, an autopilot will perform admirably. With the engine running, there is no drain on the batteries. And, with

the autopilot steering, there will also be much less drain on the crewmembers' energies.

Autopilot size   1186

Get an autopilot rated for a boat larger than yours. This way, you reduce the potential for failure of the drive unit—the motorized system that does all the work.

Below-deck autopilots   1187

Rig a separate steering quadrant or "tiller arm" on the rudderpost for your below-deck autopilot. Dick and Kay Torpin on *Thorfinn* point out that

Phil Jones and Anita Tomlin on *Sweet Pea*

When Phil Jones and Anita Tomlin started their cruise on the 35-foot cutter *Sweet Pea*, they planned to be out for a year. When we met them in the Abacos, however, that one year had stretched into two as they cruised along the coast between South Carolina and Florida and in the Bahamas. They were, however, planning to head back home to resume their careers.

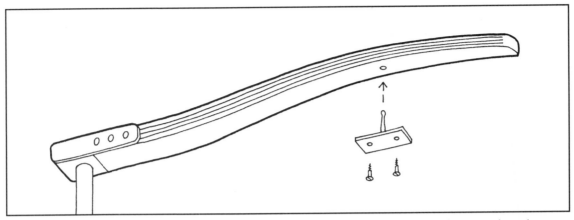

Reinforcing the pin for a tiller-drive autopilot makes a more secure installation (Tip 1,190).

the separate steering quadrant makes your autopilot independent of the wheel-steering system.

Repairing autopilots   1188

Before agreeing to have any part of your autopilot repaired, look into the cost of replacing the part—for example, the motor. You may have to spend more paying for a technician's time to repair a part than it would cost to replace it.

Steering-pedestal-mount autopilot   1189

If you have trouble with your autopilot clutch disengaging unexpectedly, Phil Jones and Anita Tomlin on *Sweet Pea* suggest rigging a piece of string with a loop in the end that you can slip over the clutch lever to hold it in place.

Tiller-drive autopilots   1190

The tiller pin for tiller-drive autopilots will often work loose over time. To solve this problem, Art Bourne on *Suits Us* lengthened the tiller pin by welding a piece to it so that the pin extends all the way through the tiller. Next, he had the pin welded to a stainless steel plate fabricated to fit snugly against the bottom of the tiller. Finally, he installed the pin using a two-part epoxy to seal the hole through the tiller against water intrusion, and secured the bottom plate firmly in place using self-tapping screws before the epoxy set up.

Tillers

Tiller backup I   1191

If your tiller breaks, the only realistic backup is a spare tiller. So, carry one.

Tiller backup II   1192

If the rudderpost fitting for the tiller breaks, the best backup is a spare fitting. Short of that, an adjustable wrench or a box or open-end wrench large enough to fit over the top of the rudderpost will provide the purchase needed to steer. You can gain leverage by slipping a length of pipe over the end of the wrench. The pipe "tiller" should be as long as the tiller it replaces. Of course, you must have these tools on board to be able to use them.

Tiller delamination   1193

Tillers tend to delaminate at the rudderpost end, because water seeps between the wood of the tiller and the metal fitting connecting it to the rudderpost. It may also seep around the bolts used to secure the fitting to the tiller. To prevent (or stop) delamination, bolt the laminates together using two or three ¼-inch machine screws with flat washers top and bottom and locknuts. First, remove the rudderpost fitting from the tiller, clean out between any delaminated sections, pour two-part epoxy glue between the laminates, and clamp them tightly. When the glue has cured, drill holes for the bolts. Fit the bolts, remove them, swab the bolt holes generously with epoxy using Q-tips, and reinstall the bolts, tightening them snugly. Before reinstalling the rudderpost fitting, swab the bolt holes for that fitting with epoxy to seal them against moisture.

Wind Vanes

For offshore passagemaking, many cruisers believe their wind vane is the most important piece of mechanical equipment on the boat—more important, even, than extra crew. A good wind vane will steer the boat tirelessly in all conditions, tell you when to shorten sail, and, in heavy weather, can make the difference between crew exhaustion and mere fatigue.

Center-cockpit boats 1194

If your emergency tiller extends above deck, rig the tiller and connect the wind vane to the emergency tiller to steer, rather than running the steering lines to your wheel-steering system.

Monitor wind vane 1195

As an alternative to the spring-loaded continuous line suggested for adjusting Monitor vanes, John and Petra Kowalczyk on *Ragtime Duet* installed two jam cleats for the adjusting line. By lifting the two sides of the loop from the jam cleats, they can adjust the vane and then put the lines back into the cleats.

Wind paddle I 1196

If your vane has a removable wind paddle, check the paddle clamps at each change of watch or on some other regular schedule, to be sure the paddle is not working loose. More frequent checks are needed in stronger winds than in light breezes.

Wind paddle II 1197

If your vane has a removable paddle, secure it with a piece of ⅛-inch braided line to the vane frame—drilling a small hole in the wind paddle near its base, if necessary. If the paddle does work loose, the string will keep it from being lost overboard.

Wind paddle III 1198

Carry a spare wind paddle—easily made from a piece of inexpensive ¼-inch lauan mahogany plywood. A coat of paint or epoxy will seal the wood.

Contributing Cruisers

Boat Name	Length	Rig	Home Port	Crew
Acamar	37 feet	Sloop	Gloucester, MA	Alan Campbell and Joan Normington
Adelante	30 feet	Sloop	Westbrook, CT	Ron and Jayne Demers
Ahoy	37 feet	Sloop	Holland	Kees Oudt and Margaretha Christoffersen
Alana	30 feet	Sloop Motorsailer	Raleigh, NC	Dan Robbins and Pam Jeffreys
Alegria	43 feet	Trawler	Norfolk, VA	Bill and Betz Hartge
Anna	22 feet	Sloop	Burlington, VT	Mike Weizenegger and Deb Bair
Annie D	36 feet	Lobsterboat Cruiser	Newagen, ME	Jon Cheston and Nancy Hauswald
Ariadne	35 feet	Cutter	Roseville, MN	Mike and Susan Carlson
Ariel	30 feet	Sloop	Kingston, Ontario Canada	David Moran
Ariel III	31 feet	Cutter	Belfast, ME	Alex and Diane Allmayer-Beck
Blue Ribbon	32 feet	Cutter	Daytona Beach, FL	Dave and B.K. Bennett

Boat Name	Length	Rig	Home Port	Crew
Blue Whale	24 feet	Cutter	Fayetteville, AR	Kim Larson and Kay St. Onge
Blue Swanny	40 feet	Cat Ketch	St. Peter Port, Guernsey, UK	Christian and Marie Le Roye
Bowstring	43 feet	Double-Headsail Sloop	Lymmington, UK	John Halley
Carpe Diem	34 feet	Sloop	Vestal, NY	Frank and JulAnn Allen
Carrie Bennett	36 feet	Ketch	East Lyme, CT	Mike and Anne Karamargin
Cetus	32 feet	Cutter	Norfolk, VA	Alex Quintard
Clarion	35 feet	Double- Headsail Sloop	Boston, MA	Tim and Judy Gray
Club Cheer	41 feet	Ketch	Philadelphia, PA	Lauren and Fran Spinelli
Copasetic	38 feet	Cutter	Newport, RI	Conrad and Kathy Johnson Jr.
Crazy Lady	41 feet	Motor Yacht	Boston, MA	Bill and Lisa Hammond
Cygnet	37 feet	Cutter	Boston, MA	Bob and Chesley Logcher
Cymba	28 feet	Cutter	Berkeley, CA	Ralph and Dorothy Greenlee
Decatur	27 feet	Sloop	Miami, FL	Mike McGivern
Defiance	43 feet	Sloop	New York, NY	Pierre Angiel
Delphini	35 feet	Cutter	New York, NY	Val and Eleni Rolan
Dessie Belle	36 feet	Ketch	Norfolk, VA	John and Carol Dingley
Diura	31 feet	Sloop	Oban, Scotland, UK	Iain and Joan Lees
Dolly	38 feet	Sloop	Merritt Island, FL	Jack and Rowena Baltar
Donna Jean	39 feet	Cutter	Sausalito, CA	Steve and Donna Thompson
Double Deuce	34 feet	Sloop	Pt. Clear, AL	William McAdams
Dreamer	38 feet	Double-Headsail Sloop	St. Augustine, FL	Roy Wilson
Dublin Dragon	37 feet	Cutter	San Francisco, CA	Jim and Ronelle Cromeenes
Dutch Maid	49 feet	Cutter	Ramsgate, UK	David and Valerie Wraight
Economy	32 feet	Lobster Boat Cruiser	Camden, ME	Paul and Barbara Wolter
Emma Goldman	41 feet	Ketch	Vineyard Haven, MA	Dennis White, Julie Robinson, Sasha and Joshua
Equinox	33 feet	Cutter	Annapolis, MD	Hal and Katie Ritenour
Escort	42 feet	Trawler	Rochester, NY	Fred Zeller
Eternity	44 feet	Cutter	Antwerpt, Belgium	Ferdinand and Jeannine Cammaerts
Flyway	32 feet	Sloop	Doylestown, PA	Dave and Phyllis Carroll
Foamfollower	37 feet	Sloop	Edinburgh, UK	Chris Autom and Alex Simcox
Genie	43 feet	Cutter	New Orleans, LA	Dave and Lynn Cunningham
Golem	42 feet	Ketch	Berlin, Germany	Holger and Christa Strauss
Grand Marjac	32 feet	Sloop	Virginia Beach, VA	Jack and Margaret Eady
Gypsy Spray	39 feet	Cutter	Boston, MA	Bob and Sally Greymont
Ho Bo V	36 feet	Cutter	Brockville, Ontario, Canada	Bill and Heidi Cornell, and Bob Atkinson
Hummingbird	37 feet	Sloop	Wilmington, DE	Bill and Joanne Weston
Impulse	44 feet	Ketch	Philadelphia, PA	Mike and Pat Davidson
Island Bound	35 feet	Sloop	Miami, FL	Cindy Stein
Jacarde	41 feet	Sloop	Hampton, VA	Jack and Carly Dethorn

Boat Name	Length	Rig	Home Port	Crew
Jewell	51 feet	Motor Yacht	McHenry, IL	Dave and Jan Miller
John Martin	37 feet 6 inches	Sloop	Rye, UK	Pete and Yvonne Seddon
Joint Venture	(not recorded)		Portland, OR	John Russell, Mary Fellows and Kate
Karina II	38 feet	Sloop	Berlin, NH	Frank and Karen Bastidas
Katie James	38 feet	Cutter	Lost River, WV	David and Kathy Rudich
Keramos	37 feet	Double-Headsail Sloop	Vashon, WA	Jeff and Donna Tousley
Kuan-yin	37 feet	Trimaran Cutter	St. Augustine, FL	Philip and Marilyn Lange
Kwa-Heri	39 feet	Cutter	Montreal, Quebec, Canada	Peter and Valerie Schulz
Lady Helen	36 feet	Sloop	Oriental, NC	Al and Helen Roderick
La Esmeralda	37 feet	Cutter	Naples, FL	Terry and Nancy Newton
L'Eau Berge	35 feet	Cutter	Montreal, Quebec, Canada	Evangeliste St. Georges
Licole	38 feet	Ketch	Road Town, Tortola, BVI	Tom Owen and Patricia Baily
Liebchen	37 feet	Sloop	Danvers, MA	William and Edna Baert
Lorelei	36 feet	Sloop	Miami, FL	Karl and Carol Jensen
Lucky Dragon	41 feet 6 inches	Cutter	Plymouth, UK	Brian and Pam Saffery Cooper
Lyra	31 feet	Cutter	Philadelphia, PA	Ralph and Doris DeGroodt
Magic Carpet	31 feet	Catamaran Sloop	North Point Creek, MD	Jim and Maggie Smith
Mariah	32 feet	Cutter	Wilmington, DE	Jim and Terry Cazer
Marie Galante	37 feet	Double-Headsail Sloop	Panton, VT	John, Mindy, Dorothy, Annie, Tom and Sarah Donnelly
Mischief	35 feet	Sloop	San Francisco, CA	Art and Kathy Halenbeck
Mooneshine	39 feet 6 inches	Cutter	Annapolis, MD	Ron and Kathy Trossbach
Moonshadow	40 feet	Sloop	Vineyard Haven, MA	David and Candia Fischer*
Mowgli	38 feet	Cutter	Baltimore, MD	Earl and Ruth Freeman
Moxie	30 feet	Ketch	U.S.A. (no home port specified)	Kirk Chamberlain and Sherrie Rausch
Orca	35 feet	Cutter	Kingston, Ontario, Canada	Guy and Joan Brooks
Packet Inn	31 feet	Cutter	Philadelphia, PA	Jack and Terry Roberts
Passport	34 feet	Sloop	Hernando Beach, FL	Jeff and Mary Ann Lawlor
Pelagic Vagrant	36 feet	Double-Headsail Sloop	Ross, CA	Dick McCurdie
Peregrine	30 feet	Ketch	Ft. Myers, FL	Ralph and Sally Pendleton
Ragtime Duet	46 feet	Cutter	Pasadena, MD	John and Petra Kowalczyk
Rosinante	34 feet	Sloop	Norfolk, VA	Win Smith
Runner	36 feet	Cutter	St. Louis, MO	John and Diane Rapp
Runinfree	40 feet	Sloop	Tacoma, WA	Bill Wittenfeld

Boat Name	Length	Rig	Home Port	Crew
Sandra	38 feet	Sloop	Stockholm, Sweden	Gunnar Dahl and Marie Louise Sterno
Sarasan	36 feet	Ketch	Newark, DE	Reade and Sarah Tompson
Sea Fever	38 feet	Ketch	Philadelphia, PA	Eugene Henkel and Bill Zeisler
Sea Wolf	42 feet	Cutter	Norfolk, VA	Sharon Sommers and Wolf Kuebler
SECO '44	44 feet	Sloop	Miami, FL	Darby Jones
Sheldro	28 feet	Sloop	Campbeltown, UK	John Robinson
Siris IV	36 feet	Trawler	Cement City, MI	Jim and Kay Stolte
Soloky	41 feet	Catamaran Sloop	Tucson, AZ	Jean Welin and Peter de Greef
Somewhere	43 feet 10 inches	Ketch	Wilmington, DE	Art and Carole Prangley
Splinter	36 feet	Double-Headsail Sloop	Barrington, IL	Wayne Koci
Stage Sea	36 feet	Sloop	Newton Ferrers, UK	Tony and Jenny Collingridge
Starbound	50 feet	Ketch	Annapolis, MD	Gordon and Nina Stuermer
Star Cruiser	37 feet	Cutter	Boston, MA	Robert and Carol Petterson
Suits Us	28 feet	Cutter	Mebane, NC	Art and Lynne Bourne
Sunrise	31 feet	Cutter	Granby, CT	John and Maureen La Vake
Sun Shine	32 feet	Cutter	Annapolis, MD	Tom and Cheryl Whitaker
Sweet Pea	35 feet	Cutter	Marietta, GA	Phil Jones and Anita Tomlin
Symphony	50 feet	Sloop	San Francisco, CA	Craig and Denise Firth*
Take Two	35 feet	Sloop	Toronto, Ontario, Canada	Ken and Penny MacKay
Tarok	37 feet	Sloop	Basel, Switzerland	Mark and Sonja Gilg
Tarwathie	42 feet	Ketch	Norfolk, VA	Dwight and Karen Rettie
The Glass Lady	34 feet	Sloop	Harpers Ferry, WV	Larry and Elaine Quayle
Themroc	40 feet	Sloop	Los Angeles, CA	Rick and Deanna Helms
Thorfinn	45 feet	Cutter	Cairns, Australia	Dick and Kay Torpin
Three Fishes B	35 feet	Cutter	Lancaster, UK	Jim, Ann, and Sarah Toms
Tiger Lily	37 feet	Cutter	Toronto, Ontario, Canada	Denis and Arleen Webster
Tournel of St. Mawes	39 feet 6 inches	Cutter	St. Mawes, UK	Robin and Pat Bowden
TranQuility	42 feet	Ketch	Philadelphia, PA	Rick and Carol Butler
Tropic Moon	42 feet	Ketch	Ann Arbor, MI	Ed and Jean Baardsen
Ty-DeWi	43 feet	Cutter	Boston, MA	David Jenkins
Westerner IV	44 feet	Ketch	Falmouth, UK	Tony and Brenda Collins
Westward	31 feet	Ketch	Seattle, WA	Dave, Vickie, Hannah and Zachary Johannes
Wild Duck	32 feet	Cutter	Golden, CO	Mike Hamilton and Barbara Davis
Wind Weaver	29 feet	Sloop	York Harbor, ME	Bill and Linda Mueller
Yellow Bird	36 feet	Sloop	Annapolis, MD	Skip and Gerri Smith
Yeti	36 feet	Sloop	Boston, MA	Hiram and Helen Connell
Yorick	36 feet	Cutter	Nieuwpoort, Belgium	Jean and Angèle Lerinckx-Parren

* Cruising with one or more small children

Index

Tip Search!

Do you have some "tips" not in this book that you'd like to share with us? If so, please write them out below, remove this page and send your tips to us. We will look forward to seeing them!

John and Susan Roberts
P.O. Box 340
Edisto Island, SC 29438

Your name _____ Boat name _____

Address _____ Boat size and rig _____

_____

_____ Boat home port _____

Where do you sail? _____

_____

Tips:

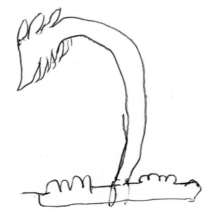